I'LL DRINK TO THAT!

by Hugh Quetton

Triumphs and blunders

from history,

with liquid mixtures

to commemorate them

CANADIAN CATALOGUING IN PUBLICATION DATA

Quetton, Hugh, 1926-
  I'll Drink to That!

ISBN 0-9696182-0-4

  1. Alcoholic beverages. 2. History —
Anecdotes. II. Title.

PN6071.D7Q4 1992   641.2   C92-090336-3

Published by HQ Services, Toronto and
distributed by Vanwell Publishing Limited,
Box 2131, Station B, St.Catharines, Ontario L2M 6P5

First edition
ISBN 0-9696182-0-4 PAPER
Printed and bound in Canada

Cover design by Kevin Richardson

All characters in the text are dead. Any resemblance to living persons
can be blamed on heredity.

DEDICATION

This might have been
a gracious acknowledgment
to the friends and colleagues
who suggested stories and found drink recipes.
But it's more in keeping with our theme
to repeat Caxton's ill-timed dedication
of five centuries ago:

To the Most Puissant, High and Mighty
Prince GEORGE, Duke of Clarence

(you'll meet him on February 18)

TO THE READER:

Pursuing the exact dates of these events showed me that different "authoritative" sources often disagree. Some authors seemed buffaloed by Pope Gregory XIII: in 1582 he pushed the calendar 10 days ahead, but some countries didn't fall into line until the 1920's. So please be tolerant.

It could have been even worse — modern scholars think Jesus was probably born a few years B.C.

Here's cheers!

H.E.P.Q.
Toronto, Friday

JANUARY 1, 1660

Putting his New Year's resolution into effect at first light this morning, Lieutenant-General George Monk turned his coat for the second time as he assembled all ranks in the little Scottish village of Coldstream. A Royalist officer in the English Civil War 16 years before, George had been taken prisoner; he agreed to join the enemy and accept a promotion. Since then he had been a member of the victorious republican forces, but now public support was swelling for restoration of the monarchy. So the general roused his 6,000 hung-over troops for the long march south to London, where they would welcome young Charles II on his return from France. As a reminder of where they had marched from, some of the soldiers were named the Coldstream Guards, while their commander was promoted Captain-General. Soon he would also be Baron Monk of Potherington, Earl of Torrington, First Duke of Albemarle, Master of the Horse and Lord-Lieutenant of Devon and Middlesex. All for keeping his New Year's resolution. You should be so lucky.

*Let **Monk's Wine** be yours tonight: In a large wineglass, stir 4 oz. white wine, 1 tsp. green Chartreuse and 2 ice cubes. Add 1 slice lemon.*

JANUARY 2, 1860

The Parisian astronomer Urbain Le Verrier considered today's annual meeting of the Académie des Sciences his best opportunity for recognition as a world authority. He had guessed that a "missing planet" was responsible for the recent disturbance of Mercury's orbit: then a country physician and amateur astronomer, Dr. Lescarbault of Orgères, said he had observed a circular black spot crossing the Sun several months before. Although the doctor's measurements lacked precision after the second-hand fell off his pocket watch, Le Verrier saw his chance for the Académie's forthcoming meeting. "Why have you kept this secret?" he roared, hastily calculating that "Vulcan" circled the Sun once every 19 days and 17 hours at a distance of 13 million miles. He presented his findings to the Académie des Sciences, but no other astronomer was sharp enough to spot the new planet. Le Verrier stuck to his opinion for the rest of his life; "Vulcan" never appeared.

*Make the **Rings of Saturn** appear in a narrow liqueur or pousse-café glass: Pour slowly, in order, ½ oz. green crème de menthe and ½ oz. crème de banane; float ½ oz. sloe gin.*

JANUARY 3, 1883

With the passenger liner *Arizona* quarantined overnight in New York City's North River, Oscar Wilde had plenty of time to plan his conversation with the customs officers who would question him this morning. The professional aesthete was 27, but when asked his age he replied "I was 26 in October", which had indeed been true for the first part of that month. Oscar had been so terribly clever all the way across the Atlantic that Captain Murray growled "I wish I had that man lashed to the bowsprit on the windward side". Now the inspector at Castle Garden customs house asked "Have you anything to declare?", and Wilde was ready with "Nothing — nothing but my genius". The customs man not having had time to rehearse his repartee, just gave Oscar a sour look, but a listening reporter wrote an invented reply for him: "That is not a thing you have to declare in this country".

*The **New York Sour** offers a friendly welcome: Shake well with ice 2 oz. rye, 1½ oz. lemon juice and 1½ tsp. sugar syrup. Strain into a Sour glass, float in 1 tbsp. red wine and top with a slice of lemon.*

JANUARY 4, 1740

A memorable wedding night in St.Petersburg, as 50-year-old Prince Mikhail Golitsyn was forced by the Empress Anna into marrying an ill-favoured serving wench, nicknamed Buzheninova because she smelt of spiced pork and onions. The empress' previous ploy in her running feud with the Golitsyn family had been to make short-statured Mikhail crouch in a palace corner and cackle like a hen. Now she decreed that the ill-suited couple should spend their wedding night in a palace of ice, built on the River Neva opposite her own heated one. Everything inside was sculpted in ice, including the marriage-bed and the slippers beneath it. Two guards were posted at the boudoir door. Their nickname for Prince Golytsin has been translated as "the frigid midget with the rigid digit".

*For a **Frosty Amour,** pour over ice in a shaker 1 oz. each Southern Comfort, vodka and apricot brandy. Add 1 dash each Parfait Amour and crème de banane. Shake well and strain into a chilled goblet. Top up with 7-Up.*

JANUARY 5, 1757

"German Geordie", Hanover-bred King George the Second of England and Scotland, was justifiably suspicious of Scottish Highlanders. Too many of them had rebelled against him, frightening his soldiers by wearing the kilt and playing the bagpipes. George had therefore prohibited both those accoutrements of war. Yet now he needed more troops to fight the French in Canada, and the son of a rebel chieftain was volunteering to raise a loyal regiment. Of course, his Highlanders would have to wear the kilt and hear the pipes. The king hesitated. But General James Wolfe himself declared, "When a Highlander gives you his word, he can be trusted". So today George signed the warrant commissioning Simon Fraser, Lord Lovat, as lieutenant-colonel. Within weeks there were 1500 Fraser Highlanders under arms, and they fought so well in Canada that the warrant was kept in force. Even now, as need arises, the current Lord Lovat, as head of Clan Fraser, raises garrisons of Fraser Highlanders to serve the descendants of George II.

Don't hesitate to raise this **Highland**: *Shake well with ice 1 oz. each Scotch and sweet vermouth, and 1 dash orange bitters. Strain into a cocktail glass.*

JANUARY 6, 1593

Antonio De Berrio, whose wife's uncle had bequeathed him the King of Spain's letters-patent to conquer and govern El Dorado, knew that there was a catch — the place had to be discovered first. Three searches for El Dorado had produced only an exceptionally detailed map of the Orinoco river basin. So today De Berrio got out of the hard part by delegating the fourth expedition to Captain Domingo de Vera. Antonio was 72 now, and he just wanted to wait quietly in Trinidad for the good news. Soon it arrived, after a fashion: Indians had assured de Vera that he was extremely close – just another fortnight's march might have got him there, but supplies were running low and he had to turn back. Before the venture could be restarted, Sir Walter Raleigh attacked Trinidad and took old De Berrio away. Neither he, nor anyone else, ever saw the fabled gold of El Dorado.

Nowadays you can find **El Dorado** *in a chilled Old-Fashioned glass. Just shake with cracked ice, in a mixing-glass, 1 oz. each white rum, Advokaat and crème de cacao. Strain into the Old-Fashioned glass and sprinkle on 1 tsp. grated coconut.*

JANUARY 7, 1785

It was a cold day over the English Channel, but Dr. John Jeffries had already thrown away his overcoat and was unbuttoning his jacket, when a providential updraft lifted the balloon from only a few feet above the water. The other balloonist, professional Jean-Pierre Blanchard, had reluctantly agreed to take the American-born passenger in return for financial help. Then at the weighing-in he had secreted lead weights inside his shirt, in an attempt to persuade Jeffries that the balloon wouldn't carry both of them from Dover Castle to the French coast. Now, thankfully, they were almost over Normandy and in a few minutes the balloon was tangled among the topmost branches of an apple tree. Dr. Jeffries climbed down to accept a dram of calvados from the farmer.

*If you have never floated free, this **Canadian Applehawk** may help: Mix 1½ oz. calvados with ½ oz. each lemon juice, lime juice and maple syrup. Shake well. Rub the rim of an Old-Fashioned glass with maple syrup and strain the drink in over ice.*

JANUARY 8, 1687

Having foresightedly composed a Te Deum in case King Louis XIV should recover from his operation for fistula, a rather surprised Jean-Baptiste Lully had to conduct it today. To be sure of the choir's attention in Paris' Church of the Feuillante, the Florentine-born musician kept time by banging the floor with a long stick resembling an overweight billiard cue. Just once he brought it down hard a bit off centre, smashing his big toe. Gangrene set in and amputation was advised, but Lully wouldn't hear of it. Next they wanted to amputate his leg, but he needed that too. A titled quack from out of town, the Marquis de Carrette, collected a substantial fee and declared that the worst was over, but he was mistaken. Jean-Baptiste's funeral mass in the Madeleine was attended by many of the nobility, but not by the Marquis de Carrette, who had prudently left Paris.

*Drink the health of their ulcer-ridden monarch with a **Louis Special**: 1 oz. each dry gin, Bénédictine and green Chartreuse. Shake well with cracked ice and strain into a cocktail glass.*

JANUARY 9, 1793

President George Washington gave François Blanchard his autograph today, but the visiting Frenchman lost more money than he could ever have made by selling the signature. Promoting the first balloon ascent in the United States, Blanchard began by charging five dollars admission to the yard of Philadelphia's Walnut Street prison; he had to reduce this to two dollars when the public estimated correctly that, if the balloon rose at all, it would be just as visible from outside. The balloonist lifted off, eventually, with the President's message "To all to whom these presents shall come", and drifted across New Jersey for 45 minutes. Then he discovered that the day's net loss amounted to $2000. Blanchard had to make several more ascents, without benefit of autograph, in order to get back to zero.

*The **Washington** lifts easily: Put 2 ice cubes in a mixing glass with 1½ oz. brandy, ½ oz. dry vermouth, 1 tsp. grenadine syrup and 2 dashes Angostura bitters. Stir well and strain into a cocktail glass.*

JANUARY 10, 1903

This was not a good morning for almost all the guests from last night's grand dinner and ball ending the Delhi Durbar. Glittering ceremonies over several days had celebrated the accession of Britain's King Edward VII as Emperor of India. To end it all, Viceroy Lord Curzon had laid on a sumptuous dinner; but now the guests' stomachs were upset. Some blamed nationalists among the native cooks. One who did not suffer, though, was David Sassoon, a leading citizen of Bombay. Not that he boasted any special resistance to gastro-enteritis, but David had taken the precaution of travelling with his own Kosher food. When that ran out he subsisted mainly on raw cauliflower, and this morning he was able to climb aboard the Bombay express in the best of health.

*Wash down a floret of raw cauliflower with a **Bombay**: Shake with cracked ice 1 oz. brandy, ½ oz. each dry and sweet vermouth, ½ tsp. curaçao and ¼ tsp. Pernod. Strain into a cocktail glass and enjoy!*

JANUARY 11, 1870

Stuck in Paris' Mazas jail this morning Pierre Bonaparte, raffish and spendthrift cousin of Emperor Napoleon III, had time to reflect on the results of trigger-happiness. While sitting at home last evening nursing a cold, he was visited by young journalist Victor Noir, representing republican editor Paschal Grousset. Pierre's assumptions of aristocracy kept him at odds with republicans at any time; now, when Noir handed him Grousset's challenge to a duel, he pulled out a revolver and fired (perhaps on the principle of shooting the second first). Victor, vanquished, staggered out of the house and expired. Bonaparte was somehow acquitted of murder; then, nearly broke after France became a republic, he managed to marry off his son to the daughter of the owner of the Monte Carlo casino, thus saving himself from a pauper's funeral.

*For a soothing **Journalist**, shake well with ice 1 oz. gin, ½ oz. each sweet and dry vermouth, 2 dashes each lemon juice and curaçao, and 1 dash Angostura.*

JANUARY 12, 1914

Another rotten birthday for Florence Dugdale, soon to become the second Mrs. Thomas Hardy. From years as his secretary, she knew that the writer had a fixation on the past: in the year after his first wife's death he had composed 100 reminiscent poems — perhaps in remorse for having practically driven her to spend much of her last year in an attic room. Annually, he would build up to an emotional climax on the birthday of Florence's predecessor, whom the 35-year-old spinster characterized as "the late espousèd saint". It might be true that on her side too, emotions toward her 73-year-old fiancé were under tight control (Virginia Woolf wrote that Florence's dog was "evidently the real centre of her thoughts"). But for heaven's sake, wouldn't Hardy ever remember that today was <u>her</u> birthday?

*The answer was No. Perhaps Florence needed a **Merry Widower**: Shake well with ice 1 oz. each gin and dry vermouth, ½ oz. Pernod, 2 dashes Bénédictine and 1 dash Angostura. Strain into a martini glass and add a twist of lemon.*

JANUARY 13, 1842

Riding a worn-out pony that could go no faster than a walk, the military surgeon William Brydon this morning came at last in sight of the mud walls of Fort Jellalabad on India's northwest frontier. Through telescopes atop the walls, British officers sighted this forerunner of their 4500-man force returning over a pass from Afghanistan. But Dr. Brydon knew something that they didn't: almost all the 4500 were dead — picked off by tribesmen after being pushed out of Kabul. General Elphinstone, as commander, had trustingly offered himself as a hostage to the Afghan leader Akbar Khan, in return for his men's safe conduct to the border. But only Dr. Brydon had been spared, fulfilling Akbar's promise to his followers: "I shall destroy the entire British force of occupation, save one man who will be sent to tell the tale!"

*The **Fort Lauderdale** cocktail (shamelessly adapted by the Americans from the Fort Jellalabad original) would have done the surgeon some good: Stir with ice 1½ oz. golden rum, ½ oz. sweet vermouth, and 1 tsp. each orange and lime juices. Strain into a large Old-Fashioned glass containing 2 ice cubes, and slide a slice of orange over the rim.*

JANUARY 14, 1437

Today's discovery of a squawking mallard ended Archbishop Henry Chichele's indecision about where to site the college that he was endowing at Oxford University. Some had advised against the town centre as unhealthy, but last night Henry dreamed that his college would stand in town and that a duck would quack from below the best location. This morning, visiting a vacant lot that he owned at the corner of High and Catte Streets, the venerable archbishop could indeed hear a faint complaint from underground. "Dygge heere!" he cried, using the spelling of the time. Soon a "schwoppinge mallarde", the size of a turkey, was discovered wedged in the drain. All Souls' College now stands there. Fellows of the college traditionally drank the health of their mascot, while singers urged them to dip their beaks in the bowl, just as the mallard had dipped his into the nutritious garbage of the town drain.

__Oxford Milk Punch__ serves a dozen Fellows: Combine in a saucepan 2 qts. milk, 8 oz. white sugar and the grated rind of 1 lemon. Stir and boil, then remove from heat and strain out the lemon. Beat in 8 oz. brandy, 16 oz. golden rum and 2 eggs until the mixture foams. Pour into warmed mugs.

JANUARY 15, 1827

Showing his faith in the experiments of Count Giovanni Aldini, dean of physics at Bologna University, Louis Chabert today put himself and a nice piece of rump steak to the test. Aldini's historical investigations had led him to promote the idea of woven asbestos suits for firefighters. When news of this reached Chabert, an amateur scientist in Paris, he constructed a suit and stepped into a brick oven, carrying the meat and breathing through a tube to the outside air. After 12 minutes he stepped out, tasted the steak and pronounced it perfect. Since Fannie Farmer allows 25 minutes for meat 1½ inches thick, Chabert's was obviously of the tenderized variety; or perhaps he was feeling rather overcooked himself.

*Hot enough to sear a steak is the **Black Stripe**: Mix 2 oz. dark rum with 1 tbsp. liquid honey in a pewter pint tankard. Fill with boiling water, stir and add a twist of lemon.*

JANUARY 16, 1586

The code took a while to decipher, but Mary Queen of Scots was in great excitement today as the first secret message arrived at Chartley Hall from supporters of her claim to the English throne. It had been wrapped around the bung of an incoming beer barrel. Mary's joy was literally unutterable, because she was detained in this English country house at the pleasure of her cousin Queen Elizabeth. An obliging brewer took the messages in and out, but unfortunately he was equally obliging to Elizabeth's intelligence service. Gilbert Gifford, the former seminarian who had set things up, was a double agent working for Sir Francis Walsingham, head of M.I. One. All the trouble Mary took to encrypt her messages was rather wasted, too — the code had been invented by that same sneaky crew, to save them time in deciphering.

*Here's the code for **Mary Queen of Scots**: 1 oz. Scotch; ½ oz. each Drambuie, green Chartreuse and lemon juice; 1 tbsp. sugar. Dip the rim of a cocktail glass first in lemon juice (shake off the excess) and then in sugar. Allow the frosting to dry. Crack 3 ice cubes and shake with the liquids; strain into the glass and decorate with a cherry.*

JANUARY 17, 1770

The wall which his novel three-wheeled steam wagon demolished today proved the end of the road for French artillery officer Nicolas Cugnot. Until now his enterprise had gone full steam ahead: the Minister of War, the Duc de Choiseul, had personally approved the first tests of the heavy *cabriot*. On a smooth parade-ground it carried two men and hauled a 12-pounder cannon usually drawn by 15 horses. But when Cugnot drove out into the cobblestoned street without the cannon, the single front wheel under the heavy engine slewed the vehicle around. The tiller was wrenched from Cugnot's hand and the *cabriot* overturned as it crashed through a stone wall. The inventor was arrested and his machine impounded, to end 150 years later in the Conservatoire des Arts et Métiers. Cugnot died a pauper in Brussels during the Napoleonic Wars, when his wagon might have played a useful part.

*Build your own **Battering Ram**: Shake with ice 4 oz. orange juice, 1 oz. each light and dark rum, and ½ oz. each lime juice and Wild Turkey liqueur. Strain into a tall glass half-filled with ice, top up with tonic, stir gently and float a slice of lime. Sip through a straw.*

JANUARY 18, 1912

Captain Robert F. Scott, 43-year-old assistant to the Second Sea Lord of the British Admiralty, today led his reduced five-man Antarctic expedition to a welcome they had hoped never to receive. Taking his turn again at pulling a sled — their motor-driven ones had all broken down — Scott hoped he was going where no man or woman had trod. But there, ahead of them, was a little cairn and a flag; and two miles further on they found a tent containing the names of their rivals, the Norwegian expedition to the South Pole. Roald Amundsen, his men and dogs had reached "Polheim" 33 days before, while the Brits were still 360 miles away on the Beardmore Glacier. Scott had sent all his huskies back to base camp, fulfilling the idea he had expressed in writing: "No journey made with dogs can approach that fine conception when men go forth to face hardships with their own unaided efforts".

*Revive the captain with a **Southern Comfort Sour**: 1½ oz. Southern Comfort, ½ oz. lemon juice and ½ tsp. white sugar. Shake with ice, strain into a cocktail glass; top with an orange slice and a cherry.*

JANUARY 19, 1865

A sweet-and-sour 58th birthday present today reached General Robert E. Lee, commanding the Army of Virginia for the impoverished Confederacy in the American civil war. He learned from President Jefferson Davis that the Confederate Congress would shortly approve a top rank, General-in-Chief, and he would be appointed. "I do not think I could accomplish much good", Lee replied, but he dutifully accepted. To the politicians in threatened Richmond, the fact that there wasn't much in the way of food or munitions to keep Lee's armies going was just the point. When the time came to surrender less than threee months later, there would be someone to do it for them, and perhaps even to be regarded as the man who lost the war. Happy Birthday, General!

*Match the general's mood with a **Bittersweet**: Stir with ice 1½ oz. each dry and sweet vermouth, 2 dashes Angostura and 1 dash orange bitters. Strain into a chilled cocktail glass; twist a sliver of orange peel and drop it in.*

JANUARY 20, 1909

Normally, George Rector would have appreciated a mention of his fashionable restaurant in *The New York Times*. But this morning its favourable review of Eugene Walter's *The Easiest Way*, which premièred on Broadway last night, disturbed him. Rector's, a two-storey edifice decorated in a mixture of Louis Quatorze and Byzantium, attracted a moneyed theatre-going crowd. George was worried by what the *Times'* review said the audience had heard last night. In the play, heroine Laura Murdock breaks away from the rich stockbroker who has been keeping her; she tries the path of virtue but finds it too narrow. In the last scene Laura cries out to her maid: "Dress up my body and paint my face, I'm going back to Rector's to make a hit!" Respectable theatregoers flocked to the play, took the hint and avoided Rector's, which within three years went bankrupt.

*To coax a **Broadway Smile**, pour carefully into a liqueur glass, in this order, ½ oz. each Crème de Cassis, Swedish Punch and Cointreau.*

JANUARY 21, 1534

King Carlos of Castile was not enthused today at the prospect of returned explorer Hernando Pizarro lugging a collection of objets d'art into the palace at Calatayud. Seeking an audience with the king, Pizarro had written on the day he landed that "nothing like the array of beauty and interest" from South America had ever been possessed by a European prince. They were leftovers from an Inca's ransom to the *conquistadores* — gold and silver filling two Peruvian rooms. Almost all of it had been melted into bars. King Carlos couldn't care less. He instructed his officials that Pizarro's offering, except for a few bijoux that he could bring in his hands, should be turned into something more useful. If future generations wanted to see the treasure of the Incas, they would have to settle for gold coins bearing the noble likeness of King Carlos of Castile.

You'll be more appreciative of a **Conquistador***: Mix 1½ oz. each golden rum and grenadine with 2 oz. each orange and pineapple juice, and 1 oz. each lemon juice and coconut milk. Pour into a highball glass over ice cubes and stir; stick in 1 chunk pineapple.*

JANUARY 22, 1879

A partial eclipse of the sun, after the night of the new moon, signalled the near-total eclipse of a poorly sited British invasion camp in northern Natal this afternoon. Cetswayo, King of the Zulus, followed tradition in never planning attacks for nights when the old moon was "dying". So it was early this morning that his 20,000 barefoot warriors assembled in a ravine, hidden by Isandhlwana Mountain from the British encampment. At noon they struck, streaming around both sides of the hill in a classic pincer. From high ground six miles away, some officers of the British force, who had gone in search of the Zulus, discerned activity at the campsite; then an eclipse darkened the sky. Only 200 of the 1300 Britons at Isandhlwana got away to tell the invasion's commander, Lord Chelmsford, what had happened. A few days earlier he had dismissed a warning relayed from Sub-Inspector Phillips of the Natal Mounted Police: "Tell the police officer my troops will do all the attacking. If the enemy does venture to attack, the hill will protect our rear".

This **Zulu Warrior** *sneaks up on you: 1 oz. each dry sherry, Lillet and Van der Hum, stirred with 2 dashes orange bitters and 2 ice cubes.*

JANUARY 23, 1791

Ralph, Earl Verney and his countess took an uncomfortable ride today from their stately Buckinghamshire home, Claydon House, which had been lavishly redesigned for them by Adam. After the general election of 1784 in which the Whiggish earl, a House of Commons MP for 31 years, had gone down to defeat, he had thrown more than the rest of his fortune into contesting a by-election. He won; but now the bailiffs had caught up with him, the furniture was to be sold and creditors were on his trail. So Ralph decided that the best thing to do was make his getaway in a heavily-curtained hearse. This proved most convenient to his countess because she was on her way to a burial, having died three days before.

Show respect for the Earl's **Cara Sposa**: *Blend at low speed for 15 seconds, 3 oz. crushed ice, 1 oz. each coffee liqueur and orange curaçao, and ½ oz. whipping cream. Strain into an Old-Fashioned glass.*

JANUARY 24, 1848

James W. Marshall, completing construction of a sawmill for entrepreneur John Sutter in California's sparsely settled Sacramento Valley, hoped this day would bring them riches. From the millrace he had picked flakes of something unknown in the region — gold! Sutter's ownership came from Mexican land grants, and on February 2 the territory was to become American by the Treaty of Guadalupe Hidalgo. So Sutter persuaded the contractor to keep the discovery secret until then. But the U.S. government was slow to allocate land rights; there was a free-for-all gold rush across the area and eventually Sutter's Mexican grants were declared invalid. Neither man grew rich. Marshall took to drink and couldn't keep hold of money; Sutter's business ventures turned sour and he spent years appealing for compensation for his lost land. He died just after the U.S. Congress failed to pass a private bill "for the Relief of John A. Sutter".

Just as short-lived as the Californians' dream is this **Golden Fizz**: *Shake well with ice 1 oz. dry gin, 1 egg yolk and ½ tsp. sugar. Strain into a highball glass, fill with soda and stir.*

JANUARY 25, 1763

A riotous and disappointing end to the benefit evening for Benjamin Victor, the elderly former theatre manager, now about to retire as adaptor of plays for London's Drury Lane. The take from this performance of Shakespeare's *Two Gentlemen of Verona* was to be his present from the management; to make sure that he got plenty, they had suspended the usual practice of letting in impecunious playgoers for half price after the intermission. Upset at this, as well as at finding that Victor had improved the Shakespeare with two scenes of his own invention, the audience became restive and began smashing the benches and chandeliers. Soon there was no light, no play and, since the customers demanded their money back, no benefit for poor Benjamin Victor.

At least they named a cocktail for Victor: 1½ oz. sweet vermouth and ½ oz. each gin and brandy. Stir well with cracked ice and strain into a cocktail glass.

JANUARY 26, 1826

Thomas Jefferson, 83-year-old ex-President of the United States, was $100,000 in debt and often without sufficient cash on hand to pay the grocery bill, so today he sent grandson T. Jefferson Randolph to the Virginia legislature to see whether a state lottery could be organized for his benefit. The legislators delayed for some time before granting approval, for Jefferson had recently refused on principle their offer of an interest-free loan from public funds. When the lottery was finally launched it proved an instant disappointment and was cancelled; Jefferson's showplace home, Monticello, had to be sold at auction to pay his debts when he died a few months later. The ex-president might have taken this philosophically: soon after leaving office he had written, "Having myself made it a rule never to engage in a lottery.....I can with less effect urge it on others".

*Sometimes principles must be compromised in an **Emergency**: Shake 2 oz. dry gin with 1 oz. frozen concentrated orange juice. Pour into a cocktail glass and sprinkle with nutmeg.*

JANUARY 27, 1914

The new American ambassador to Germany learned today how to squelch a royal snub. In the foyer of the Berlin Opera James W. Gerard, a New Yorker whose appointment was his consolation for losing election to the U.S. Senate, was meeting the Berlin diplomatic corps and minor German royals at a gala in honour of Kaiser Wilhelm's birthday. Among them was King Friedrich Christian III of Saxony; he maintained his own little court at Dresden, but the United States had not accredited Gerard to it. To show his pique, the king ordered that the ambassador be presented to him; then, because he had not officially "received" Gerard, he declined to shake hands. In line behind the American stood the wife of the Turkish ambassador; the king tried the same trick on her. The lady, familiar with diplomatic upmanship, just stepped around him and seized the hand stuck behind his back. She shook it vigorously until the embarrassed kinglet begged her to stop. He was, deservedly, the last king to rule Saxony.

*A **Perfect Lady** is always composed — like this: Shake well 1 oz. gin, ½ oz. each peach brandy and lemon juice with white of 1 egg. Strain into a cocktail glass.*

JANUARY 28, 1889

By 11 o'clock last evening it was clear that General Georges Boulanger, France's former minister of war and a vehement critic of the present government, had won a stunning victory in his Paris bye-election. There were said to be 100,000 supporters in the streets, ready to have the heroic "man on horseback" seize the reins of government. They expected him to leave the Restaurant Durand and lead them to the presidential Elysée Palace. But for some reason Boulanger stepped into a hired carriage and drove quietly away. Discreet agents were sent out from the Elysée and now, at 1:15 in the morning, the Préfet de Police himself appeared at the door of the meeting room: "The general has gone to bed". "To bed!", exclaimed president Sadi Carnot. "Yes, with a lady — not his wife". "*Alors*", said the relieved Carnot ambiguously, "he has set us a good example".

*For an unambiguous **Playmate**, mix ½ oz. each brandy, Grand Marnier, orange juice and water. Add 1 white of egg and 1 dash Angostura; shake well, strain into a large wineglass and top with a twist of orange peel.*

JANUARY 29, 1587

Rather an embarrassment for Robert Dudley, created Earl of Leicester as one of her favourites by Queen Elizabeth, to have to report today's events to his royal mistress. Commanding 5,000 infantry in the Netherlands against the Spaniards who were now threatening to invade England, Leicester had put two of his best captains in charge of the forts of Zutphen and Deventer. When his Dutch Protestant allies complained that both men were Roman Catholics like the Spanish enemy, Leicester replied that he would stake his life on their loyalty. This afternoon one of them, Sir William Stanley, opened the gates of Deventer and joined the enemy with 1200 men; a few hours later the other, Rowland York, gave up his fortifications and handed Zutphen to the Spaniards. Leicester signed his report to the Queen as her "most unhappy servant".

Leicester may have felt like a **Prize Idiot:** *Build 1 oz. each vodka and crème de banane into a highball glass over 2 ice cubes. Add 2 dashes fresh lemon juice and 1 dash grenadine; stir in 4 oz. 7-Up. Decorate with a wedge of lemon, a green cherry and straws.*

JANUARY 30, 1877

When he was discovered this evening gilding the floor of his London bedroom, the interior designer Tom Jeckell was muttering something about peacocks. Obviously his mind had been unhinged by a traumatic visit to 49 Princes Gate. There, the cocky and innovative artist James McNeill Whistler had just shown him some "slight improvements" being made to Tom's designs in the mansion of shipping magnate Frederick Leyland. Whistler, lying on the floor of a room which he had repainted in dazzling blue and gold, was touching up the ceiling with a brush on the end of a fishing rod. Jeckell had to be taken to the lunatic asylum where he would spend the remaining four years of his life. Mr. Leyland was rather ambivalent about the "improvements". Whistler wrote "he is utterly ignorant of art; he is only a millionaire". The Peacock Room ended in a Washington art gallery.

If, like Tom Jeckell, you have an urge for **Yellow Fingers,** *here you go: Shake well with ice 1 oz. each gin and blackberry brandy, ½ oz. each banana liqueur and 35% cream. Strain into a champagne saucer.*

JANUARY 31, 1909

Until he was sentenced to prison today, Parisian chemical engineer Henri Lemoine had persuaded almost everyone that his secret formula would produce jewel-quality diamonds from a powder. After a demonstration in which Lemoine pulled a diamond from the furnace in his basement laboratory, directors of the mighty De Beers consortium bought time by advancing him 66,000 pounds. Meanwhile they arranged for a technical expert to mingle with the "other directors" at a final demonstration. He knew that Lemoine's 1800-degree Celsius temperature would soon melt a diamond, and reasoned that the Frenchman was sneaking a ready-cut stone in and out of the furnace at the end of the experiment. So he put in a diamond too, in a little crucible. Lemoine's reaction when the expert's diamond was liquefied sufficed for De Beers to bring fraud charges. Paris laughed at *notre alchimiste* duping the business magnates, but the diamond men enjoyed the last laugh, during the six years of Lemoine's prison sentence.

The **Liar's Martini** *tells the truth about gin: stir with ice 1½ oz. gin, ½ oz. dry vermouth and ¼ oz. each sweet vermouth and orange curaçao. Strain into a cocktail glass.*

FEBRUARY 1, 1666

Held in protective custody in the Jasmine Tower of his own capital fort at Agra, the widowed Moghul emperor Shahjahan was on a particular downer today. He had taken an overdose of aphrodisiacs after overhearing two concubines mock his declining prowess. In fact he felt terminally unwell, his only consolation the thought that he would soon be resting in a grand black mausoleum opposite the Taj Mahal. Under his orders an international team of artisans had spent 17 years building the white marble Taj, two miles down the Jumna river, as a tomb and memorial for his wife Mumtaz. As he lay dying this evening he could look through the open stone grillework and see it. But Shahjahan's own planned tomb never was built on the other bank: his son Aurangzeb, who had deposed and imprisoned him, decided to save time and money by placing the old folks together, where they still lie in the Taj Mahal.

The **Shah's Reward** *(with a spare for Mumtaz) calls for 1½ oz. each crème de cacao and coffee liqueur, blended with 4 oz. milk, 1 pinch salt and 8 oz. crushed ice. When it becomes creamy, pour into tulip glasses and drink straight-up.*

FEBRUARY 2, 1901

Queen Victoria had never travelled so fast in her life! Royal trains were normally held to 40 miles per hour, even on the long journeys north to Balmoral Castle. But today the aged empress remained silent as her "special" made up a 10-minute delay between Portsmouth and London's Victoria Station. Her son Bertie had ordered the speedup; by going as fast as 80 miles an hour they were able to make connections through London, and get the Queen to Windsor in time for service in the Chapel Royal. This was rather important because the service was in her honour: on such occasions Victoria insisted on punctuality. But this time, being late might not have mattered too much — she had been dead for over a week.

You can enjoy travelling ***Express*** *without that disadvantage: Stir with ice 1 oz. each Scotch and sweet vermouth, and 1 dash orange bitters. Strain into a martini glass.*

FEBRUARY 3, 1912

A most irritating end to the evening for retired Admiral Lord Charles Beresford, now member of parliament for Portsmouth and leader of a government mission to Tsarist Russia. A formal dinner had been arranged in Moscow, at the palatial riverside home of the sugar magnate Kharitonenko. Beresford was accompanied by the young Russian naval officer who had been allocated to him as escort and interpreter. In mid-meal this aide was called to the telephone. On the line was his mistress, simply letting him know by Long Distance that their affair was over. Without putting the receiver down, the young officer drew his service revolver and shot himself in the head, leaving Lord Beresford to find his way around Moscow by himself.

Those who can't wait choose a ***Russian Espresso:*** *Combine with ice 1½ oz. vodka, 2 tsp. coffee liqueur and 3 drops lemon juice. Shake well, strain into a chilled martini glass and add a twist of lemon.*

FEBRUARY 4, 1650

The elderly philosopher René Descartes, staying at the Swedish royal court as the guest of Queen Christina, suspected today the intentions of the substitute physician treating him. A few days ago René had caught a chill when Christina obliged him to travel in bitter cold to meet her. Remorsefully she had offered her guest the services of her personal physician, Dr.Ryer, but he was away; Descartes had to accept the ministrations of Dr. Johann van Wullen, his worst enemy at court. "Spare French blood!", he shouted as the doctor set about bleeding him. "If I must die", he added, "I shall do so more peacefully if I don't see you." Descartes thought he was suffering only from rheumatism, but within a week death changed his mind.

*This **Swedish Treatment** shouldn't hasten your end: Put 3 ice cubes in a mixing glass with ½ oz. each gin, brandy and cherry brandy, and 1 dash orange bitters. Stir well, strain into a cocktail glass and top with a twist of orange peel.*

FEBRUARY 5, 1831

After unintentionally grounding Gunboat No.2 on the muddy bank of the Scheldt today, Lieutenant Jan Joseph van Speyk of the Dutch Navy had to move quickly before independence-minded Belgians could come from Antwerp to board it. Dutch occupation forces were holed up in the town's citadel and eight gunboats were supposed to be guarding the approaches, but this left lots of space for Belgian patriots to move around. Soon an armed band of them aporoached along the riverbank; Lieutenant van Speyk rushed to unlock the door to his gunpowder store. When he opened it, his pistol somehow discharged. Since the resulting explosion blew the lieutenant and most of his crewmen to bits, it was uncertain whether his action was heroic or accidental. The Dutch have expressed their opinion in bronze: the lion at the base of the Egmont-aan-Zee lighthouse represents van Speyk. In front of the Royal Naval College at Willemsoord stands all that was left of his gunboat — the mast.

*To cool a **Hot Deck**, put cracked ice in a shaker and cover with 1½ oz. rye whiskey, ½ oz. sweet vermouth and 1 dash ginger essence. Shake well; strain into a chilled cocktail glass.*

FEBRUARY 6, 1797

Field-Marshal Count Peter Suvorov learned today the Tsar's reaction to his criticism of changes in army regulations, such as the shorter marching step. Suvorov had pointed out that this would be an excellent way to cover three-quarters of the distance toward the enemy. Equally snappish, Tsar Paul arranged for a note to be published in today's military gazette: "Field-Marshal Count Suvorov, having said that in the absence of war there is nothing for him to do, is hereby excluded from the service." The 67-year-old soldier went to his country house, buried his uniform and decorations, and refused to open a letter from the Tsar (who had meanwhile changed his mind). He pointed out that it was "addressed to Field-Marshal Count Suvorov, who no longer exists."

*The **White Russian Mule** comes from a blender in which you mix at high speed, for 10 seconds, 2 tbsp. each vodka and white crème de cacao, 2 oz. vanilla ice cream and 1 oz. ice chips. Serve straight-up in a Sour glass.*

FEBRUARY 7, 1845

William Lloyd, an unemployed youth with an apparent aversion to early blown glass, today picked up a large Babylonian sculptured stone in the British Museum and brought it down on a glass case containing the unique Portland Vase. This vessel, which for some 1800 years had depicted in elegant relief the marriage of Peleus and Thetis, shattered into 200 pieces. It was on loan from the Duke of Portland, so the museum authorities were satisfied simply to have Lloyd pay a fine of three pounds for breaking their display case. The duke declined to prosecute for the breaking of his less replaceable vase, but he did ask the museum to have the 200 pieces put back together. That job took a full year. This was, declared Sir Frederic Madden, a senior museum official, "the result of exhibiting such valuable and unique specimens of art to the Mob".

*Get it all together with a **China Smash**: Shake well with ice 2 oz. golden rum, 1 tsp. curaçao, ½ tsp. each grenadine and passionfruit juice, and 2 dashes Angostura. Strain into a highball glass containing 2 ice cubes; decorate with 1 sprig mint.*

FEBRUARY 8, 1601

While changing his shirt today Robert Devereux, Earl of Essex, decided that he had overestimated the quantity and the quality of his friends. Upset at losing favour at the court of Queen Elizabeth, the 33-year-old earl had started on horseback from his palatial home beside the Thames, leading 200 armed men to try and gather the London populace in a show of support. But the citizens just stood and watched. Despite the winter chill, Essex perspired freely; eventually he dismounted to put on a fresh shirt at the house of a friendly sheriff. The sheriff promptly scuttled out the back door. Returning home with only one companion, the earl went onto his roof and soon saw barrels of gunpowder being unloaded at the waterside. If he didn't surrender, the house would be blown up. Essex decided that he would rather go on living, and did, for another 17 days.

*Keep your head, and your **Coronet**: Stir with 1 ice cube 2 oz. gin and 1 oz. ruby port. Strain into a martini glass and add a twisted spiral of lemon peel.*

FEBRUARY 9, 1801

Nobody in Europe was more relieved by today's signing of the Treaty of Lunéville than the renowned geologist Déodat Dolomieu. Invalided home the previous year from Egypt, where he had been resident scientist with a French military force, Dolomieu had the bad luck to be shipwrecked in the Gulf of Taranto and then cast by the Kingdom of Naples into a particularly foul Messina prison. When he threatened to die on the authorities, his jailer allowed that "I only have to answer for your bones". In the margins of a Bible the prisoner began composing his *Philosophie de Minéralogie*; before he reached Exodus, the French victory at Marengo enabled Napoleon to dictate terms at Lunéville to Austria and Italy. One of the first conditions was the release of Dolomieu. As an added humiliation, the name of the mountain range separating the two defeated countries would honour the Frenchman who had identified its special content — the double carbon of lime and magnesia that we call Dolomite.

*Treasure your **Liberty**: Stir well with ice 2 oz. applejack, 1 oz. white rum and 2 dashes sugar syrup. Strain into a cocktail glass.*

FEBRUARY 10, 1910

An unforgettable day for the flag officer of HMS *Dreadnought*, pride of Britain's battle fleet, as he received the Emperor of Abyssinia on a surprise official visit in Weymouth harbour. Nothing had appeared in the newspapers, but the Foreign Office telegram made it clear that every courtesy should be extended. So it was lucky that the flag officer, Commander William Fisher, did not recognize beneath layers of greasepaint two undergraduates — his cousin Adrian Bell and wealthy man-about-town Horace deVere Cole, who was starting a career in practical joking. They conversed in disguised Latin tags which passed for Amharic among the ships' officers, but had to decline a drink that might have smeared their Abyssinian complexions. After Mr. deVere Cole, unsatisfied by the small audience, got word to the newspapers, questions about security were asked in Parliament. "I am glad", the hoaxer wrote, "to think that I have been of help to my country".

*Here's a well-prepared **Visitor**: Shake well with ice ½ oz. each gin, Cointreau and crème de banane. Add 1 white of egg and 2 dashes orange juice; shake again and strain into a chilled Sour glass.*

FEBRUARY 11, 1898

"I prefer to be a dead gentleman than a living blackguard like your father", the son-in-law of Standard Oil tycoon John Flagler wrote to his wife today from an El Paso hotel. Then Prince James the First of Trinidad, or Baron James Harden-Hickey, or plain Jim Hickey to his mother in San Francisco, achieved his aim with an overdose of barbiturates. Until two years ago, he had been standing proud against the rival claims of Brazil, Portugal and Britain to the rocky, uninhabited islet of Trinidad, 700 miles east of Bahia. After his marriage to the Flagler heiress, Jim granted himself a title and planted a flag on Trinidad during a cruise on his father-in-law's yacht. But when he sent stamps out with his princely profile, James the First ran foul of international recognition of Brazil's rights. His wife's family told him to stop embarrassing them. Asked about the suicide note, "blackguard" John Flagler could only offer: "among other eccentricities he had a tendency to melancholy, which made him say strange things".

*A temporary cure may be found in the **Asylum**: Over 3 ice cubes in a large Old-Fashioned glass, pour 1 oz. each Pernod and dry gin; splash on 3 dashes grenadine and stir gently.*

FEBRUARY 12, 1760

With the admission price set at a hefty two pounds sterling, Mrs. Cornelys' masked ball at Carlisle House, in London's Soho Square, was said to attract a fast crowd. Tonight, none was faster than 24-year-old Joseph Merlin, a Walloon who earned his living making musical instruments but was seeking attention for his recent invention of roller skates. Young Joseph had just come to stay at the Count de Firentes' house across the square, and Mrs. Cornelys agreed to his offer to enliven the subscription dance in return for a ticket. Merlin made a grand entrance to the Carlisle House ballroom, playing the violin as he swayed along on his skates. Unfortunately the knock-kneed stem-christie which he used for braking carried him straight into a large wall-mirror, later valued by Mrs.Cornelys at 500 pounds. Right now it was worth much less, being in pieces, along with Merlin's violin.

Knickbeinig is the German for knock-kneed. This drink must be the cure. Mix 1 oz. each Bénédictine, curaçao and kirsch in a glass, then pour into a champagne flute. Separate 1 egg and float the yolk on the liquid. Beat the white until it forms peaks. Float it on and add 1 dash Angostura. Spoon up the white and toss back the rest!

FEBRUARY 13, 1278

Tough luck today, for 59-year-old Franciscan monk Roger Bacon, that the late Pope Clement IV's successor didn't share his admiration for Roger's scientific inventiveness. His latest device should have shortened the next Crusade: take along a great solar reflector and focus it on the the the Arabs occupying Jerusalem. This would incinerate them and make Israel safe for Christianity. Small-minded critics complained that (a) Roger would have to wait for a sunny day, and (b) the rest of Jerusalem would also burn down. Worse, to the new Pope Nicholas III messing with God's resources was the work of the Devil; he quickly acceded to a request by Jerome, head of the Franciscans, that "this dangerous doctrine be totally suppressed". So today poor Roger was cast into jail and told to stop scribbling. Released after 14 years, he managed one more manuscript and died. As they used to say at the time, "publish and perish".

Show your sympathy with **Roger**: *Shake well with ice 1½ oz. each gin, peach nectar and orange juice, and 2 dashes lemon juice. Strain into an ice-filled highball glass.*

FEBRUARY 14, 1876

Elisha Gray had never met Alexander Graham Bell, and the documents that the two inventors signed today were far from Valentines. During the afternoon Gray filed at the United States Patent Office in Washington a "caveat" or notice of intention to patent the telephone. His invention was not quite complete — that is, it would transmit the tone of each syllable but not the words. Unfortunately, a lawyer for Bell had checked in only a few hours before to file Bell's caveat for <u>his</u> telephone. Gray wrote his competitor in a generous personal letter, "I do not.....claim the credit of inventing it"; but later he regretted the words, and died an embittered man. Many others decided, after the telephone became a commercial success, that they had thought of it first. Bell fought off 600 court challenges, including some from ultra-persistent Daniel Drawbaugh, who modestly listed himself as "one of the greatest inventive geniuses of this age".

*To make a **Loudspeaker** for each end of the line, stir well with ice 1½ oz. each gin and brandy, and ½ oz. each lemon juice and Cointreau. Strain into 2 cocktail glasses.*

FEBRUARY 15, 1851

Today's snowy visit to the little Seneca Falls, N.Y. post office by two cousins of the postmaster's wife set off a new fashion trend. Mrs. Dexter C. Bloomer happened to be editor of a women's magazine, and she saw immediately that the ankle length pantaloons which her cousins were wearing under short skirts were just the thing to replace long dresses dragging in the snow and mud. On a transatlantic trip the two ladies had heard of the English feminist, Helen Weber, plowing fields in a similar outfit. In the next issue of *The Lily*, Amelia Bloomer recommended that timid readers might start by wearing the pantaloons for housework; she herself wore them everywhere and started a trend among the advanced. But soon the dress designers fought back with the hoop skirt — so outrageous and unwieldy that it made an instant fashion hit and temporarily eclipsed "bloomers".

*It's a shame to disguise **American Beauty**: Mix ½ oz. each sweet vermouth, brandy, grenadine syrup and orange juice with ¼ tsp. crème de menthe. Shake with ice and strain into a martini glass.*

FEBRUARY 16, 1588

Comfortably settled in southwestern Spain, the Duke of Medina-Sidonia tried today to excuse himself from what sounded like a hyperactive naval expedition out of Lisbon. When the previous commander had died, only a week before the Spanish Armada was due to sail, King Philip II decided that the tactful duke was the man to supervise the fleet's ambitious sea-captains in their assault against England. He had not anticipated the duke's excuses in today's letter: "I am always seasick, and always catch cold", he assured the king's private secretary. "I cannot feel that I ought to command so important an enterprise." When Philip insisted, the duke proved right on all counts and lost 22 of Spain's biggest fighting ships. Then, having been relieved of his command, the Duke of Medina-Sidonia was able to retire to his family seat, where he had not even a distant view of the sea.

*Settle the duke's stomach with a **Calm Voyage**: Blend at low speed, for 10 seconds, ½ oz. each light rum, Galliano and pear syrup, 2 tsp. lemon juice, ½ egg white (raw!) and ½ cup crushed ice. Pour into a pre-chilled champagne saucer.*

FEBRUARY 17, 1864

Along with the eight men who turned the cranks propelling his submarine just below the surface of Charleston harbour, Confederate army lieutenant George Dixon enjoyed a brief moment of success this evening. In trials the unique CSS *H.L.Hunley*, adapted from a cylindrical iron boiler 40 feet long, had shown a disturbing tendency to sink and not to rise again. But her newest commander was determined to torpedo one of the U.S. Navy ships blockading the city. Filled with 95 pounds of powder, the ram torpedo was on a rod fixed to the *Hunley*'s bow at surface level. Thus at 8:45 the "rotten log" which sailors on the steam-sloop USS *Housatonic* had watched proceeding toward them struck and sank their ship. If it was any consolation, the shock was also too much for the *H.L.Hunley*, which was never seen again.

*For a similar effect, try this **Torpedo**: Combine with ice in a shaker 1½ oz. calvados, 1 tbsp. brandy and a few drops of gin. Shake well, strain and serve over ice.*

FEBRUARY 18, 1478

Prince George, Duke of Clarence, went to the cellar tonight for his last drink of the evening. The cellar was in the Tower of London and pleasure-loving, 28-year-old George was there for calling his brother a bastard. This was regarded by the brother in question, King Edward the Fourth, as not just ill-mannered but a threat to his throne. So he had a Bill of Attainder worked up against George, whom the Court of Chivalry obligingly popped into the Tower. It gave the young prince lots of time to study the chess manual which William Caxton had dedicated to him. Then somehow tonight, George ended up head first in a 120-gallon barrel of strong, sweet Malmsey wine. What a way to go! It has since been suggested that the barrel had only contained wine on its way from Greece to England, and was now filled with water; but drowning in his bath would surely have been too dull an end for fun-loving George, Duke of Clarence.

*You too can go **Head-over-Heels**: Put 4 ice cubes in cocktail shaker. Pour over them 1½ oz. vodka, 1 tsp. sugar syrup, juice of 1 lime and 3 drops Angostura bitters. Shake until a frost begins to form, pour the drink (ice and all) into a highball glass, and top up with chilled champagne.*

FEBRUARY 19, 1913

It was no coincidence that General Victoriano Huerta had dressed formally this evening, for he had good reason to suspect that before midnight he might succeed to the presidency of Mexico. Knowing of a military plot brewing against President Madero, Huerta had declined to join it and played instead the part of a loyalist. Then, when the rebels attacked, he convinced Madero that the government could only hope for a stalemate. The president and vice-president both resigned. Under Mexico's constitution the presidency now devolved upon the secretary for foreign affairs, with whom General Huerta had reached an agreement. In front of Congress the obliging fellow took on the additional responsibilities of president; then, after naming Huerta to the next post in line, secretary of the interior, he resigned. At this, a dinner-jacketed figure detached itself from a doorway and stepped forward to assume the presidency. It was Victoriano Huerta, Mexico's third president in 24 hours.

*Keep a trick like that under your **Sombrero**: Pour 1½ oz. Kahlùa over 1 ice cube in a small Old-Fashioned glass, then carefully float on 1 oz. light cream.*

FEBRUARY 20, 1814

Late tonight the astounding news of Napoleon's capture reached Dover from France as a secret in the mind of "Colonel de Bourg". Clothed in the distinctive red jacket of a general's a.d.c., he chartered a chaise to take him to London and asked the ostler to have a note rushed to the admiral commanding at Dover. Others must have sneaked a look at his note, for at the Stock Exchange next day the bid price for British Treasury bonds rose by 20 percent in a ferment of trading. Only at closing did questions begin to be asked, especially regarding Lord Cochrane, who had been buying the bonds for two weeks and unloaded them all during the day. On the morrow the news turned out to be false, and "Colonel de Bourg" turned out to be Charles de Berenger. He had donned his costume in a house rented by Lord Cochrane. The pair were sentenced to spend an uncomfortable lunch hour in the pillory outside the Exchange.

*The evening of their coup, Lord Cochrane doubtless said "**Cheers, Charley**" and each enjoyed a double: Whirl together in a blender 6 oz. each gin and frozen lime juice, 1 oz. cherry juice, 4 dashes Angostura and lots of cracked ice. Strain into wineglasses and top with maraschino cherries.*

FEBRUARY 21, 1846

The 21-year-old Alexandre Dumas lost his sweetheart today as she married a nobleman, but soon found a way to write about her for profit. Marie Duplessis, who had slept around with sufficient selectivity to qualify as a courtesan, chose to take the Vicomte Edouard de Perregaux as her bridegroom in London. Dumas wrote to say goodbye, but Marie never replied. Soon she took off on a new string of lovers, including the composer Franz Liszt; but she was dying of tuberculosis. This inspired Dumas to write *La Dame aux Camélias*, which was such a success that it was adapted to the theatre and provided the juicy lead role of *Camille* for tragic actresses. At the auction of Marie's effects, Alexandre contented himself with a thin gold chain, his memento of their broken love.

*Alex had time to mix a lifetime supply of **Parfait Amour**: Grate 1 oz. lime rinds and ½ oz. lemon rinds; put in a pot containing 1 oz. pounded rosemary sprigs and 1 gallon cooking alcohol. Seal the pot and store for 2 weeks. Then soak 7 cups white sugar in 1½ qt. water until dissolved and pour into the pot. Stir in ½ oz. each ground cloves and caramel; float 1 oz. orange blossoms. Bottle, and sip at leisure.*

FEBRUARY 22, 1905

Many East Indian gentlemen, intrigued by a British officer's tale of the theft of a historic Moghul jewel, turned up at today's biggest London auction. The rose-pink Agra Diamond was the last lot in Christie's sale of Henry Streeter's stock by the late Bond Street jeweller's estate. The Agra now weighed 31 carats, lighter but better cut than when it had been swiped from the King of Delhi in 1857. During the Indian Mutiny, according to Streeter's confidential information from the late Marquess of Donegall, some British officers had secreted the diamond in a horseball that they thrust down the throat of a regimental mount. Back in Blighty, the purloined jewel changed hands a few times and today was finally on the block at a reserve price of 1,000 pounds. Quickly the bidding rose to 5,100 pounds, for which a Herr Meyer took it away to his Berlin gemmery, and no questions asked.

*The **Diamond Fizz**, sparkling and costly, takes 1 oz. dry gin, 1 tsp. each sugar and lemon juice, and a lot of stirring. Strain into a champagne tulip and fill with champagne!*

FEBRUARY 23, 1913

Readers of the *Chicago Tribune* received fair warning today of what was coming their way. Harriet Monroe, its fait-tout art and poetry critic, had returned from the modernist show of paintings at New York's 69th Regiment Armory ready to excoriate "the most hideous monstrosities ever perpetrated in the name of long-suffering Art". Marcel Duchamp's *Nude Descending Staircase, #2* particularly intrigued the paper's editors: when the exhibition reached Chicago they printed a diagram showing "how to find the nude". Duchamp nonetheless managed to sell it in the States for $325; and the American Association of Painters and Sculptors had to turn visitors away from the exhibition because the rooms were so crowded.

*Even in drinks one must keep **Up-to-Date**: Stir briskly 1 oz. each rye and dry vermouth with ½ oz. Grand Marnier and 1 dash Angostura, in an Old-Fashioned glass containing 2 ice cubes. Top with a twist of lemon peel.*

FEBRUARY 24, 1809

Richard Brinsley Sheridan, the British playwright who had also long been a member of Parliament, was called out from the House of Commons this evening with the message that something belonging to him was burning. It turned out that the Drury Lane Theatre, luckily empty during Lent, was afire. At great expense to Sheridan it had been erected only 15 years before, replacing "Old Drury Lane". Tonight's news would worsen his shaky financial position; but the extravagant playwright, after hurrying over and seeing that it was now too late to save anything, repaired to a nearby watering-hole. Acquaintances marvelled at his composure. "But surely", responded Sheridan, "a man may be allowed to take a glass of wine by his own fireside?"

*Call for a **Fireman**: Shake well with cracked ice 2 oz. dark rum, ½ oz. grenadine, ½ tsp. sugar and the juice of 2 limes. Strain into a highball glass over 2 ice cubes, then top up with soda.*

FEBRUARY 25, 1899

Retired Major James Richie, now in striped-pants uniform at a large London department store, knew that rival Harrod's had recently taken delivery of a gasoline-powered Daimler delivery van. So this Saturday, he asked E.H.Sewell of The Motor-Car Company for a Daimler demonstration. Sewell was happy to show off a big open touring car to the major and three colleagues. Its effortless handling under load took them quickly up Grove Hill, in suburban Harrow. Then, as *The Times* reported, the Daimler left Harrow "at a pace that attracted attention". It particularly attracted the attention of Major Richie and his fellow-passengers, who were swept overboard as the car turned sharply into Roxteth Park Road. Sewell and the major were rewarded, however, with a plaque at the corner. It commemorates the first automobile accident in Britain to kill both driver and passenger.

*Major Richie's memory was kept alive at the Army & Navy Stores by his successor, **Major Bailey**: Muddle in the bottom of a julep glass 1 tsp. finely powdered sugar, a few drops unsweetened lime juice and some mint leaves. Fill with crushed ice, add 2 oz. dry gin and stir briskly to frost the glass.*

Alfred Ely Beach, the New York engineer who had patented a typewriter, invited politicians and journalists to inspect a larger project today. Noting the growing traffic congestion from his office opposite City Hall, Beach had leased the basement of Devlin's Clothing Store nearby to construct a trial length of subway line (but prudently omitted to seek a city license). His workmen dug until they completed a tunnel nine feet in diameter and just over 100 yards long. A rotary blower propelled the single car from one end to the other, then reversed to draw it back. To reassure his guests, Beach had the passengers' waiting room elegantly done in above-ground style, with a grand piano, fountain, goldfish tank and murals. But building owners, fearful for their foundations, threw roadblocks in Beach's way until he ran out of financing. More than 40 years later, subway constructors dug right into his waiting room. A plaque on the spot, in City Hall station, honours far-sighted Alfred Ely Beach.

*Beach's passengers enjoyed one helluva ride for 104 yards when he shouted **Blast Off** !: Shake well with cracked ice 1½ oz. Southern Comfort, 1 oz. grapefruit juice, ½ oz. lime juice, white of 1 egg and 1 tsp. sugar. Strain into a Sour glass and top with a cherry.*

Even when he stopped thrashing and screaming this morning in the bunk to which he had been tied, 21-year-old harpooner James Bartley of Gloucester, Massachusetts was unable to tell his shipmates on *Star of the East* much about life inside a whale. Off the Falklands an exceptionally large sperm bull had stove in the boat from which Bartley, standing in the bow, had harpooned it. A luck flip of the 80-footer's tail knocked him into its mouth — lucky because few sperm whales would have had a gorge large enough to slide through. Jim Bartley had been given up for dead when the 100-tonne monster was hauled aboard *Star of the East* and cut open; but there, covered in whale blood and several thousand shrimp, was the unconscious sailor. The skin of his hands, neck and face, bleached dead white by acids in the whale's stomach, never regained natural colour during Bartley's remaining 18 years; and he never went to sea again.

*Your **Atlantic Flip** is less life-threatening: Shake well together 1 oz. gin with ½ oz. each Cointreau, lemon juice and grenadine syrup, with the yolk of 1 egg. Add cracked ice, shake well again and strain into a small Old-Fashioned glass.*

FEBRUARY 28, 1844

During today Captain Stockton of the armed sloop *USS Princeton* had conducted a VIP demonstration of the huge new "Peacemaker" gun, which spat a 22-pound cannonball from its 14-foot barrel. The guests included newly-inaugurated President James Polk and his fiancée, along with Thomas W. Gilmer, Secretary of the Navy. After dinner and drinks, Gilmer went on deck. When he called for another round he was at first misunderstood, but finally the Peacemaker was reloaded too. Captain Stockton, leaving the President smooching below, came topside to fire the gun himself. Just as well that he did, since this put him directly behind the Peacemaker's trail, rather than among those standing to its port side. When the big gun's barrel burst, several spectators lost their lives and offices, including the Secretary of the Navy.

*Soften the shock with a round of **Princetons**: 1½ oz. gin, 2 tsp. port and 2 dashes orange bitters. Shake with ice and strain into a cocktail glass. Top with a twist of lemon.*

FEBRUARY 29, 1872

Arthur O'Connor, a forgetful youth, could have kicked himself when the pistol he fired at Queen Victoria turned out to be unloaded. Yard helpers were at work as the royal carriage scrunched past on the gravel outside Buckingham Palace, and the 17-year-old great-nephew of the Fenian Feargus O'Connor appeared in his street clothes to be one of them. Then he stepped forward and aimed at the Queen's head. Although her two grown sons, Arthur and Leopold, were with her, it was the faithful ghillie John Brown who grabbed O'Connor by the throat and thereby earned the only Victoria Devoted Service gold medal ever awarded. In her journal the Queen sensibly noted: "Not enough police. We shall have 3 inside the gardens".

*If this is a **Leap Year**, celebrate with a friend as Harry Craddock, the Savoy Hotel bartender, did on February 29, 1928: Shake well with cracked ice 2 oz. gin, ½ oz. each Grand Marnier and sweet vermouth, and 1 dash lemon juice. Strain into 2 cocktail glasses and twist a sliver of lemon peel over each.*

MARCH 1, 1835

Thomas Carlyle wouldn't learn the bad news for nearly a week, but most of the bulky first section of his *The French Revolution* manuscript went up in flames today. He had lent it to the young sociologist John Stuart Mill, and it had landed on the sittingroom floor of Mill's girlfriend Harriet Taylor. Her maid had used most of the pages for firelighting. At least, that was the story spread by Mrs.Carlyle after Mill visited to break the news. He suggested she go and chat with Harriet, waiting in the hansom cab, while he had a private word with her husband. Carlyle, looking out the window, had guessed an elopement was being planned; he learned different. Modern psychologists have posited that Mill, perhaps unconsciously, left the manuscript where it might be destroyed; for he had planned to write a history of the same subject. Instead, he married Harriet, while Carlyle sat down to rewrite *The French Revolution* from scratch.

*This **Classic** is meant to disappear: Shake with ice 1½ oz. brandy, and ½ oz. each lemon juice, maraschino and orange curaçao. Strain into a martini glass, adding a twist of lemon peel.*

MARCH 2, 1792

With a good sense of public relations, Dr. Joseph-Ignace Guillotin wanted his new invention to be associated in the public mind with anyone but himself. Sanson, the official executioner, and Tobias Schmidt, a clavecin maker who had submitted low bid on constructing the invention, had already declined to have their names immortalized either. So this afternoon the three of them called on the royal physician, Dr. Antoine Louis, at the Tuileries to get authoritative agreement that the mechanism should be effective but painless. Dr. Guillotin suggested that "Louison" would be a name for the invention which would bring credit on his colleague, and Dr.Louis promised to recommend it to the Chamber of Deputies. But they were both disappointed. For the remaining 22 years of Guillotin's life people would grimace and rub their necks whenever they met on the street the inventor of the Guillotine.

*Join his compatriots in giving J.I. the **Cold Shoulder**: 1 oz. brandy, ½ oz. each sweet vermouth and white crème de menthe are shaken with ice and strained into a martini glass.*

MARCH 3, 1906

Trajan Vuia, the Romanian-born inventor, didn't succeed today in making the first 100-metre flight in Europe in a heavier-than-air craft, which would have won him a substantial money prize. Nor did he get near the 25-metre mark, which would have earned him rather less. But he did have a more comfortable ride than formerly: *Vuia I* sat on a four-wheeled cart equipped with pneumatic tires — an innovative idea which had come to Trajan after finding that his projected flights were mainly runs along the ground. The bumpy fields which he had chosen as a takeoff site, at Montesson northwest of Paris, were close enough to the St.Germain forest that there was some concern about the trees. But not to worry. Two weeks of trying did get the *Vuia I* up for its longest hop ever — 13 metres. The plane destroyed itself on landing.

*This more successful **Aviator** comes in a cocktail glass: Shake with 1 ice cube 1 oz. each sweet vermouth and medium sherry. Strain into the glass and add a twist of lemon peel.*

MARCH 4, 1849

David Rice Atchison, the Senator from Missouri and president *pro tem* of the Senate, dearly needed to stay awake this Sunday to control the fate of the nation. The country's presidential term would end at noon on the 4th, as prescribed, but the President-elect, old Zachary Taylor, had decided that it would be only proper to postpone his inauguration from the Sabbath until noon tomorrow. This meant that the new Vice-President was equally unable to assume office, which under the line of succession left poor David Rice Atchison holding the bag. He would have appreciated the honour more if the Senate had not kept him in the chair all night until 7 a.m., enlivening its discussions with drink-warmed oratory and the occasional thrown punch. Terrible things were happening overseas, but fortunately the transatlantic cable had not yet been strung, so Atchison and his nation spent a peaceful 24 hours.

*Enjoy your **Sabbath Calm**: Shake with cracked ice 2 oz. cream, 1 oz. each brandy, port and black coffee, 1 egg and ½ tsp. sugar. Strain into a goblet; sprinkle with nutmeg.*

MARCH 5, 1815

Pear-shaped Louis XVIII was not disturbed today to learn that a former Emperor of France had disembarked at a Riviera port. Years of comfortable exile in great English country houses had insulated him from the dangers of Napoleon Bonaparte, successor to the revolutionaries who had cut off Louis' eldest brother's head. Now Napoleon, from his exile on the little Mediterranean island of Elba, had landed near Cannes and was gathering support as he marched north toward Paris. But Louis told a group of foreign ambassadors "This event will have as little effect upon the tranquillity of Europe as it does upon my mind." He sent Marshal Michel Ney off to bring "the Corsican" back in a cage, but Ney and his soldiers were swung by old comradeship to join Napoleon. It was Louis who had to be carried downstairs from the royal apartments in the Tuileries, his gouty foot sticking out in front, and to be hurried out of France until foreigners could again restore his reactionary monarchy after Waterloo.

*The **King's Peg** was quite long and narrow: Combine in a champagne tulip 2 ice cubes, 2 oz. brandy and 6 oz. chilled champagne. Stir gently.*

MARCH 6, 1872

Arthur Orton became himself again at the end of this 103rd day of his London court challenge to the Trustees of the Tichborne Estate. After emigrating to Australia Arthur had spotted an advertisement for information about Sir Roger Tichborne — who, everyone except his mother assumed, had been lost at sea some years ago. Arthur decided to be happier as a baronet in Britain than a butcher's helper in Wagga Wagga. He seemed well on the way after old Lady Tichborne, in a darkened sickroom, gratefully acknowledged his presence. But she soon died in a reduced mental condition, and the Trustees refused to see slim, classically educated Roger in a 330-pounder with uncertain diction. Today the jury heard the evidence of a jilted sweetheart from East End Wapping and turned Arthur down. Arrested for borrowing on pretensions, he was convicted of extortion and sentenced to 14 years. But Arthur's friends had the last word: his headstone reads "Sir Roger Charles Doughty Tichborne."

*Send Arthur back to Wagga Wagga and shake hands with a **Kangaroo**: Pour 1½ oz. vodka and ½ oz. dry vermouth over ice in a mixing glass. Stir well, strain into a cocktail glass and top with a zest of lemon.*

MARCH 7, 1914

Everything went downhill for Prince Wilhelm zu Wied after he was welcomed today at the Adriatic port of Dürres to rule the ungovernable principality of Albania. The little Balkan country, recently detached from the Ottoman Empire, was so riven by sectional differences that it had taken five foreign ambassadors weeks of leafing through the Almanach de Gotha for a sufficiently impartial Royal to put on the throne. They discovered Wilhelm in the fine print on page 527. His winning qualifications were a studied ignorance of politics and extreme hesitancy in most of the languages current in Albania. But after an uneasy five months, Wilhelm heard that World War I had started and announced that "it would be advisable for me to spend some time in the West". Six years later the Albanians elected a council of regents to look after things until their Prince should come back. But Wilhelm had lost interest: he never returned, not even to abdicate.

*Your **Adriatic** relies on that luscious liqueur from the Marasca cherries which grow on the Albanian coast: Pour 1½ oz. dry gin and ½ oz. Maraschino over ice in a small Old-Fashioned glass. Stir and drink.*

MARCH 8, 1810

The 18-year-old Austrian princess Maria-Luisa finally went through the betrothal ceremony today, despite her reservations about this divorced suitor, more than twice her age, who had chosen the eve of his previous wedding's anniversary for the occasion. For one thing he had been an officer in the French revolutionary army, while her grandmother was the now headless Marie Antoinette. The bridegroom was too important these days to travel and meet Maria-Luisa in person, but he had sent a stand-in bearing a nice present — a miniature portrait of himself framed by 16 diamonds. In return he was awaiting a substantial cash dowry. Luckily, Maria-Luisa didn't find out until later that she was Napoleon's second choice. The No.1 offer, a Russian princess, had been accompanied by such difficult territorial negotiations that Napoleon decided it would be simpler to marry someone else and just take over Russia later.

*The **Napoléon** cocktail is said to have ended his stomach-clutching pose: Shake with ice 3 oz. dry gin and 3 dashes each orange curaçao, Dubonnet and Fernet Branca bitters. Strain and sip. On to Waterloo!*

MARCH 9, 1792

Louis XVI, still managing to hang in there as *Roi des Français* nearly three years after the Revolution, watched with misplaced relief today as the friendly smith François Gamoin completed concealing an iron safe within a passage wall outside the royal bedroom in Paris' Tuileries palace. Louis, an amateur locksmith himself, had taken an interest in Gamoin's work at Versailles in the old days. Recently, though, he had been corresponding secretly with people outside the country who might invade France and overturn the Revolution. It seemed wise to hide their letters. But regrettably, the locksmith decided that publicizing this job might help his career. When 108 compromising letters were brought out as evidence against Louis, he could only remember receiving 38 of them, but numbers didn't really matter. Marie Antoinette burned her correspondence, and a lot of good it did her.

Welcome this more reliable **Royalist**: *Stir together in a Sour glass 1 oz. dry vermouth, ½ oz. each bourbon and Bénédictine, and 1 dash peach bitters. Drink straight-up.*

MARCH 10, 1890

This was Blue Monday for Henry de Groux, the Belgian painter of religious subjects. He was mortally offended while previewing a exhibition being put on by his art group, *Les Vingt*, to find one of his works hung next to some done by the inmate of a French mental asylum. Henry resigned and took his painting away, rather than be so closely associated with "an abominable pot of sunflowers" and an equally splashy picture of vines. But another member, Anna Boch, did appreciate one of them enough to pay 400 francs for *Red Vineyards at Arles*. This rather surprised its creator, Vincent van Gogh, because he had never before sold a publicly shown painting. He never would again, either. Four months later he had quit the asylum and was dead of a self-inflicted gunshot wound.

Cure a Blue Monday with a **Sombre Lundi**: *Shake well with cracked ice 1 oz. vodka, ½ oz. Cointreau and ½ oz. Parfait Amour. Strain into a chilled martini glass.*

MARCH 11, 1871

After his golden dream overnight, the Sixth Earl Poulett communicated urgently today with the champion jockey Tommy Pickernell in the hope of making it come true. In his dream the earl's horse The Lamb, with Pickernell up, had won a great steeplechase. There would be racing at Liverpool 10 days hence, when a public holiday would celebrate the wedding of Princess Louise. Luckily Pickernell was free to ride. At the end of the first circuit only 10 of the 25 starters were still running; then two horses fell in front of The Lamb, but he jumped them and finished first. This would have been far more profitable to Earl Poulett if he had not been telling everyone about his dream. By the time he placed bets on his own horse the odds had dropped and he made almost nothing.

*This **Golden Dream**'s a winner too: Shake together with ice 1 oz. each Galliano, Cointreau, orange juice and 35% cream; strain into an Old-Fashioned glass.*

MARCH 12, 1644

There was great satisfaction today for fearless, earless William Prynne as he turned the tables on Archbishop Laud, Primate of All England. Seven years earlier, outspoken Puritan Prynne had been noted for two pet peeves: the shameless way in which women cut their hair, and the power-hunger of the Church of England hierarchy. It was the latter peeve which had landed him first in court at Laud's complaint, and then in the pillory to have his ears publicly removed. This time Prynne was the prosecutor and Laud was in the dock, on trial for treason. Prynne more than evened the score: the archbishop's ears, along with the rest of his head, were soon afterwards removed by the axeman on London's Tower Hill.

*Imitate poor pilloried Prynne with a **Squarehead**: Stir 1 oz. each brandy, dry gin and sweet vermouth in a highball glass with 2 ice cubes. Fill with soda and garnish with a twist of lemon peel.*

MARCH 13, 1899

Although the Clifton suspension bridge, outside Bristol in western England, had recently been the scene of a suicide attempt, Larry Donovan knew a safe way to dive the 245 feet to the River Severn. He spread the word through the taverns of Bristol town; on several evenings those in the know crowded to the centre of the span, but coincidentally found the police patrolling it. Finally this evening, two of Larry's friends drove a pony-trap to the middle, and as it stopped a bulky form was seen toppling over the guardrail. Shortly afterward, Larry Donovan emerged on the riverbank below and asked to be taken to the infirmary, where he was pronounced in perfect health. His resilience surprised many, and must have pleased the directors of The Clifton Suspension Bridge Company. It had collected one penny per pedestrian on each occasion that Larry had publicized as the night of the dive.

You would need at least one **Bristol Bracer**: *Pour 2 oz. vodka and 1½ tbsp. undiluted, unsweetened grapefruit juice concentrate into a highball glass containing 3 ice cubes. Top up with tonic water, stir gently and add a cherry.*

MARCH 14, 1757

Insolent and self-righteous, but far from cowardly, British Admiral John Byng today knelt on a cushion on the quarter-deck of his flagship <u>Monarque</u> and was judicially executed for cowardice. His leaky, ill-provisioned warships had failed to follow a superior French force off Minorca, allowing them to capture the island and its garrison. Byng blamed his lack of supplies and repairs on King George II, who had been ordering British defence allocations to be used in Hanover, his own birthplace and other kingdom. A court-martial found Byng technically guilty, but its strong recommendation for mercy almost nullified the verdict. Still, rather than discredit the king and themselves, the government ignored the recommendation. So the "cowardly" admiral knelt to be shot, only agreeing to be blindfolded because his steady gaze was unnerving the firing squad.

No sad scenes on your **Quarter-Deck**: *Shake well with cracked ice 1½ oz. dark rum, ½ oz. sherry and 2 tsp. lemon juice. Strain into a cocktail glass.*

MARCH 15, 44 B.C.

Although this was a public holiday Julius Caesar, recently voted *Dictator Perpetuo* by Rome's Senate, had asserted his power by calling a meeting of its members for today. Arriving, he was pleased to note the large attendance, with most senators even carrying their little leather-sheathed styli in case there might be wax documents to sign. What Caesar couldn't note was that several had replaced their styli with even sharper instruments. His young fourth wife, Calpurnia, had urged Big Julie to heed the warning of a soothsayer, and only this morning the academic Artemidoros had told him to watch out. Caesar paid no attention. Now, as Senator Lucius Cimber presented a petition he reached chummily around the chief's shoulder and stabbed him in the back. Other members of the anti-dictator group joined in with enthusiasm. Most of them soon regretted it: Caesar's death plunged Rome into 13 years of civil war.

*This **Bloody Caesar** is far from fatal: Shake well with ice 1½ oz. each vodka, tomato juice and clam juice, 1 tbsp. lemon juice, 5 drops Worcestershire and 2 drops Tabasco. Strain and serve straight up in a Sour glass; add 1 dash each salt and pepper.*

MARCH 16, 1914

Perhaps foreseeing that any French jury would take a sympathetic view of her *crime passionel*, Parisienne Henriette Rainouard Cailloux today eliminated troublesome, sharp-penned editor Gaston Calmette, of the daily *Le Figaro*. The loyal young second wife of the minister of finance had been upset by the newspaper's continual attacks on her husband's honesty and general morality; her indignation peaked when *Le Figaro* promised a "comic interlude" which she suspected would include her letters to Cailloux before his first wife divorced him. When a lawyer told her no court action would be possible until the letters were published, Henriette took matters into her own hands, along with a revolver. After a little target practice in the basement, she went off to the *Figaro* office, confronted the nuisance and shot him, getting four of six rounds into the target. The jury let Henriette go free; and the letters were never published.

*Try one shot with the **French 75**: Shake with ice ½ oz. each gin and lemon juice and ½ tsp. sugar syrup. Strain into a champagne tulip containing 2 ice cubes, and top up with chilled champagne.*

MARCH 17, 1909

Because soldiers of Britain's Irish Guards were celebrating an important anniversary today, they missed the other Guards regiments' field exercise, the least arduous one ever — it involved no marching. The War Office had been persuaded by motoring enthusiasts, led by Colonel Arthur Du Cros,MP, to try a troop movement from London to the island's invasion-prone south coast. Owners of 286 cars, mostly open tourers, drove in convoy, wearing the necessary goggles, gloves and furlined overcoats. The troops made do with standard uniforms, but at least they had been instructed to hold down their peaked caps with the recently introduced chinstrap. Following the convoy were 20 Napier trucks to take care of "the plentiful mishaps and punctures which are the life of the road". None of the trucks broke down, which pleased Colonel Du Cros immensely — his family firm, distributors of Napiers, sold them to the Army.

*The **Colonel Chinstrap** won't blow your cap off: Stir in a lowball glass 1 oz. vodka, ½ oz. each Mandarine liqueur and sweet vermouth, 1 dash lemon juice and 1 ice cube. Decorate with 1 slice each orange and lemon.*

MARCH 18, 1847

Tough economic times reached a new low point this morning for Henri-Clément Sanson, Executioner of Criminal Judgments in Paris. He had inherited from his father and grandfather the prestigious appointment to pull the string on the guillotine, but over the past seven years there had only been 18 of the short-order jobs — hardly enough to keep body and head together. Now the authorities were telling Henri to have the equipment ready for another one tomorrow. This would bring in 3500 francs, <u>if</u> he could just get the guillotine back: he was so far in debt that a major creditor had taken it as security. So Henri went to the Palais de Justice and asked for a cash advance. The Minister of Justice, who knew how much it cost to keep a prisoner fed, okayed the payment. Sanson reclaimed his machine, the event went off successfully and almost everyone concerned felt better.

*Fight back with a **Corpse Reviver**: Shake well with cracked ice ½ oz. each brandy, white crème de menthe and Fernet Branca bitters. Strain into a martini glass.*

MARCH 19, 1831

A bright idea had struck English immigrant Edward Smith, but today it struck back. Commercial banks with vaults were in their infancy, and nobody in the United States had yet gotten around to doing what Edward did: make a key to fit the door of New York's City Bank, then break into its vault and take the money. In the unlikely event of being caught, he would use the clever alias of "James Smith" so that his own name would remain untarnished. Everything went well and Edward (or James, as it turned out) managed to run through nearly $60,000 of the $245,000 he had found waiting in the bank, before his spectacular spending habits inspired questions. These were followed by a trial, ending in today's sentence of five years' hard labour in Sing Sing.

*Your **Long Green** will be more honestly made than James's (or even Edward's): Pour 2 oz. crème de menthe over ice cubes in a highball glass. Fill with soda and stick in a sprig of mint.*

MARCH 20, 1857

Before finding anything to criticize in their recently-deceased neighbour Samuel Zimmerman, other leading citizens of Clifton, Ontario gathered today to memorialize his "dreadful and untimely fate". This had resulted when Sam, a Pennsylvania-born banker and railway entrepreneur, was seated aboard the train from Toronto last week when it plunged through the trestle bridge over the Desjardins Canal. The memorializers innocently attributed the disaster, in which 58 other people had also been carried to their death, to "the melancholy dispensation of an inscrutable Providence". In plainer language it turned out that Zimmerman, as prime contractor for the railway's construction, had settled for substandard timbers which broke under the unusually heavy train. The directors of the Zimmerman Bank (not, one assumes, in a reference to divine retribution) ascribed the boss's demise to an "Act of God".

*This **Bridge** won't let you down: Pour over 2 ice cubes 1½ oz. white rum and 1 oz. each dry vermouth and pineapple juice. Stir in 1 tsp. grenadine syrup; strain into a martini glass.*

MARCH 21, 1829

The Duke of Wellington, who had been used to conducting battles with massed artillery, was faced with a more personal test of marksmanship this morning. Recently, as Prime Minister, he had challenged his political opponent Lord Winchilsea to a duel; rather than kill him, the Duke hoped to crease his leg. "Dammit, don't put him so near the ditch!", he shouted, afraid that Winchilsea might topple in and drown. But when the order to fire was given, Wellington saw that his opponent had kept his hand at his side. Declining to aim straight in such circumstances, the Duke fired wide, tipped his hat to the seconds and to his opponent, mounted his horse and cantered away.

*Just say **Bang!**: Stir in a pot, over low heat, 1 pint each hard cider and warm brown ale. Add 4 oz. sugar, 2 oz. Scotch and 2 tsp. powdered ginger; stir again and pour into warmed mugs.*

MARCH 22, 1820

Commodore Stephen Decatur, American hero for his wartime and anti-pirate exploits, and now in middle age a member of the Board of Naval Commissioners, today showed his final contempt for fellow-Commodore James Barron. Having been suspended from active duty for allowing British officers to remove deserters from his frigate *Chesapeake,* Barron now suspected Decatur of blocking his return; he had been provoked by the Commissioner's sneering disclaimers into challenging him to a duel. In a Maryland gully just across the District of Columbia line, they faced each other at only eight paces distance — agreed by Decatur because his older opponent was so nearsighted. But meanwhile Barron's eyesight had improved, for he got his man first shot. Stephen Decatur died content at 41, no doubt: he had recently told a friend, "I shall feel ashamed to die in bed".

*Nearsighted or not, you can score a **Bullseye**: Pour 2 oz. hard cider and 1 oz. brandy into a highball glass containing 2 ice cubes. Fill with ginger ale and stir gently.*

MARCH 23, 1743

Some Christian spokesmen had protested at the blasphemy of presenting George-Frideric Handel's new "Sacred Oratorio" this evening on a London stage usually reserved for frivolous plays, but King George II of England was determined to attend. *Messiah* had been sung only in a small Dublin theatre, while today's performance had been booked in the Theatre Royal. However, it lasted longer than the king expected; after nearly two hours he felt the need to find a bathroom, and stood up. Many other members of the audience thought it only respectful for them to rise also, and soon everyone was standing. At that moment the chorus burst into their triumphal Hallelujah Chorus. The king, mistakenly thinking that this signalled the approaching end of the oratorio, decided to wait on his feet. Ever since, British audiences have commemorated the incident by standing during the Hallelujah Chorus.

*Your **Oratorio** is happily much shorter: Stir with ice cubes in a jug, 1 oz. vodka and ½ oz. each Dubonnet and orange curaçao. Strain into a chilled martini glass.*

MARCH 24, 1910

Half the populace of Venice seemed to be crowding the steps of the Assize Court this morning, awaiting in vain the arrival of a Russian aristocrat who had been called as a character witness for his wife. The voluptuous Countess Marie Tarnowska was on trial for using one lover to help her dispose of two others. Arranging her divorce, her lawyer had unwisely fallen for his client. They took out heavy life insurance on Count Paul Komarowsky, then convinced lovesick young Nicholas Naumoff that Marie was about to ditch him for the older man. Naumoff obligingly tracked him to Venice and shot him. But under arrest the youth told all. If, incredibly, Marie's husband had agreed to appear as a character witness, she surely would still have ended in the Trani penitentiary, watched over by nuns. After doing her time, Countess Tarnowska was banished from Italy, where such trifling in matters of the heart is unacceptable.

*Join in the **Carnival of Venice**: Stir with ice 1 oz. dry gin and ¼ oz. each Grand Marnier, Campari and dry vermouth. Strain into a chilled cocktail glass and add a cherry.*

MARCH 25, 1844

This Monday morning Phineas T. Barnum was pleased to see that his American chutzpah had paid off with a promotion in Britain's prestigious Court Circular, which lists the royal family's appointments and distinguished visitors. After showing off the Connecticut midget "General Tom Thumb" at Buckingham Palace on the weekend, Barnum asked the official who wrote the Court Circular if he was getting a listing. Rather taken aback, the functionary suggested that Barnum try drafting it himself. Thus readers of today's *Times* found, sandwiched between "The Royal Dinner Party" and "A Cabinet Council", a puff for Tom Thumb's "clever imitations of Napoleon" which had "elicited the approbation of Her Majesty and the Royal Circle". Thenceforth Barnum advertised "General Tom Thumb's Farewell Levées under the PATRONAGE of The QUEEN".

*Good luck with your **Barnum**: Combine 1½ oz. gin, ½ oz. apricot brandy, ½ tsp. lemon juice and 2 dashes Angostura. Shake well, then pour over shaved ice in a brandy snifter.*

MARCH 26, 1699

Willem Bosman, a Dutch trading-post manager on the Guinea Coast, assumed that his readers were unlikely to meet the animal which, until today, no other European had recorded seeing. He felt free to describe the furry West African mammal as "the most disagreeable-looking in the whole Earth", adding that he couldn't look at it without shuddering. Just what it was about *Periodicticus Potto* — a shy and slow-moving tree climber — that roused Bosman to such insults is hard to tell. Perhaps he was turned off by the potto's vertebrae, which stick out through the skin of its back. On the other hand it may have been simple envy, since a potto can do several tricks that Bosman couldn't, such as sleeping rolled up on a branch. And what *Periodicticus* thought of Willem Bosman's looks is not on record.

*Nothing disagreeable about **The Jungle** when you share it with an attractive companion: Stir with 1 ice cube 2 oz. dry gin, and 1½ oz. each sweet vermouth and medium sherry. Strain into chilled martini glasses.*

MARCH 27, 1902

Several hundred wealthy Chicagoans were flattered to receive in today's mail an invitation bearing the British royal coat of arms. It bade them attend the coronation of Edward VII, then scheduled for June, and was accompanied by a card of instruction about dress for the ceremony in Westminster Abbey. "Peers of the Realm will wear capes of crimson velvet edged with minever", and so on down the ranks. Of particular interest in Chicago would be the category "Titled Nobility of America": Merchant Princes, Coal Barons and Lords of Finance. These should carry, respectively, tape measures, coal scuttles and stock tickers, and wear "golf capes edged with two and one-half rows of rabbit skin." By now the guests might be excused for a certain scepticism, which hardened when they read the punchline. Toasts to the newly crowned monarch should be drunk in whiskey from Denehey's, a Chicago distiller.

Denehey's is difficult to find now, so your toast is a **Royal Smirk:** *Shake with cracked ice 1 oz. each dry gin, applejack, grenadine and lemon juice. Strain into a small Old-Fashioned glass and decorate with a cherry.*

MARCH 28, 1888

Carrying the telegram for London, Captain Herbert Ward today saluted his expedition commander and stepped into the canoe on the Upper Congo. It would take four months to bring an answer via São Thomé on the coast, but that didn't matter to Major Edmund Musgrave Barttelot, an impatient martinet. Tired of waiting to meet an Anglo-American exploration team, he was only going through the motions of asking permission to go find them. By the time Captain Ward returned with London's refusal, the major's search party was hundreds of miles away. But his impatience proved his undoing. At 4 o'clock one morning a Manyema porter's wife began beating a drum to celebrate the Festival of the Moon. Armed with the steel-tipped cane which he used to prod people who upset him, Major Barttelot rushed into her tent, bellowed "This drumming must stop!", and was promptly despatched by the woman's husband with a well-aimed bullet.

Jungle Juice calls for exotic ingredients: 1½ oz. Pisang Ambon, ½ oz. each Genevers gin and Mandarine liqueur are well stirred in a highball glass with 2 ice cubes, 3 oz. orange juice and 3 dashes lemon juice. Decorate with a slice of fresh pineapple and a cherry.

MARCH 29, 1848

Before leaving his mills on the Niagara River this evening, James Clark Street made his regular inspection of the machinery which activated the production of flour, lumber and woollen cloth. Street was rather proud of his inherited business, which in 1786 had been the first to make commercial use of the water on the Canadian side of the river. But he discovered that the wheels were not turning at anything like the normal rate. Indeed, by 5 a.m. the millrace was empty. Then it dawned on James Clark Street that ice had jammed Lake Erie where it debouches into the Niagara. It stayed that way for 30 hours, while locals picked relics of the War of 1812 from the dry riverbed. Then with a great rumble the ice-jam broke; Niagara Falls, and Street's mills, rolled again.

*The **Icebreaker** takes only 15 seconds to get things flowing smoothly: Combine in a blender 2 oz. each tequila and grapefruit juice, 1 tbsp. grenadine, 2 tsp. Cointreau and a little crushed ice. Blend for 15 seconds and strain into a 5-oz. Sour glass.*

MARCH 30, 1858

Turning five years old today, Vincent Willem van Gogh was put through an embarrassing annual ceremony by his parents. When their first-born had died some years before, Theodorus and Wilhelmina van Gogh had decided that their next boy should bear the same names. Coincidentally, the new Vincent Willem came into the world on his deceased brother's birthday. Every Sunday he could not fail to notice the first Vincent's grave: Theodorus, as pastor of the little Protestant church of Groot Zundert, had chosen a place right next to the church door. But today was special — the official anniversary visit by the family to the grave of Vincent Willem van Gogh. It was a birthday treat that his namesake never forgot.

*Wish the young man a **Happy Birthday**: Build into a highball glass nearly full of cracked ice 1 oz. Genevers gin, ¼ oz. pale rum, and 2 dashes each Triple Sec, peach juice and pineapple juice. Top with champagne and a slice of lemon.*

MARCH 31,1889

In a unique topping-off gesture at 2 o'clock this afternoon, the energetic engineer Gustave Eiffel, who had just climbed the north pier steps of his new tower in half an hour, proudly unfurled a 25-foot-long *tricolore* flag. Emile Chautemps, president of the Paris municipal council, and a few others strong of wind and muscle, saluted. But across town, despair rose in the heart of author Guy de Maupassant, who had called the Eiffel Tower "this giant skeleton, casting its long shadow like an ink-blot" over his city's beauty. Now, already showing signs of the syphilitic *folie de grandeur* which would put him in an asylum, Maupassant suggested that one might visit the tower's restaurant "out of disgust and curiosity, to eat the canteen-like food amid the mingled sweat of the common herd scattering their fleas".

*To foam at the mouth Maupassant-style, mix a **French Foam**: Combine in a highball glass ¼ oz. each brandy and kirsch, 1½ tsp. sugar syrup and 3 drops Angostura. Stir well, add a scoop of lemon sherbet and fill with iced champagne.*

APRIL 1, 1903

This was the day of final disappointment for Emma and Etta Wrong, the aeronautic pioneers of Canada's east coast. They had come from Naufrage, New Brunswick to the remote Newfoundland promontory of Doggie Prey to test their first self-propelled flying machine. With the equipage of willow and gutta-percha fully assembled, they headed it into the west wind. The sisters had hired Homer Nodds, the Burin Peninsula Strongman, to wind the propeller, for the power unit of fully-stressed elastic bands could snap it back to break an arm. But they forgot one thing: to hold down the fuselage. When Homer paused for breath, the double-knotted rubber exerted all its force. He held on tight to the propeller; the machine began turning over, crushing both wings. Soon a pile of splintered willow and limp rubber bands lay on the cliff top. Sadly, the Wrong sisters told Homer to push it over the edge. They couldn't remake the aircraft before December 14 (q.v.), and resigned themselves to having the episode related as an APRIL FOOL.

*The **Newfie Bullet** goes down fast: Stir ½ oz. each lemon juice and honey; add 2 oz. each dark rum and shaved ice. Mix well, strain into a small Old-Fashioned glass and top with a cranberry (that's the bullet).*

APRIL 2, 1801

Vice-Admiral Horatio Nelson was rightly miffed today when Admiral Sir Hyde Parker, commanding their operation against the Danish fleet off Copenhagen, hoisted Signal 39, "Cease Action". As an order for his own vanguard squadron Nelson had just run up Signal 16, "Engage More Closely". Since joining the Royal Navy at the age of 12, he had earned a reputation in 104 engagements for winning battles while losing an arm and most of the sight in one eye. Now, with his remaining left hand Horatio raised a telescope and declared "I am allowed to be blind — I don't see the signal". Although four ships, including his own, ran aground, the enemy fared even worse: their flagship blew up. In the truce that was called, the Danes agreed to stay in port for 14 weeks; by then an armistice had been signed. Admiral Parker was relieved of his command and Horatio Nelson named in his place.

*You may drink the **Bloody Nelson** with one eye closed: Put in a shaker with cracked ice 1 oz. each dark rum and Southern Comfort, 2 oz. sweetened lemon juice and 1 dash grenadine. Shake well and strain into a cocktail glass.*

APRIL 3, 1863

Setting a world record in his moccasins but losing today's 12-mile run on handicap, the 37-year-old native American Deerfoot regretted having given 100 yards to the much younger Yorkshire farmer Lang, known as "The Crowcatcher". In a period when Victorian newspapers were chary of publicizing a professional race on Good Friday, only a handful of spectators turned up at London's Brompton track. Deerfoot, who had perfected his seven-foot stride in upstate New York using his other name Louis Bennet, overtook Lang but faltered at the end to lose by just half a yard. Second prize was only five pounds sterling, but Deerfoot's one-hour distance of 11 miles 970 yards remained a world record for 90 years more.

*Close the gap with **Half a Yard of Flannel**: Beat 2 eggs with 1½ oz. sugar in a wide-mouthed pitcher. Add 2 oz. dark rum, and 1 dash each ground nutmeg and ginger. Stir well. Heat 2 pints of ale without boiling, then slowly stir into the mixture. Pour into pre-warmed mugs.*

APRIL 4, 1865

U.S. Major-General George H. Stoneman was used to having his orders obeyed right down the line of his Civil War cavalry division, but today he suffered a small psychological reverse as the advancing Union army left Mount Airy, North Carolina. Seeking to draft an auxiliary labour force, General Stoneman had a lottery drum prepared for the names of all male residents of Surry County aged 18 and over. One of the draftees was 53-year-old tobacco farmer Eng Bunker; his twin brother Chang, more fortunate, escaped having his name drawn. This posed a problem for the Army because the Bunkers were the original Siamese Twins, now retired from exhibition. Not even General Stoneman planned to sever the six-inch band of flesh which united them. Luckily the Civil War was drifting to its end, thus reducing the likelihood of drafting other Siamese twins.

*A **Twin Sin** is surprisingly acceptable: Combine with ice 1 oz. gin, 1 egg white, 2 tsp. each sweet vermouth and orange juice, and 3 dashes grenadine. Shake well and strain over 1 ice cube into a small Old-Fashioned glass.*

APRIL 5, 1795

Fleshy, fastidious George, Prince of Wales had reluctantly accepted having his official marriage arranged with a suitable princess, in this case his first cousin Caroline of Brunswick, whom he had never met. Putting aside thoughts of Maria Fitzherbert, to whom he was already secretly married, George waited in London today for his fiancée's coach to arrive from Greenwich. He might not have been so resigned to the match had he known that his equerry, Lord Malmesbury had just discovered that the princess lack breath appeal — due no doubt to her habit of chewing on a raw onion. Now, when at last Caroline entered and knelt before him, the Prince raised her and very briefly embraced her. Rapidly withdrawing several paces, he whispered to an aide, "I am not well; pray get me a glass of brandy". Then he bolted from the room. "My God!", the princess exclaimed to Malmesbury, "is he always like this?" He was, and she was, and after four months they separated forever.

Prince George's Cocktail helps to make other people more appealing: Combine with ice 1½ oz. light rum, 1 tbsp. Grand Marnier and 2 tsp. lime juice with ice. Shake and strain into a cocktail glass; add a twist of lemon.

APRIL 6, 1896

King George of the Hellenes, although not a Greek by birth, had a patriotic idea to raise the international standing of his country's athletes. Today he was to inaugurate the first running of the Olympic Games since 394, but before doing so he took the opportunity to celebrate the 75th anniversary of Greece's successful revolt for independence from Turkey. This had the happy result of alienating the Ottoman government. George's Olympic committee would not have to entertain any Turkish athletes, and that would ensure that no Turk placed ahead of a Greek in the Games. The athletes who did turn up came from 10 foreign countries and they beat the Greeks in most events, but there was not a Turk among them. Next year Turkey got its revenge by beating Greece in a one-month war. It was a non-Olympic year.

*Everyone benefits from the **Esprit Olympique**: Shake well with ice 2 oz. brandy, 1 oz. each vodka and orange juice, and ¼ oz. Triple Sec. Strain into an Old-Fashioned glass.*

APRIL 7, 1784

Living in Florence with an unrecognized king had lost its appeal for Louise-Caroline-Maximilienne-Emmanuelle, nominal Queen of Scotland and England; so she welcomed the arrival today of official permission to cease sharing bed and board with the sagging, hard-drinking 63-year-old ex-Bonnie Prince Charlie. Even after an enforced 38-year holiday abroad, her husband managed to retain his hauteur: "WE, Charles, legitimate King of Great Britain, on the representations made to Us ... that she wished to reside at a distance separated from Our Person ... do permit her to live in any town she may consider convenient." Louise had, as it happened, already left Florence for Rome, where her young poet friend Count Vittorio Alfieri was much more fun, besides knowing how to write in the first person singular.

*Charles solaced his retinue with **Florentine Punch**: Chill two bottles each rosé and marsala, 1 bottle brandy and 4 oz. lemon juice. Pour them over an ice block in a punchbowl. Add 2 oranges thinly sliced. Stir well and refrigerate for 1 hour before serving.*

APRIL 8, 1826

John Randolph of Roanoke, the patrician senator from Virginia, wished he hadn't worn such a thick buckskin glove for his duel today with Henry Clay, whom he had provoked by describing him as "So brilliant, yet so corrupt, that like a rotten mackerel by moonlight he shines and stinks." Randolph's second, Colonel Tattnall, had already pulled the hair-trigger safety catch on the pistol, so the moment Randolph grasped it the bullet fired, just missing his own right foot. Clay's second, General Jessup, thought this a good reason to call off the duel and save his principal's life: firing before the signal was a definite no-no, even if sometimes rather effective. The duel went ahead, but only after Clay had told Randolph "I would not hurt you for the world", leaving people to wonder what the duel was for. They both missed.

*This **Flintlock** will merely warm you: Combine with cracked ice in a mixing glass 1½ oz. bourbon, ½ oz. calvados, 1 tsp. lemon juice and 1 dash each grenadine and white crème de menthe. Shake well and strain into a small Old-Fashioned glass.*

APRIL 9, 1747

Reputed to possess the shortest neck in Scotland, 80-year-old Simon Fraser, eleventh Lord Lovat, underwent a special custom-fitting before today's event in London. The high-shouldered Highland chieftain had encouraged rebellion in the Stuart cause against the British throne, which now seated Hanoverians exclusively. Worse, at his Castle Dounie the clan chief had sheltered the fleeing Bonnie Prince Charlie, the very night after last year's disastrous defeat at Culloden. So today Lord Lovat was on his brief public journey from the Tower of London to Tower Hill, where a special execution block had been carved to accommodate his short neck. En route, a viewing stand collapsed and many spectators were injured. "The more mischief, the more sport!", cried the incorrigible rebel lord.

*High spirits can be caused by **Ould Mon's Nourrishment**: Mix 2 oz. Scotch and 7 oz. thin cream in a mixing-glass; add 1 lightly beaten egg and 1 tsp. icing sugar. Shake with shaved ice, strain into a highball glass; sprinkle with freshly grated nutmeg.*

APRIL 10, 1750

On the rare occasions when English champion Jack Broughton lost a boxing match he was a game loser, but after today's event he discovered that his principal backer was a poor sport. The royal Duke of Cumberland liked to see people beaten up, and his enjoyment was heightened if he had bet against them. In this case Jack Slack of Norfolk had challenged the champion. The duke was used to Broughton winning and placed his money accordingly. But the match was barely under way when Slack conked the champion so hard between the eyes that he was temporarily blinded; in 14 minutes it was all over. The Duke of Cumberland claimed that Broughton had thrown the fight, and withdrew the financial support that kept the ex-champion's fisticuffs academy going. But Broughton had the last laugh, if a little late — his appreciative countrymen buried him in Westminster Abbey.

*Jack Slack's **Powerhouse Punch** should be distributed among several guests: Dissolve in a jampan 8 oz. sugar in 1 qt. water; add 1 bottle each white rum and brandy, 1 qt. lemon juice and 3 oz. apricot brandy. Stir well, let stand for at least 1 hour, then pour over ice in a punchbowl.*

APRIL 11, 1889

Thomas A. Edison's agent in London, Colonel Gouraud, was anxious to corral well-known British men of letters to speak into the newly developed phonograph. He was concentrating on those who didn't appear to have long to live; today's effort with 77-year-old Robert Browning resulted in a memorable recording but only partial success. The poet, although ailing and sliding toward his death later in the year, still came to the studio determined to recite all 60 lines of *How they brought the good news from Ghent to Aix.* "Ready?", went his recorded enquiry, and then he launched into

"I sprang to the stirrup, and Joris, and he;
I galloped, Dirck galloped, we galloped all three......"

The aged poet's voice faltered. "I forget it", he said.

*A **Potted Parrot** could have recited it better: Shake well together 2 oz. each white rum and orange juice with 1 oz. lemon juice, 2 tsp. orange curaçao and 1 tsp. each almond extract and sugar syrup. Strain into a 5-oz. Sour glass over cracked ice and garnish with a sprig of mint.*

APRIL 12, 1858

Celebrating the completion of renovations at his licensed establishment this evening, Torontonian John Quinn didn't exclude himself when ordering several rounds on the house. It took the barman some time to convince John that the wild spring storm raging outside was actually rocking the building, for it had once been the substantial summer residence of Governor-General Lord Sydenham. But Quinn's Hotel sat on a sandy peninsula jutting out into Toronto Harbour; soon water began seeping over the doorsills, and the prudent innkeeper joined his guests on a hasty return to the city. Next morning, coming out to survey the damage, Quinn couldn't find his hotel. It had been replaced by a 500-foot-wide channel separating the mainland from the newly created Toronto Island.

*Let the **Spring Tide** wash your cares away: Stir with ice 2 oz. dry vermouth and 4 oz. cranberry juice. Strain into a small Old-Fashioned glass and top with a strawberry.*

APRIL 13, 1868

Her Britannic Majesty's consul, Charles Cameron, was finally delivered from Ethiopian house arrest today by the gallant Lieutenant-General Sir Robert Napier, who rather than travel alone had brought along 12,000 soldiers, 5,018 mules and ponies, 1,839 camels and nearly as many pack-bullocks. Learning that Ethiopia's ill-tempered King Theodore was keeping Cameron in the mountain stronghold of Magdala, Queen Victoria had written to say that she was not amused, but Cameron was too scared of the king to show him the letter. Then two Foreign Office functionaries were sent to find out why their queen had received no reply. Theodore seized them too. General Napier, having taken eight months to arrive, had the good grace to sit down and write a long letter. The Queen created him Lord Napier of Magdala.

*Hard to believe that the general would have chosen this mixture to represent **Empire Glory**, but there you are: Shake with ice 2 oz. rye, 1 oz. each lemon juice and ginger wine and 2 dashes grenadine syrup. Strain into a chilled cocktail glass.*

APRIL 14, 1852

Herbert Spencer, the editor of *The Economist* who had yet to make his name as a philosopher, was deemed to have failed today in an important life project. He executed the first step correctly, dropping on one knee before his companion, Mary Ann Evans. The place Herbert had chosen, a terrace overlooking the Thames, was shaded by trees but in clear view of the government offices in Somerset House. From its windows, clerks of the Excise Office followed the game, and soon it was apparent that Herbert had lost. Mary Ann, who would be better known as the novelist George Eliot, went off and lived with someone else's husband. In later life, as an old bachelor, Herbert would deny that she had turned down a formal proposal. But the clerks pointed to a fatal omission in the role-playing: in his nervousness, Herbert had forgotten to remove his hat.

*This **Spencer** is usually successful: Shake well together 1 oz. gin, ½ oz. apricot brandy and 1 dash each orange juice and Angostura bitters. Strain into a cocktail glass; add a cherry and a zest of orange.*

APRIL 15, 1912

It had been <u>such</u> a tiring morning for Henry Sleeper Harper, scion of the American publishing family. First, the steward on the liner to New York had insisted that Henry get up at the Godawful hour of 1:30 a.m. to climb into a lifeboat, along with his Pekinese dog Sun-Yat Sen and the Sudanese servant Hamad Hassah, who had been Henry's impulse purchase in Egypt. Then, an uncomfortable several hours rocking about in mid-Atlantic had done nothing for his digestion. Now they couldn't see the *Titanic* any more, and the sleep-starved Mr. Harper was being dumped in a deck chair aboard the *Carpathia*, a decidedly inferior vessel. But walking toward him and looking well breakfasted was his New York friend and fellow socialite, Louis Ogden. Harper rose to the occasion: "Louis!" he exclaimed. "How do you keep yourself looking so young?"

*Only denizens of the first-class bar made the **Passenger List**: Shake well with cracked ice ½ oz. each of brandy, dry gin, green Chartreuse and Parfait Amour, plus 1 dash Pernod. Strain into a cocktail glass.*

APRIL 16, 1821

Napoleon Bonaparte, rewriting his will today as a prisoner on Saint Helena while suffering from hepatitis, fainting fits and a diet rich in mercury, still had enough spirit to outwit the British authorities. Calling him General instead of Emperor, they insisted that his dynasty had ended. So for public consumption Napoleon wrote a will leaving his belongings on the island to three senior aides. But he really wanted his 10-year-old son Napoleon, nicknamed *l'Aiglon* (The Eaglet), to inherit Napoleonic glory. In a secret codicil, to be opened by his aides only after they left Saint Helena, he wrote: "I gave everything ....to Bertrand, Montholon and Marchand. It was a device to foil the English. I wish my effects to be disposed of as follows.....". Napoleon died three weeks later, leaving to his son the Sword of Austerlitz which he had carried at that bloody victory on the first anniversary of his coronation.

*Excellent for a mercurial stomach is the **Digestif Impérial**: to 1½ oz. dry gin add 2 dashes each curaçao and Dubonnet, and ½ oz. Fernet Branca digestive. Shake with ice, strain into a cocktail glass; top with zest of lemon.*

APRIL 17, 1907

Louis Botha, Prime Minister of the Transvaal, was noted chatting at length with Winston Churchill before tonight's dinner in London, where the Prince and Princess of Wales were entertaining delegates to the Imperial Conference at Marlborough House. General Botha now held an honorary commission in the British Army, but eight years earlier he had headed a commando of Boers fighting the British in South Africa. In heavy rain his men had ambushed a supply train near Estcourt; among their prisoners was a young English newspaper correspondent — Winston Churchill. By now Churchill was in his thirties and a rising member of Parliament, Under-Secretary for the Colonies. Another guest asked whether the two had met in South Africa. "Ah yes", replied Botha, "he and I have been out together in all weathers!"

*A more cheering **April Shower** is made as follows: Pour 1 oz. each cognac and Bénédictine over 2 ice cubes in a tall glass. Stir in 2 oz. orange juice, top up with soda and serve with a straw.*

APRIL 18, 1906

When he arrived in San Francisco as a guest star of the touring Metropolitan Opera, Enrico Caruso installed himself and his valet in the newly-completed Palace Hotel, said to be the most expensive in town. So he was understandably a bit miffed when, at 5 o'clock this morning, the $7 million establishment began to quiver. For more than a minute it was rocked by the San Francisco Earthquake; Caruso, discovered clinging to his valet, was led down to the street with only one suitcase from his uninsured travelling wardrobe. The Met lost most of its props, cancelled this afternoon's performance of "Carmen" and had to stop the tour. Caruso received his full contract payment; but while sitting on his suitcase in the street he vowed never to return to San Francisco, and he never did.

*The **Earthquake** should be shaken like Caruso's hotel: Combine 1½ oz. tequila, 1 tsp. grenadine syrup, 2 dashes orange bitters and 3 oz. crushed ice. Shake, strain into a highball glass, add ice and top up with soda. Garnish with a sprig of mint.*

APRIL 19, 1861

Professor Thaddeus Lowe, who had really only wanted to test wind-flows, ended up in jail this evening, tired and puzzled. Lifting off from Cincinnati under the huge gas-filled *Enterprise*, Lowe had hoped the prevailing wind would carry him to Philadelphia. When instead, nine hours later, he landed at Pea Ridge, South Carolina, he found that President Lincoln had declared a blockade of the South and that the Civil War was under way. Luckily a local official who knew Lowe from college days vouched for the professor's harmlessness, sprung him from arrest and secured him a safe-conduct back North. Lowe got his own back on the Rebels by having himself attached to General McLellan's army as "Chief Aeronaut". From captive balloons, his team spotted enemy troop movements and telegraphed ranging instructions to Union artillery officers on the ground.

*If a balloonist asks **Which Way?**, here's the answer: shake well with ice ½ oz. each Pernod, brandy and anisette, then strain into a chilled cocktail glass.*

APRIL 20, 1775

Only this morning could Israel Bissel convince the inhabitants of Worcester, Massachusetts that the American Revolution really had begun. Yesterday he had been confident of carrying a vital message all the way from Watertown to New York City. Entrusted to Izzy by a member of the colonists' Committee of Safety, the message related that British regulars had fired on Massachusetts militiamen at Lexington and were on their way to seek out weapons stashed at Concord by rebellious citizens. All true patriots were enjoined to supply the messenger with fresh mounts as he needed them. Unforeseeably last night, as Bissel entered Worcester 38 miles from home, his horse dropped dead of a heart attack. In vain did Izzy try to exchange it for a live one: there were no suckers in Worcester. He had to wait overnight.

*This **New England Stirrup Cup** might have helped him convince a party of eight: Dissolve 3 tbsp. brown sugar in 3 tbsp. water. Over a block of ice in a punchbowl, pour the sugar syrup, 12 oz. golden rum, 6 oz. pineapple juice and 3 oz. lime juice. Stir well; ladle into highball glasses containing shaved ice. Garnish with spirals of lemon and serve with straws.*

APRIL 21, 1894

Reginald Golding Bright, an aspiring playwright, got back at George Bernard Shaw tonight, but even then Shaw enjoyed the last word. Shaw, already a well-known critic, had given Bright his unfavourable opinion of a play submitted for comment. Now Shaw himself had turned to playwriting and was assured of a stage for his *Man and Superman* at London's Avenue Theatre. Throughout tonight's première, hissing seemed to come from the gallery where Bright sat. When the curtain came down, calls of "Author!" brought Shaw to the stage amid loud applause. When it died, Bright could be heard shouting "Boo!" Shaw bowed in his direction: "I quite agree with you, sir, but what can we two do against so many?" Later, finding that the culprit was an acquaintance, Shaw claimed that he had addressed him as "my dear fellow".

*For an unopposed **Opening**, shake well with ice 1 oz. Canadian whisky and ½ oz. each grenadine and sweet vermouth; strain into a chilled cocktail glass.*

APRIL 22, 1846

Benjamin Haydon, the painter of vast heroic canvases who had confided to his diary "I am of the Napoleon species", reacted angrily to the discovery that a midget (dressed, coincidentally, as Napoleon) was out-drawing his London exhibition of classical scenes in the ratio of 120 to 1. The advertisement he placed in today's *Times* sarcastically praised "the exquisite feeling of the English people for High Art .... B.R. Haydon, who has devoted 42 years to elevate their taste, was honoured by the visits of 133½, being a reward for two of his finest works". Charles Dickens, who had visited both concurrent shows at the Egyptian Hall in Piccadilly, wrote when Haydon committed suicide a short time later: "No amount of sympathy ought to prevent one from saying that he most unquestionably was a very bad painter".

Drown such sorrows in an **Artists' Special**: *Shake well with ice 1 oz. each Scotch and medium sherry with 2 tsp. each lemon juice and gooseberry syrup. Strain into a small Old-Fashioned glass.*

APRIL 23, 1838

They had to break up the *Sirius's* cabin furniture yesterday and stuff it into the boilers after the coal ran out, but the satisfaction of steaming up New York harbour today after nearly three weeks at sea made it worth while to Junius Smith. The Connecticut-born Londoner intended his British & American Steam Navigation Co. to be the first to start a regularly scheduled transatlantic service under power. But while he was having the *British Queen* built for the purpose, Smith learned that the rival Great Western Steam Ship Company's new *Great Western* was ready to leave Bristol and claim the honour. So he quickly leased the smaller, slower *Sirius* from its Cork-London run and gained the four days he needed to overcome the handicap. It was a close thing: *Sirius* got hung up on a sandbar last night and dropped anchor only two hours before *Great Western* arrived.

Your turn to hold the Atlantic **Blue Riband**: *Stir vigorously in a small Old-Fashioned glass 1 oz. each dry gin and white curaçao, with ½ oz. blue curaçao.*

APRIL 24, 1916

To Nebraskans supporting Henry Ford for the Republican presidential nomination in their upcoming primary, today's news was welcome, for it linked him with the prospect of cheaper automobile travel. Trailed by reporters to the home laboratory of Louis Enricht at Farmingdale, Long Island, Henry acknowledged that he was there for a demonstration of the inventor's water-mixed green fuel. Enricht said he didn't want to risk having it analyzed, or to answer any technical questions, until his patent came through. Henry Ford kept his opinion to himself, but it could be deduced when, a few days later, the inventor claimed that Maxim Munitions were going to buy the rights instead. It took a letter to the press from Sir Hiram Maxim himself to squash that one. In the end, Henry Ford was not nominated for president, and Enricht's green fuel was not heard of again.

*May your **Green Hope** have a happier ending: shake with cracked ice 1 oz. vodka, ½ oz. green curaçao, ¼ oz. crème de banane, and 1 tsp. each lemon and grape juices. Strain into a cocktail glass and add a cherry.*

APRIL 25, 1862

Today *The Times* was to do an advance review of the final volume of the Earl of Stanhope's biography of William Pitt the Younger. Stanhope had drawn extensively on a manuscript from one of his great-uncles, Pitt's brother-in-law. But now he decided that he had misinterpreted the handwriting in a significant line. It seemed that Pitt, instead of declaiming on his wartime deathbed, 56 years before, "How I love my country!", might have groaned "How I leave my country?" (presumably in an upward direction). Lord Stanhope, chagrined to think of the letters to *The Times* if he got it wrong, hastened to take pen in hand to his publisher and the newspaper. To ensure that the quotation was properly printed to cover both eventualities, he insisted that it read "How I love [leave] my country".

*If you need a **Last Thought**, let this be it: Gently stir together 1 oz. each brandy and champagne, both of which have been well chilled. Pour into a chilled cocktail glass.*

APRIL 26, 1537

Being clapped in jail today for continued insolence to the new governor was an unpleasant surprise for the brothers Hernando and Gonzalo Pizarro. With fewer than 300 soldiers they had held the Andean capital of Cuzco against thousands of Peruvians led by the Inca, Manco. This month the hard-pressed Spaniards were saved when one-eyed Diego Almagro brought a strong force and routed the Inca's warriors. But then Almagro declared that he carried the King of Spain's authority and would take charge, if the Pizarros didn't mind. Because they did mind, Almagro had them smoked out of their fortified house and stuck in jail. One of his advisers quoted the proverb *el muerto no mordía*, but Almagro risked being bitten. He should have listened: next year the Pizarros' followers turned the tables, took control and executed him for treason.

*Join the conquistadores in downing an **Inca**: Shake well with ice ¹/₂ oz. each dry gin, dry sherry, dry vermouth and sweet vermouth, with 1 dash each orange bitters and sugar syrup. Strain into a cocktail glass.*

APRIL 27, 1813

When Zebulon Pike, at the age of 27, had led an expedition across the western Territories of the young United States, it was gratifying to have the men name after him the highest mountain they sighted. Today, however, Pike's pique overtook his pleasure at a military success. After being brevetted brigadier-general at Sacketts Harbor on the south shore of Lake Ontario, he had taken a force across the lake to attack the Canadian Fort York. The attack went so well that a white flag appeared at the fort; Pike turned to talk with his aides. At that moment the fort's powder magazine blew up, showering the area with rocks. One of these hit the temporary brigadier-general in the back, and he never learned that Congress ratified his promotion three weeks later.

*Celebrate the posthumous promotion with a **Pike's Picon**: Pour 4 oz. chilled red wine, ¹/₂ oz. Amer Picon and 1 tsp. grenadine into a large wineglass. Add 1 ice cube. Stir well, twist a sliver of orange peel over and drop it in.*

APRIL 28, 1159

A highly satisfying day for Gregorio Papadeschi dei Guidoni, Pope Innocent II, as he began winding down the second Lateran Council. Its closing canons showed that the 100-plus bishops from European monarchies had been well briefed by the Establishment. First they outlawed chivalric tournaments, which had been depopulating the upper classes since they were the only ones allowed to compete. Then the bishops outlawed the newfangled crossbow. Using this equalizer, any old peasant could knock a knight off his horse with a well-aimed bolt. Unfortunately, the prohibition was taken seriously only by those major Christian monarchies which had sent delegates to the Rome convention. It turned out to be an excellent way to lose Crusaders and others in their encounters with the outsiders, who had not read the minutes of the meeting. The crossbow soon made a comeback.

*Permission granted to try your own **Crossbow**: Put ½ oz. each gin, Cointreau and crème de cacao in a small Old-Fashioned glass with 1 ice cube. Stir, then aim down the throat.*

APRIL 29, 1812

Every member of the Cercle Philharmonique of Sisteron, in southeastern France, insisted on standing godfather at the baptism of little Louis, son of their colleague Antonio Jullien. They all wanted their names attached to the newborn, who would in time become the "Paganini of the Alps" (according to his father, anyway). Louis' career peaked as a conductor in England, where a jewelled baton was handed to him on a silver salver at each concert. Less successful at staying solvent, he fled to Paris to escape creditors and died in a lunatic asylum. There was no room on his headstone to list all the names of Louis Georges Maurice Adolphe Roch Albert Abel Antonio Alexandre Noé Jean Lucien Daniel Eugène Joseph-le-Brun Joseph-Barème Thomas Thomas (yes, a different one) Thomas-Thomas Pierre Arbon Pierre-Maurel Barthélemi Emanuel Vincent Luc Jules-de-la-Plane Jules-Bazin Julio-César JULLIEN.

*One **Godfather** should be enough to digest: 2 oz. bourbon and 1 oz. Amaretto, built into an ice-filled Old-Fashioned glass.*

APRIL 30, 1899

Naval officials in Madrid received good war news tonight by cable from their colonial governor-general in the Philippines, Don Fermín Jaudénez. A few hours ago, he reported, six U.S. warships which had sailed into Manila Bay were quickly engaged by 11 Spanish vessels protecting the outer harbour of the port of Manila. Now the Americans had disappeared from view (it was already early morning in the Philippines). Don Fermín had no radio communication with the Spanish fleet, so he wired home his best guess, via the undersea link to Hong Kong: the Americans seemed to have withdrawn badly hurt. In reality Commodore Dewey, the U.S. commander, had inflicted heavy damage and suffered none; now he wanted his sailors to have a good breakfast before going back in. When the Spaniards surrendered soon afterward, Dewey demanded to use the cable, but Don Fermín replied politely that it appeared to have been cut. His optimistic invention misled the world's capitals for a whole week.

*The **Commodore** recommends this before a hearty breakfast: Combine 1 oz. each of bourbon, crème de cacao and lemon juice with ice. Add 2 dashes grenadine, shake well and strain into a small Old-Fashioned glass.*

MAY 1, 1851

What a surprise for Western eyes to see! Just as the more traditionally dressed international diplomats were taking their places for today's official opening of the Great Exhibition in London's Hyde Park, in wafted a gorgeously caparisoned Chinese mandarin. He prostrated himself before Queen Victoria. "Is he on the list?", whispered the Lord Chamberlain. Nobody within calling distance could be sure, and it would be wiser to play it safe. The mandarin was placed in a distinguished non-political seat, between the Archbishop of Canterbury and the aged Duke of Wellington. He embarrassed nobody and the opening was a great success. Next day, less elegantly attired but admitting to the name Hee Sing, the mandarin could be found at his usual place of business — the docks in London's East End. He guided tourists around a Chinese junk for a shilling a head.

__East and West__ meet in this highball glass: Half-fill with shaved ice, then pour on 2 oz. arrack and top up with bitter lemon.

MAY 2, 1839

Cyrus McCormick would never have guessed it today, but it was good luck that nobody at the auction wanted to buy the rights to the grain reaper he had patented five years ago. Since then, Cyrus had failed to commercialize the invention and he went back to helping his father run a pig-iron furnace. After iron prices collapsed in the wake of the Panic of 1837, creditors took most of the family's assets; the remaining goods were put up for bids. Now, because the reaper patent didn't interest anyone, Cyrus puttered about refining the prototypes. Soon he was able to offer a version that seemed an improvement on the competing Hussey reaper. Four years later McCormick's annual sales exceeded Hussey's by over 1000 per cent — 29 against two. And his successor company, International Harvester, now sells a lot more than that.

The McCormicks traditionally celebrated with a **McBrandy**: *Shake well with cracked ice 1½ oz. brandy, 1 tbsp. apple juice and 1 tsp. lemon juice. Strain into a brandy snifter.*

MAY 3, 1810

Fear of testicular hypothermia seemed of more concern to Lord Byron than his general fatigue on completing this afternoon's current-hampered, 70-minute swim across the mile-wide Dardanelles separating Europe from Asia Minor. Flopping ashore at Abydos, he found his friend Hobhouse reading Ovid's account of the mythical Leander's similar successful effort. "I doubt whether Leander's conjugal powers must not have been exhausted!", commented the poet, whose first attempt at the crossing had ended in failure. On this second one he was accompanied by Lieutenant William Ekenhead, who beat him across the strait from Systos by five minutes. But Ekenhead, not being titled, an author or even notoriously randy, swam quietly in and out of history.

Sink or Swim? Find out by stirring with ice 1½ oz. brandy, ½ oz. sweet white vermouth and 1 dash Angostura. Strain into a cocktail glass.

MAY 4, 1830

Simon Bolìvar, Liberator of Colombia, was sorely embarrassed today. Congress, sitting at his capital of Bogotà, had promised their 47-year-old president an annual pension of 30,000 pesos. But growing criticism of his near-dictatorship forced him to resign, and now Congress claimed to be unable to find the money for a pension. Planning to move to Caracas in Venezuela, Bolìvar lacked the cash to get there but feared assassination if he stuck around Bogotà. Over the next three days he was lucky to find buyers for his horses and jewellery, which brought in 17,000 pesos. Then yesterday's Liberator was escorted by an armed guard to Venezuela, where the inhabitants were more appreciative and named their currency the Bolìvar.

*Bid farewell to **El Presidente**: Shake gently with ice 1½ oz. white rum, 1 tbsp. dry vermouth and 2 dashes each orange curaçao and grenadine. Strain into a small Old-Fashioned glass over 1 ice cube.*

MAY 5, 1862

French Brigadier-General Comte de Lorencez, sent by his government to establish French supremacy in Central America, discovered today that the natives were capable of contradicting him. Yesterday he had cabled to the Minister of War at Paris, "We have over the Mexicans such superiority of race, of discipline, of organization that tomorrow, at the head of 6,000 of my choice troops, I shall attack, and I consider that Mexico is mine!" But this morning, when Lorencez approached the city of Puebla by way of its forts, it took only 2,000 Mexicans under Ignacio Zaragoza to defeat him. The city responded by changing its name from Puebla de los Angeles to Puebla de Zaragoza. Lorencez went back to France and was never given another command.

*Commemorate the victory with a **Mexican Flag**: Shake with ice 2 oz. tequila, 1 tbsp. sugar syrup and 2 tsp. lime juice. Strain into a champagne saucer. To complete this patriotic potion, pop in 1 tsp. vanilla ice cream surmounted by a red cherry and a green grape.*

MAY 6, 1569

England's first state lottery closed with deep embarrassment to its organizers today, after taking in only one-twelfth of the amount projected. Since the game had been rigged more to boost Queen Elizabeth's treasury than to enrich her subjects, the queen urged local officials to push the tickets. "This matter hath not been as well advanced as it was looked for", she admonished the Lord Mayor of London. The promised cash prizes had to be reduced, although the grand winner still did get 1300 pounds' worth of "good tapestry, meet for hangings", in return for a 10-shilling ticket. Like everyone else, he had to wait six weeks after the lottery closed to learn the lucky numbers: the inexperienced organizers had mixed in the 29,505 winning numbers with the 370,495 blanks, and each one had to be picked out by hand.

Help the British treasury by drinking to **Queen Elizabeth**: *Shake well with cracked ice 1 oz. gin, ½ oz. each Cointreau and lemon juice, and 1 dash Pernod. Strain into a cocktail glass and decorate with a cherry.*

MAY 7, 1898

As soon as he reached the U.S. Department of the Navy this morning, Under-Secretary Theodore Roosevelt handed his resignation to his sedate and proper boss, John D. Long, so he might dash off to take part in the Spanish-American War. Then, walking through the offices to say goodbye, Roosevelt spotted decoders at work on a cable from Hong Kong. During a naval engagement off Manila a week earlier, the lines from there had been cut, and now 40 reporters were camped outside Secretary Long's office waiting for any news. Roosevelt saw enough of the decoding to learn that the Americans had won the battle; he passed the news to those waiting in the corridor and went on his way. Two hours later Secretary Long, having as usual first advised the President and then composed a press release, called in the few reporters who remained. But by then, newsboys on the street outside were already shouting "Extra!" and giving the public his story.

Dispel any sense of urgency with a **Cablegram Cooler**: *Crack 2 ice cubes and shake them with 1 oz. rye, ½ oz. lemon juice and 1 tsp. sugar. Strain into a goblet, top up with ginger ale and decorate with a spiral of orange peel.*

MAY 8, 1902

Convicted murderer Auguste Henri Ciparis found a unique way to earn his pardon today, after the sudden disappearance of almost every other inhabitant of St.Pierre, at the north end of the Caribbean island of Martinique. Volcanic Mont Pélée, directly behind the town of 30,000, erupted at 8 o'clock and shot a tide of glowing ash down the slope at a speed of 20 metres a second. The people of St.Pierre were smothered or asphyxiated, but the 25-year-old stevedore's solitary cell had only a tiny grating in the door and this stopped most of the flow. Ciparis was found three days later, suffering such unpleasant burns that the authorities kept him alive as a curiosity. Later he was able to earn money as a sideshow exhibit, which after all provided greater life expectancy than the alternative.

*Let this **Volcano** burn itself out: into a parfait glass pour 1 oz. apricot brandy, then float in 1 oz. Southern Comfort and set a match to it. Let the glass cool before serving.*

MAY 9, 1913

Anthony Comstock, Secretary of the New York Society for the Suppression of Vice, had spent 40 years keeping dirty pictures away from those who wanted to see them; so he was angered today to observe, on a canvas in the window of Braun's gallery, a French wench bathing stark naked. Comstock expressed his gratitude to public-spirited Harry Reichenbach for bringing this to his attention, then raised a public storm. But Braun's continued defiantly to expose *Matinée de Septembre* to the thousands who now came to gawk. Comstock could not guess that Harry Reichenbach had planned it that way, nor that Harry's more tangible reward was a commission on the painting's sale to a wealthy visitor from Imperial Russia. Hidden during the Revolution, *Matinée de Septembre* eventually returned to New York. Perhaps Anthony Comstock's ghost visits the Metropolitan Museum of Art for a closer look.

*Immerse yourself in a **September Morn**: Shake with ice until frothy 2 oz. light rum, juice of ½ lime, 1 egg white and 3 dashes grenadine. Strain into a Sour glass.*

MAY 10, 1775

Lieutenant Jocelyn Feltham of the British garrison at Ticonderoga, on Lake Champlain, would normally put his breeches on to welcome male visitors; but this morning he was carrying them over his arm as he peered out his bedroom door to see what all the noise was about. His visitors didn't mind: "Come out of there, you damned skunk!" was the greeting from an intruder on the staircase, dressed in a homemade uniform of green and yellow. It was Ethan Allen, leading 83 Green Mountain Boys, volunteer militiamen from the New Hampshire Grants whose main enemy until then had been the colonial administration of New York. This morning they had turned their attention to the British regulars, and so Lieutenant Feltham had time to reflect, as he was escorted prisoner to Hartford, that the American Revolution must really have begun.

More to Jocelyn's taste was **Colonial Tea Punch***: Squeeze 12 lemons into a punchbowl; add their peel, with 1 qt. strong cold tea and 12 oz. sugar. Let steep for 1 hour. A quarter-hour before serving, add a block of ice and stir in 1 qt. dark rum with 2 oz. brandy.*

MAY 11, 1745

By 11 o'clock this morning, Captain Lord Hay of the First Guards needed a drink. Five hours ago his battalion had started toward the Belgian village of Fontenoy; now, after a long uphill march the leading line crested a rise and found itself less than 100 yards from the French enemy. With the muskets of the time, marksmanship over that distance depended greatly on luck, so Lord Hay was only slightly foolhardy to step forward, raise his flask and cry "*Messieurs les Français, tirez les premiers!*" But the French weren't about to be sucked in: at a previous battle they <u>had</u> fired first, too soon to be effective, and were still going through the 24 ordered movements of reloading when they were overrun. This time, threrefore, the English had to fire first, and lost the battle. But Lord Hay managed to put away his flask and survive for another 33 years.

Lord Hay's batman had doubtless mixed him a **First Regiment Punch***: Have batman heat water almost to boiling. Stir well in a tumbler 1 oz. each Scotch and Irish, 1 tsp. sugar, 3 dashes lemon juice and 3 oz. hot water.*

MAY 12, 1826

James M.W. Turner, one of the more original British painters of his time, proved at today's preview of the Royal Academy's annual exhibition that he had a streak of sportsmanship too. He found his splashy view at Cologne, "Arrival of a Packet Boat", in prestigious company: it had been hung between two works by the president of the Academy, Sir Thomas Lawrence. But these were precisely-limned formal portraits and Sir Thomas, attending the same private viewing, was mortified to see them upstaged by Turner's innovative work. Quickly Turner consoled him by getting some lampblack and watering it down to make a grey wash. This he spread over the lurid sky of Cologne. Sir Thomas was alarmed and rather embarrassed, but "It will wash off", said Turner.

Brighten your life with a **Yellow Sky**: *Shake well with ice 1 oz. each apricot brandy and Pernod, and 1 tbsp. yellow Chartreuse. Strain into a chilled, small Old-Fashioned glass.*

MAY 13, 1904

Sorry at the death of his second young wife, and even sorrier at the prospect of not siring a line of Marquesses of Donegall, 79-year-old George Augustus Hamilton, the Fifth Marquess, decided to advertise in the *Daily Telegraph* for a suitable child-bearer. The new wife for the "anonymous peer", the advertisement pointed out to the *Telegraph*'s well-heeled readers, would have to bring enough money to enable their heir to carry on in proper Marquessian style. Soon the successful applicant appeared: Violet Twining, daughter of a rich Nova Scotia merchant. Fulfilling her side of the bargain Violet produced, nine months after the wedding, Edward Arthur Donald St.George Hamilton. Just in time, for the old Marquess, having done his bit, expired today. Although the seven-month-old baby carried on as Sixth Marquess, he failed to live up to his father's hope of a dynasty, leaving the title to a cousin.

The **Heir Apparent** *is always welcome. Both parents deserve one: Put 6 ice cubes in a wide-mouthed jug; shake on 6 dashes each orange bitters and white crème de menthe. Pour in 3 oz. brandy, stir well and strain into cocktail glasses.*

MAY 14, 1874

This was a second deeply disappointing day for David Roger, captain of the first McGill football team to visit a United States university. Practice sessions against Harvard had revealed one disconcerting difference between Canadian rugby and the American "Boston" game: in the States a player could pick up the ball only if he was being pursued. The fairest solution seemed to be to play it both ways — first half Canadian style, second half American. At half time the Harvard captain, Henry Grant, said his team had so enjoyed running with the ball that they'd be willing to carry on by the same rules. The Americans won, three goals to none. David Roger, to his lasting regret, agreed to continue with Canadian rules in today's return match. So the Redmen tried again to win at their own game, and again failed to score.

*Show your sportsmanship by downing a Harvard **Crimson**: Shake well with cracked ice 1½ oz. gin, 2 tsp. lemon juice and 1 tsp. grenadine. Strain into a cocktail glass and float ½ oz. port.*

MAY 15, 1800

Phlegmatic old King George III found what he caught of the double feature at Drury Lane quite interesting this evening, mainly because the leading lady, Dorothea Jordan, happened to share the master bedroom of a large suburban house with his son William, Duke of Clarence. But there was one disturbing moment. When George entered the royal box and stood, as usual, to bow to the audience, all eyes were on him. An ex-cavalryman called Hatfield chose this moment to climb on his bench in the pit and fire two shots at the king. He hit the woodwork instead, and George raised his opera glasses to survey the scene while Hatfield, who had suffered head wounds serving his country in the 15th Light Dragoons, was led away and later judged insane. Then His Majesty found the intermission so tedious that he dozed right off.

*Imitate the royal snooze with a **Sleepyhead**: Pour 2½ oz. brandy into a snifter, add 1 ice cube and 3 torn mint leaves, then top up with ginger ale and drop in a twist of orange peel.*

MAY 16, 1917

The inventor Nikola Tesla was described as "a man difficult not to offend"; the offence was probably mutual when, immediately after shaking hands with someone, he rushed to the nearest washbasin. This evening, Tesla was to be awarded the American Institute of Electrical Engineers' Edison Gold Medal at its annual convention in New York City. But when the meeting adjourned after dinner to reassemble for presentations in another hall, he was not to be found. Tesla was brooding about Thomas Edison, who had gained much greater public recognition than himself, sometimes for developments from Tesla's own discoveries. Eventually he was spotted on the sidewalk, trying to locate a taxi. He had to be cajoled into returning to pick up the medal bearing Edison's likeness — and the $10,000 that went with it.

*This **Gold Medal** is its own reward: Stir with 1 ice cube in an Old-Fashioned glass, 2 oz. orange juice, 1 oz. gin and 1 dash Angostura.*

MAY 17, 1875

This turned out to be a gloomy day for the renowned racehorse Chesapeake, and a surprising one for his owner, Price McGrath. Price had chosen a colt with an inferior record to pace Chesapeake in the first running of the Kentucky Derby at Louisville. The colt, Aristides, was supposed to get the best out of Chesapeake by forcing the pace and then falling back, exhausted, as the champion forged ahead. But after the first mile Aristides, fresh from the training grounds of upstate New York, showed no desire to let Chesapeake take over for the final half. The intended winner just couldn't catch up. Nor could any competing horse, so McGrath waved on the young pacer's jockey to take the race in 2 minutes 37¼ seconds. He collected a $2850 purse for Aristides' effort. Chesapeake didn't even place.

*The **Kentucky** cocktail combines 1¼ oz. pineapple juice with 1 oz. bourbon. Shake them with cracked ice and strain into a chilled martini glass.*

MAY 18, 1619

When he was sentenced today to "perpetual imprisonment" for spreading doctrines unacceptable to the strict Calvinists governing the Netherlands, the jurist and diplomat Hugo Grotius flashed back "I know no permanent punishment but Hell!" That, however, was before he had seen the guest rooms at the Castle of Loevestein. Soon Hugo, who had entered Leiden U. at the age of 11, figured out an ingenious means of escape and got word of it to his wife, the resourceful Maria van Reigersberch. After 22 months, she persuaded the prison governor that Hugo's continuous studying was ruining his health: she was sending a chest to take his books away. Instead, of course, Grotius climbed into the chest and was carried out by the complaisant carters. At a friend's house he dressed as a mason, then took boat for Brabant and ended in Paris, where Louis XIII pensioned the "Jurist of the Human Race".

*Take the time to fill a **Boxcar**: Line the rim of a champagne saucer with water and press it in sugar. Combine with ice 1½ oz. each gin and Cointreau, 1 tsp. lime juice, 1 eggwhite and 2 dashes grenadine. Shake well and strain into the glass.*

MAY 19, 1850

This evening Honoré de Balzac, the Parisian author whose bourgeois family had appropriated the honorific "de" in a quest for social status, was looking forward to showing his upper-crust Polish bride the home he had bought in her name. After their tiring journey from Dresden, Balzac hoped to relax in a haze of domesticity: relatives had prepared the house, leaving the old manservant François in charge. But repeated ringing and knocking brought no one to the locked gate, and the Balzacs were obliged to have a locksmith do his work before a curious crowd. Inside, they found a shambles: François had gone berserk. He had to be bolted into an upstairs room, while the newlyweds spent the night waiting for attendants from a lunatic asylum to come and take the old man away.

*A better welcome awaits in the **Bride's Bowl**: Boil 2 cups sugar with enough water to make a syrup; stir in 1 qt. pineapple juice, 2 cups lemon juice and 1 pint pineapple chunks. Add 3 bottles golden rum and refrigerate for several hours. When ready to serve, pour over a block of ice in a punchbowl. Add 2 bottles soda water, stir gently and float ½ pint of strawberries.*

MAY 20, 1881

Although the American Bible Society's annual meeting had reaffirmed last week that "the only copies to be circulated by the Society shall be the version now in common use", the English Revised Version of the New Testament was selling briskly on this official day of publication. Boosted by Queen Victoria, who had just accepted her advance copy, "official" publishers Eyre and Spottiswoode advertised their editions at from 15 cents to 10 dollars; but American publishers urged readers to "bypass the British Monopolist". One of them offered the Gospels at 2 cents each, all four for 7 cents — or one could plunge and spend a dime for the complete Book. A reader willing to wait another 24 hours would do even better: the *Chicago Tribune*, with considerable pious fanfare, published the whole New Testament as a free 16-page supplement.

Whether or not you're a B.S. member in good standing, you can enjoy **Heaven**: *Put in a shaker 4 oz. pineapple juice, 1 oz. amber rum, and ½ oz. each coffee liqueur and crème de cacao. Shake like hell, then strain into a highball glass over 2 ice cubes.*

MAY 21, 1914

Such an annoyance for high-flying Princess Anne von Löwenstein-Wertheim to miss her Paris luncheon date, after ensuring that she was the first person to charter a British aircraft for a private overseas trip. The English-born widow had been ready at 7 this morning, climbed into the Handley-Page at Hendon in northwest London, and urged the pilot onward despite the drizzly weather. But fog over the Channel isolated the Continent, and the H.P.7 had to land in a field near Eastbourne. The princess, a good sport at heart, soon forgave Frederick Handley-Page his rotten airplane and commissioned one which would fly the Atlantic. This project being frustratingly delayed by such things as World War I, she tried again at age 62. But after taking off toward Newfoundland in a single-engined monoplane, Princess Anne was never heard from again.

Use a liqueur glass for your **Princess**: *Pour in 1½ oz. apricot brandy, then gently float ½ oz. whipping cream.*

MAY 22, 1611

Nicholas Bacon of Redgrave got his money's worth today in buying the first English baronetcy to be issued in over 200 years: he simply had to pay £365 down and the remaining £730 in easy instalments. King James I recognized that his treasury needed the money, for it had recently been explained to him that the year's revenue of £427,000 would not cover the year's expenses of £490,000. So word was passed around that any person of good repute could apply to become a Baronet. Oh yes, and you needed enough land to bring in rents of £1000 a year. Then your heirs would be Sirs forever, or until the rules changed again. After Nicholas Bacon, 74 other gentlemen took the hook. They gave the royal treasury such a healthy boost that the king decided to sell titles for full Barons, at 10 times the price.

*Meanwhile you can make **Honourable** at little cost: Combine 1 oz. each bourbon, dry vermouth and sweet vermouth in a shaker; strain into a small Old-Fashioned glass containing 1 ice cube.*

MAY 23, 1888

Henry Morton Stanley thought it best to register today's discovery in writing as he led an East African expedition through the European-run district of Equatoria. Stanley insisted to natives of the Ruwenzori foothills that the white substance covering two high peaks of their range was not salt. Some of his associates had passed that way earlier and reached the same conclusion, but Stanley wanted to spring the discovery on the world in his next book, *In Darkest Africa*. So he wrote to the Governor of Equatoria, Austrian-born Emin Pasha. The Governor kindly replied "Let me be the first to congratulate you on your most splendid discovery of a snow-clad mountain." During his 12 years in the region Emin Pasha had passed the same mountain several times, but he was notoriously nearsighted. *In Darkest Africa* sold 150,000 copies in its first year, and British mapmakers showed those twin peaks of the Ruwenzori as Mount Stanley.

*Your turn to discover a **Stanley**: 1 oz. each dry gin and rum, with ½ oz. each lemon juice and grenadine. Shake well with cracked ice and strain into a cocktail glass.*

MAY 24, 1862

It was lucky that John Fowler, chief engineer of London's new underground Metropolitan Railway, decided to go ahead with his V.I.P. preview today, despite the passenger coaches not being ready. Open wagons provided standing room for those notables who had accepted his invitation (others shared the view of old Prime Minister Palmerston, approaching 80, who said he preferred to remain above ground as long as possible.) Although open sections of the railway let out some smoke from the coal-burning locomotives, so much was left in the tunnels that holes soon had to be bored to the roadway above, causing surprise and alarm to pedestrians. Why was John Fowler lucky? Well, less than a month later a sewer burst through the tunnel wall, flooding a length of the Metropolitan Railway to 10 feet with what the newspapers politely described as "refuse".

*For a refuse-free **Metropolitan**, stir well with cracked ice 1½ oz. each brandy and sweet vermouth, ½ tsp. sugar syrup and 1 dash Angostura. Strain into a cocktail glass.*

MAY 25, 1857

Foresighted British Colonel George Campbell today was finally able to outfit his 52nd Regiment, the Oxford Light Infantry, the way he had planned. Stationed at Sialkot in the Punjab, Colonel Campbell had taken note of the restlessness which seemed to be affecting troops of Indian regiments nearby. With a foreboding of trouble, he decided to make his own men less conspicuous, and asked around in Urdu for *khaki* ("earthy" or "dusty" coloured) cloth. This he ordered made up into battledress, with the men keeping their bright dress uniforms for parades. Less than two months later Campbell's initiative paid off when the Indian Mutiny began. Yet the dull cotton khaki could not be officially approved for another 25 years — Queen Victoria described it as "a sort of café-au-lait shade, quite unsuitable for uniform".

*An **East India** may make you feel less conspicuous: Shake well with ice 1½ oz. brandy, 1 tsp. each red curaçao and pineapple juice, and 2 dashes Angostura. Strain into a small Old-Fashioned glass over 1 ice cube.*

MAY 26, 1919

World War I had been over for six months but W.G.Tarrant, a building contractor in Weybridge, Surrey, was still determined to show that his huge triplane bomber, the Tarrant Tabor, would today outfly anything the RAF had in service. The massive machine had been enlarged over five years of construction until it stood 75 feet high. A pyramid of six engines amidships was counter-balanced by an extra half-ton of lead in the nose. So far the Tabor hadn't left the ground but now Captain Rawlings, Tarrant's senior manager and an ex-naval flier, taxied across the field using only the lower engines. Then he gave full throttle to the upper ones. "The machine pitched bodily forward", reported *The Times* next day, "and almost buried its main parts in the ground, smashing and grinding its way six or seven feet into the soil". Thus Tarrant lost both a good manager and a rotten airplane.

*One **Nosedive** will not prove fatal: Shake well with ice 1 oz. gin and sweet vermouth, 1 tbsp. green chartreuse and 2 dashes orange bitters. Strain into a martini glass; add a twist of lemon.*

MAY 27, 1899

Edward H. Harriman, stockbroker, railroad builder and now multimillionaire chairman of the Union Pacific, wanted nothing to hold up his scientific expedition today. Its destination was Alaska, but the special train of five Pullman cars was stuck in Portland, Oregon after crossing the continent from New York. Harriman wanted to get aboard the expedition's luxuriously-outfitted cruise ship at Seattle, 400 miles north; but the lines of the Northern Pacific Railroad were frustrating his plan, crowded as they were with passenger and freight trains. Luckily there was a friend at the Northern. His name was J.P.Morgan. Harriman's telegraphed message to his fellow-multimillionaire had the desired effect: the Northern Pacific trains were ordered onto sidings, and the private convoy swept through.

*To get the feeling of a **Millionaire**, squeeze 1 lime into a mixing glass containing cracked ice; add 1 oz. each sloe gin, apricot brandy and rum, and 1 dash grenadine. Stir well and strain into a cocktail glass.*

MAY 28, 1779

Today saw the first of two bits of bad luck to strike Sir Charles Bunbury, president of England's Jockey Club. During the spring meeting at Epsom, in Surrey, Bunbury had agreed with Edward, 12th Earl of Derby, that next year the club should include a new annual race, a one-miler for colts and fillies. But how should it be listed in the schedule? Sir Charles suggested naming it for one of themselves; Edward agreed, so they tossed a coin. Bunbury lost. Then his wife ran off with Lord William Gordon. But Sir Charles soon forgot such petty aggravations: at next spring's meeting, even if they hadn't named the new race after him, Bunbury's horse Diomed won it, in the first running of the Derby.

*At least a drink was named in his honour — the **Sir Charles**: Put 3 ice cubes in a highball glass. Pour in 1½ oz. port, ½ oz. each brandy and orange curaçao or Mandarine, and 1 tsp. sugar syrup. Stir, garnish with a slice of orange and serve with a straw.*

MAY 29, 1453

The Byzantine emperor Constantine the Last thought he had the defence of Constantinople sewn up tight this morning. The attacking Turks were using their fearsome Basilica cannon to throw 400-pound granite rocks more than a mile into the city, but their aim was lousy. Then they discovered that a postern, left open by Constantine for a sortie, was equally useful for an entrée. The Janissaries — youths from conquered countries who were paid off in plunder — stormed in and took the city for King Mehmet. Constantine, knowing the Janissaries were not noted for kindness, begged at least to have a Christian cut his head off; it would feel more appropriate. Mehmet agreed, then called for the head and had it appropriately exposed atop a column in front of the largest Christian church.

*You can follow in the **Barbarians' Tracks**: Put in an ice-filled shaker 1 oz. Scotch with 2 tsp. each of gin, rum, crème de cacao and cream. Shake the mixture and strain it into a cocktail glass, topping with a twist of lemon peel.*

MAY 30, 1894

Handsome, blond Theo Weiss regretted after this evening ever having confided to Beatrice Rahner that his hypnotic-eyed, black-haired older brother was really Harry, the Great Houdini. With her mother, Beatrice went to see the young magician's show from the front row of her Brooklyn high school auditorium. It became a difficult evening to forget because Harry Houdini, during his "wine into water" trick, tipped a jar over and spilled liquid onto Beatrice's dress. After an introduction like that it was natural that they should get married within the fortnight. Luckily Beatrice had already been on stage as one of the Floral Sisters, so being sawn in half was just a different act. She became one of the Houdinis instead, for the next 32 years. By then, people were tired of hearing her brother-in-law say "I dated her first, you know".

*There's magic in **Harry's Pick-me-Up**: Shake well with ice 1½ oz. brandy, 1 tsp. Grenadine and the juice of ½ lemon. Strain into a champagne tulip and fill with champagne!*

MAY 31, 1902

Even braver than Walter C. Baker, the manufacturer of an electric racing car, was his mechanic and electrician, Charlie Denzer. As Baker drove through the cleared outer-suburb roads of Staten Island, New York today, Charlie had to crouch behind him and regulate the voltage of a dozen acid-filled lead batteries while the Baker Torpedo tried to beat the record for the flying mile. They survived the journey through two bends and across a double set of streetcar tracks, but when the Torpedo veered off line and hit a tree stump its crew was trapped under the jammed cockpit cover. They remained unhurt until an enthusiastic policeman, using his billyclub to break open the cover, gave Charlie Denzer a great lump on the head.

*The nervy electrician could have used this **Battery Charger**: Stir with cracked ice in a highball glass 1 oz. Pernod and 1 tbsp. Grenadine; top up with soda.*

JUNE 1, 1847

The embarrassment was mutual for Karl Marx and the executive of the League of the Just, starting a week-long meeting in London. The assembled English, French and German socialists knew Karl's work in organizing Communist Correspondence Committees, and wanted him to join them and give new international direction to the cause. But there was a hitch: he was living in Brussels after being obliged to leave France, and the Marx household at 42 rue d'Orléans was short of cash. Luckily another European delegate was able to tell the London group of Karl's plans for a movement to rock the world. They thought this such a good idea that before the meeting ended they changed the name of the organization to the Communist League.

*The **Red Flag** is served straight up. Combine with ice 2 oz. Irish, 1½ oz. each clam and tomato juices, 1 tsp. lime juice and 3 drops Worcestershire sauce. Add a pinch of pepper, shake gently and strain into a Sour glass.*

JUNE 2, 1809

Friends of the late Joseph Haydn conquered their qualms tonight in the hope of bringing yet more honour to the composer. An eminent Austrian surgeon, Dr. Franz-Joseph Gall of Vienna, had a thing about measuring skulls to determine brainpower, and he had convinced Haydn's friends that no sculpture would do nearly as well for his purpose as the man's head. Since Haydn had been buried a few days before, this posed a problem, but the friends stole into the graveyard and out with the head. Dr. Gall was delighted, and declared that Haydn's brain was "immense". After keeping the skull for many years, he presented it to the Society of Friends of Music in Vienna. Not until 1954 was it reunited with the rest of Haydn.

*Trust yourself to this **Headshrinker**: Chill your tequila. Shake well with cracked ice 2 oz. orange juice, 1 oz. each lemon juice and grenadine, ½ tsp. salt and 10 drops Tabasco. Strain into a chilled Sour glass. Now toss back 1 oz. cold tequila; the mixture is a chaser!*

JUNE 3, 1896

Portly 54-year-old Edward, Prince of Wales, suffered a slight sartorial embarrassment on Epsom Downs today but turned it to his advantage. His horse Persimmon had just won the Derby by a neck, from St.Frusquin, in the record time of 2 minutes 42 seconds. The prince, whose proudly correct dress included elastic loops under the instep of his boots to keep his trouser-bottoms looking neat, lumbered across the muddy paddock to congratulate jockey Johnny Watts. At that moment one of the elastics broke; Edward bent down and folded the bottom of the royal pantleg up to keep it out of the mud. Within a few days, tailors were besieged by gentlemen asking for "turn-ups", thus starting a useless fashion that endured through more than half of the twentieth century.

*Celebrate the Prince's victory by a **Horse's Neck**: Into a highball glass containing 2 ice cubes, stir 1½ oz. Canadian whisky and 1 dash Angostura. Top up with ginger ale and decorate the rim of the glass with a spiral of lemon rind.*

JUNE 4, 1813

Disappointed by his disobedient crew, Captain James Lawrence of the United States Navy today lay wounded below decks while the enemy towed his ship away. Lawrence had taken command of the *Chesapeake* only three days earlier, and was determined not to lose her to the attacking British *Shannon* outside Boston harbour. Mortally wounded, and about to be carried below, he told the crew "Don't give up the ship!", adding either "fire her until she sinks" or "blow her up instead". Whichever way it was phrased, his men misunderstood and failed to carry out the order. Captain Lawrence did not have long to regret this, for he died soon afterwards in a Halifax, Nova Scotia hospital; but his ship served the Royal Navy for another seven years.

*The **American Flag** is a pousse-café: With great care, pour into the centre of a narrow glass in this order, 1 oz. each grenadine, blue curaçao and sweet cream.*

JUNE 5, 1884

Six months after retiring from the U.S.Army, General William Tecumseh Sherman didn't expect to be bothered again today about the Presidency. He had written that any man of 64 who wanted to be President "must be an ass or a madman". But as he sat in the library of his St.Louis home a telegram from Chicago was delivered, signed by one of the Republican party's professional politicians. Rather than nominate one of their own type, "Your name is the only one we can agree on. You will have to put aside your prejudices". Sherman had the messenger wait while he composed this reply: "I will not accept if nominated and will not serve if elected". So the old pols had to run one of their own, James G. Blaine, and lost the election.

*The general's retirement tipple is now known as the **Sherman**: Shake with cracked ice 1½ oz. apricot brandy, 1 tbsp. orange juice and 4 dashes orange bitters. Strain into a chilled cocktail glass.*

JUNE 6, 1505

Although this was Friday, traditionally the unluckiest day of the week to start a job, the city council of Florence had been pressing Leonardo da Vinci to get going on his mural of the Battle of Anghiari. They pointed out that on another wall in the Palazzo Vecchio his young rival, Michelangelo Buonarroti, was well along with a similar work. So at 1 p.m. Leonardo reluctantly set brush to wall with a new formulation of paints. Almost immediately the sky clouded over with a torrential thunderstorm that he took as an ill omen. Sure enough, when he tried to dry the paint with heat from torches, some colours melted and ran down the wall. Half a century later the hall was remade and a new wall stuck on top of Leonardo's work, so now nobody knows what remains.

*Would a **Mona Lisa** stop the runs? Shake well together ½ oz. each Amer Picon, orange curaçao and Bénédictine with 1 tsp. whipping cream; pour into a cocktail glass and sprinkle with cinnamon.*

JUNE 7, 1879

The electric arc-lights which were turned on today in the salons of Paris' Palais de l'Industrie brightened the lives of almost everyone. The *Annual Register* marvelled that with the new lighting "six burners, covered in crystal glass, sufficed to illuminate hundreds of pictures". An exception to the general enthusiasm was the outspoken septuagenarian Dr. Erasmus Wilson, whose expertise in subjects as diverse as dermatology and Ancient Egypt had earned him a fearsome reputation. When a newspaper opined that gaslight's yellow tinge was "more agreeable to the eye than the dazzling whiteness of the electric light", Wilson agreed. During a similar display at the Trocadéro a year earlier, he had pontified: "With regard to the electric light, much has been said for and against it, but I think I may say without fear of contradiction that, when the Paris Exhibition closes, electric light will close with it, and no more will be heard of it."

Glow gently with this **Trocadéro**: *Stir briskly over ice 1½ oz. each dry and sweet vermouth with 2 dashes Grenadine. Strain into a small Old-Fashioned glass.*

JUNE 8, 1895

"Diamond Jim" Brady, the extroverted railroad-equipment salesman and New York escort of actress Lillian Russell, chose this Saturday to show off the electric automobile which had just arrived from the Woods carriage factory in Chicago. The custom-made "town coupé", being rather taller than it was long, resembled a telephone booth on wheels. For his drive down Fifth Avenue, Brady sat in the booth while the driver — a mechanic hired away from the Woods factory — perched outside ahead of it. As they approached Madison Square so many carriages and wagons stopped, and so many pedestrians crowded around, that Brady couldn't proceed. With his customary good humour he stepped out, crossed the street to the Hoffman House and drank lemon soda until the police had sorted out the mess. Brady thanked them, but the reply was a letter telling him to drive only in the evening, and be sure to keep his machine out of the way of regular horse traffic.

Diamond Jim enjoyed **Lillian Russell** *and so will you: Pour carefully into a pousse-café glass, in this order, 1 oz. each Crème de Rose, Crème de Violette and 35% cream. Rich!*

JUNE 9, 1914

Readers of the British weekly *John Bull* had their hearts warmed today by the news that the £25,000 first prize in the magazine's sweepstake on last week's Derby had been won by an old blind lady of Toulouse. Its publisher, Horatio Bottomley, had his heart warmed too. To avoid any silly arguments, he had hired a boat and been rowed three miles out on Lake Geneva before personally drawing the tickets for all the horses entered for the Derby. The name of Hélène Glukad appeared on the stub of the ticket drawn for the winning horse, Durbar II. This was a happy coincidence, to say the least: Madame Glukad was, under another name, the sister of a Bottomley employee. Now the *John Bull* announcement of the old lady's good fortune added that she was so afraid of being pestered by strangers that she had left Toulouse for an undisclosed location. Wherever she was, Madame was grateful and generous: she returned £24,750 of the prize to the *John Bull* office.

*To celebrate that **Derby Rum Fix**, dissolve 1 tsp. sugar in 2 tsp. water in a highball glass. Add 2 oz. white rum, ½ oz. lemon juice and 1 tsp. crème de menthe. Fill glass with crushed ice, stir; garnish with 2 torn mint leaves. Sip through a straw.*

JUNE 10, 1817

All the publicity that Caraboo, the escaped slave girl, had managed to engender came to an abrupt stop today when her former landlady decided to be helpful. Speaking and writing a language not formerly encountered in the Gloucestershire village of Almondsbury, Caraboo had appeared on Maundy Thursday in vaguely Asiatic garb. Dr. Wilkinson, the noted scholar from nearby Bath, admitted to the *Chronicle* that "all the assistance to be derived from the Polyglot Bible .... does not enable us to ascertain either the nature of her language, or the country to which she belongs." Reading this, the former landlady of one Mary Baker was prompted to write that all young Mary really wanted was five pounds to ship steerage to Philadelphia. So the money was found and "Caraboo" sailed from Bristol on the *Robert & Ann*, in company with various cheeses, two fowling pieces and a bedstead.

*Like Caraboo, you can make a **Sensation** among eight new acquaintances: Put a block of ice in a punchbowl and pour on 5 oz. each Cointreau and brandy, along with juice of 1 lemon. Just before serving, add 2 bottles champagne and 12 strawberries.*

JUNE 11, 1860

Leaving the railhead at Inverness today, the Earl of Caithness steered his new three-wheeled Thomas Rickett road steamer north through the Highlands toward his family seat, Borrogill Castle. The earl had some rather necessary help from a stoker standing on the rear platform of the 2½-ton vehicle. On level ground, hard stoking might result in a speed approaching 20 miles an hour, but this hilly 140-mile journey took two days. Approaching Borrogill the steamer had to climb the road up the massive Ord of Caithness, which rose by 1000 feet in five miles. The earl was a determined fellow. "All this", he reported, "I got over without difficulty". The stoker's comments were not recorded.

The whisky that shares its name with the earl's stoker is the main ingredient in his noble steersman's **Scotch Holiday:** *Shake well with ice 2 oz. The Famous Grouse, 1 oz. each cherry brandy and lemon juice, ½ oz. sweet vermouth and ½ white of egg. Strain onto ice in a chilled Old-Fashioned glass and garnish with a slice of lemon.*

JUNE 12, 1832

Colour-blind John Dalton was an eminent man of science, but the two standards he had to reconcile today were more ones of taste. Oxford University had chosen the annual meeting of the British Association for the Advancement of Science as the occasion to make Dalton a Doctor of Civil Law. The award of this honorary degree called for a brilliant scarlet robe, but Dalton was a Quaker committed to inconspicuous clothing. Still, he succeeded in finding a way to go through with the ceremony, meeting the university's dress code while satisfying his own conscience. Being colour-blind, Dalton was able to tell a fellow-recipient that the scarlet robe appeared to him as a "proper Quaker drab".

Today's not-so-drab drink is the **Quaker:** *Shake together with ice 1½ oz. brandy, ½ oz. golden rum, ¼ oz. lemon juice and 1 tsp. raspberry syrup. Strain into a chilled cocktail glass; twist a piece of lemon peel over and drop it in.*

The Bavarian mental specialist Dr. Bernhard von Gudden had advised his capricious new patient, King Ludwig the Mad, to go easy on the food and drink, but at 4:30 this afternoon the king ordered a second huge luncheon. This he washed down with one glass of beer, two of spiced wine, three of Rhine wine and finally two of arrack. Then, today being *Pfingstsonntag*, he suggested they tiptoe through the peonies from his fairytale castle of Schloss Berg to the nearby shore of Lake Starnberg. The doctor, his patience exhausted by the king's nonstop questioning, still felt it his professional duty to go along. It's not certain who pulled whom into the lake, but when their bodies were found at 10 p.m. Ludwig's watch had stopped at 6:54. Dr. von Gudden's showed 8 o'clock, but it was a standing joke that he never remembered to wind it.

Share their walk as far as the **Lakeside**: *1 oz. crème de cacao, well stirred with ½ oz. each of brandy, crème de menthe and Cointreau. Pour over ice in an Old-Fashioned glass.*

A tasty dish brightened the end of this wearying day for Lieutenant-General N. Bonaparte; fearing indigestion he refused to eat until a battle was over. Things had gone wrong at the Piedmont village of Marengo when his French force of 30,000 men was nearly defeated by more numerous Austrians. Then at 5 o'clock General Desaix' corps came up from reserve and turned the tide of battle. Bonaparte was sufficiently pleased to call his personal chef Dunand to field headquarters near Alessandria. But the supply wagons were miles away and Dunand had to set the orderlies to foraging the neighbourhood. They brought in only a small hen, four tomatoes, three eggs and six crawfish from the Orba, along with a saucepan and some cooking oil. From all this, plus a little brandy from the general's flask, Dunand composed a dish that earned him Napoleonic praise — and a listing in the Larousse Gastronomique for Poulet Marengo.

The follow-up is an **After Dinner**, *prepared at field temperature: Shake well together 1 oz. each apricot brandy and curaçao, then pour into a sherry glass.*

JUNE 15, 1894

After singing *Lohengrin* this evening with the brothers Jean and Edouard de Reszke as her co-stars at London's Covent Garden, 33-year-old Nellie Melba received a pleasant surprise as she supped at the Savoy Hotel with her current paramour, the Duc d'Orléans. The hotel's chef, Auguste Escoffier, had been brought in four years earlier by César Ritz to draw fashionable diners to the Savoy with his original approach to haute cuisine. Tonight, to thank Melba for a pair of opera tickets she had given him, Escoffier fashioned a Lohengrin-style swan of ice, and set between its wings a delicious new iced peach dessert. With Nellie's modest assent he thereafter added it to the menu as Pêche Melba.

Improve your voice with a **Brandy Melba***: Shake well with ice 1½ oz. brandy, ½ oz. lemon juice, ¼ oz. each peach and raspberry liqueurs and 2 dashes orange bitters. Strain into a chilled cocktail glass and add a slice of brandied peach.*

JUNE 16, 1487

It seemed rather a comedown today for young Lambert Simnel to be condemned to wash dishes, after having only recently been crowned King of England and Ireland. Trouble was, there was already a live king, working out of London under the name Henry VII, so Lambert's coronation had had to take place in Dublin. At 16, the son of an Oxford tradesman, he had attracted attention as the lookalike of an imprisoned claimant to the throne, Edward of Warwick, and been coached by enemies of Henry VII. Lambert rather fancied the royal robes and such, but found himself unwelcome in England. In fact, those who were promoting his cause lost their only battle today, and Lambert was taken away to be a scullery boy in Henry's kitchens.

Considering the alternative, Lambert was quite a **Happy Youth***: Place 1 lump sugar in a chilled champagne tulip. Add 1½ oz. orange juice and ½ oz. cherry brandy; fill with champagne.*

JUNE 17, 1872

Despite Johann Strauss Jr.'s chronic motion sickness (in trains he used to sit on the floor drinking champagne, as if that would help), the promise of $100,000 in gold coins carried him across the Atlantic. The first element of his money's worth was conducting this evening's grand World Peace Concert in Boston. The city was celebrating the centenary of its premature declaration of independence, and 100,000 Bostonians crowded the Common to hear the 20,000 choristers and instrumentalists. A hundred sub-conductors awaited Strauss' signal; then the audience was blasted off its collective fanny by the roar of a cannon. As Strauss related it, the sub-conductors started "more or less together". Seven concerts later, he was ready to recross the Atlantic and pick up his coins from a Vienna bank.

*The **Blue Danube** shows you the real colour of that river: Stir 2 oz. each Scotch and lime cordial with 2 ice cubes in a highball glass. Fill with soda and top with a slice of lemon.*

JUNE 18, 1887

The painter Paul Gauguin had lost his construction job with a French engineering consortium trying to build the Panama Canal, and was living from hand to mouth on the island of Martinique. So he was encouraged today to be offered a split guava for nothing, even though its end had been squashed. This bit of generosity came from a pretty 16-year-old, and Gauguin was about to take the fruit when a local lawyer standing by grabbed it and threw it away. "She has bewitched it by crushing it against her breast", he explained. "If you ate it you would be at her disposition." Gauguin, who was not only hungry but had recently left his wife, might not have minded at all.

*The **Guava Tempter** can attract a party of five: it calls for 13 oz. rosé and 7 oz. each guava nectar and coconut milk. Mix well, chill in freezer until almost frozen and pour into tulip glasses.*

JUNE 19, 1867

Max Hapsburg, everyone agreed, had loads of charm. He sorely needed it today at Querétaro, in Mexico — the country to which he had been enticed by the offer of a job as emperor, with a salary of about one-seventh of the national tax revenue. Mexico's conservative Church party had made the deal with Max's brother, ruler of Austria-Hungary, who had always felt more comfortable with his charming sibling at a distance. But soon the new Emperor Maximilian found that most Mexicans would like this gringo even farther away. Which explains why, early this morning, Max was being stood before a wall outside town. Before reaching it he dug in his pocket for gold coins bearing the imperial profile. Handing them to members of the firing squad, the urbane emperor exclaimed "What a glorious day! I have always wanted to die on such a day as this!"

*When it comes your time to say **Adios Amigos**, this is a quick way: Shake with ice 1 oz. light rum, ½ oz. each gin, dry vermouth and brandy, and juice of ½ lime. Strain into a large cocktail glass.*

JUNE 20, 1855

Alfred Tennyson, the longhaired Poet Laureate of Great Britain, found himself rather out of his element during today's formal ceremonies in the Museum of Oxford University. He was to be awarded an honorary doctorate, and everyone had in mind the stirring verses which he had submitted to the *London Examiner* about last autumn's Charge of the Light Brigade against the Russians. Appropriately, therefore, the poet was escorted up the aisle of the great hall by two officers recently returned from the Crimea, Sir John Burgoyne and Sir George de Lacey Evans. They were trim and upright; Tennyson slouched along between them in his well-known irregular shuffle, wearing a floppy academic gown and borrowed white gloves several sizes too large. From the gallery an undergraduate called down, "Did your mother wake you early, Alfred dear?"

*Recreate Tennyson's feelings with a **Doctor Funk**: Squeeze the juice of 1 small lime over 1 ice cube. Add 3 oz. golden rum, ½ oz. lemon juice, 1 tbsp. Pernod and 1 tsp. each grenadine and white sugar. Shake well, strain into a highball glass over 2 ice cubes and fill with soda.*

JUNE 21, 1791

The white velvet upholstery in the huge long-distance six-horse coach could offer only physical comfort today to Louis XVI as he was trundled back to Paris. Yesterday the plump monarch had tried to slide out of France and an uneasy co-existence with revolutionaries. He was dressed as the servant of a "noble foreign lady" who, he hoped, wouldn't be recognized as Marie Antoinette. But their attention-getting green and gold *berline* was delayed for four hours: the combination of five passengers, heavy trunks and a full toilet had begun to break the traces. After observing the "servant" at length, particularly from the side which appeared on coins, the owner of a horse relay station sent his suspicions ahead to Varennes. There Louis found the bridge across the Aire blocked by angry citizens. His return to Paris under escort was the last trip he would take in comfort.

*For internal comfort, try **White Velvet**: Shake well with ice 1½ oz. dry gin, ½ oz. Maraschino and 1 oz. milk. Strain into a cocktail glass.*

JUNE 22, 1893

Admiral Sir George Tryon, commanding Great Britain's Mediterranean fleet, liked to make his captains practice running maneuvers, and today he did so for the last time. Enroute to North Africa with the fleet sailing in two parallel columns, the admiral ordered the leading ships to turn inward and head back through the lines. These were his own flagship *Victoria*, largest in the whole Royal Navy, and the four-year-old battleship *Camperdown*. Nothing happened for a minute, so impatiently he signalled *Camperdown*, "What are you waiting for?". Both captains then obeyed the order, with the result that the ships charged straight into each other. Admiral Tryon had forgotten that these modern battleships had such a wide turning circle. The official enquiry into the accident had to be conducted posthumously.

*To remember the difference between **Port and Starboard**, pour ½ oz. grenadine into the bottom of a pousse-café glass; then carefully float on 1½ oz. green crème de menthe.*

JUNE 23, 1314

Crossing the Bannock Burn on horseback today, hot-headed Humphry de Bohun thought he saw a simple way to settle the dispute over who ruled Scotland. He and his cousin the Earl of Hereford were leading the forces of England's King Edward II to relieve Stirling Castle, besieged by Robert the Bruce. The castle's governor had agreed to surrender this last English stronghold if the siege couldn't be raised by tomorrow, St. John the Baptist Day, so Humphry was reconnoitering for the big breakthrough. Suddenly he spotted Robert the Bruce himself only 100 yards away, also reconnoitering on horseback; Humphry charged in. The Scotsman, however, chose to fight with a heavy battle-axe, with which he split Humphry's uncertified helmet and its contents so hard that the axe-handle broke. Next day he finished the job by pushing the English across the Bannock Burn and out of Scotland.

*Celebrate with a **North of the Border Julep**: Crush 3 mint leaves with 1 tsp. sugar and 2 tsp. water in the bottom of a frosted goblet. Fill with crushed ice, add 2 oz. Canadian whisky and stir gently. Sprinkle with 2 torn mint leaves.*

JUNE 24, 1902

King Edward the Seventh felt decidedly unwell, and it was only two days before his scheduled coronation. The doctors diagnosed appendicitis; but "I must go ahead with the coronation even if it kills me!", exclaimed the 60-year-old monarch. Then he changed his mind. At 12:30 p.m. the operation commenced and within 40 minutes the royal appendix was successfully extracted. Soon the king awoke; next day's newspapers averred that his first words were of concern for the nation. That may have been so, for Edward was not ready to hand over to the Prince of Wales, heir to the throne. This was his surviving son Prince George, whose trousers were pressed sideways to preserve the creases. What the king actually said was "Where's George?"

*Was the gruesomely-named **Appendectomy** cocktail created in commemoration, or for its effect? Take a chance for four patients: Shake 6 oz. gin, 1½ oz. lime juice, 1 oz. Grand Marnier and 1 egg white. Strain over ice into chilled Old-Fashioned glasses.*

JUNE 25, 1906

Evelyn Nesbit, one of the original Floradora showgirls, had elevated her language after marrying Harry Thaw and his inherited wealth. So when, at dinner tonight in the rooftop nightclub atop Madison Square Garden, she saw a discarded lover giving her the eye, she simply whispered "Harry, that 'B' is here again." Harry's response was to escort Evelyn to the door. Then, after strolling past the table where the "B", architect Stanford White, was dining, he turned and shot him. The defence lawyers pleaded insanity — hindered or perhaps helped by Harry's press statement that "I am not crazy now and I was not crazy when I shot Stanford White". He spent the next seven years in a prison for the insane; Evelyn, just to show her appreciation, divorced him.

*The **Floradora Cooler** treats hot blood: Stir well in a 12 oz. glass 2 oz. gin, ½ oz. raspberry syrup, ½ tsp. sugar and juice of 1 lime, with cracked ice. Pour in 2 oz. each chilled ginger ale and soda.*

JUNE 26, 1789

John Paul Jones, yesterday's hero in American naval circles, reached the end of his career today as he was effectively cashiered by the Empress of Russia. Having joined her navy as a rear-admiral, Jones had commanded a fleet which decisively beat the Turks in the Black Sea last summer; but many well-placed Russians at Catherine the Great's court were jealous. They framed him by getting a 12-year-old butter delivery girl to say he had raped her in his apartment. Kontradmiral Pavel Ivanovich Jones was obliged to take two years' leave of absence outside the country. He never returned, for when the two years were up he was dying in poverty in Revolutionary Paris.

*For nostalgia, nothing beats the **Balalaika**: Equal parts of vodka, Cointreau and lemon juice (1½ oz. each will induce a good case of nostalgia) are shaken with ice and poured over an ice cube in a small Old-Fashioned glass.*

JUNE 27, 1743

George the Second, the last British monarch to accompany his troops into battle, spent part of today wishing that he hadn't, and the troops agreed. After slogging through a marsh to face the French near Dettingen, Germany, they were out of precise formation. George rode up and down bellowing at them gutturally (his first 31 years had been spent in Hanover) to dress their lines. But then some musketeers came under French fire and decided to return it, making the king's horse bolt from the field out of control. By the time he came back the French had had enough and were marching away. This was a great relief to Britain's Secretary of State, Lord Carteret, who had been dragged along and sat through the battle quivering in his coach. He and the king then sat down to a supper of lukewarm mutton, which reminded George so much of home cooking that he agreed to return to England and leave the fighting to the generals.

*This **Crazy Horse** is under your control: Shake with 1 ice cube 1 oz. Scotch and ½ oz. each crème de banane and Fraises des Bois. Strain into a tulip glass and top up with champagne. Decorate with slices of lime and orange, and 1 sprig mint.*

JUNE 28, 1161

When England's King Henry II planned the stone and brick labyrinth in his new park at Woodstock, the main idea was to keep his domineering wife Eleanor from reaching the middle of it. Today she found out why, by getting there. In the secluded bower with the 28-year-old monarch was his current best friend, Rosamond de Clifford. The queen, who had traded in her previous husband for Henry by means of annulment, was underjoyed. The rumour of the time had her forcing the girl to drink poison, but someone must have diluted the recipe, for Rosamond actually spent the rest of her life in Godstowe Nunnery. Then, because news moved so slowly, it took 15 years for the Bishop of Lincoln to discover that she had been buried in consecrated ground. Rosamond was moved to the nunnery outbuildings and, fortunately, re-interred.

*If, like Queen Eleanor, you have reason to exclaim **Oh Henry!**, pour 1 oz. each Scotch, Bénédictine and ginger ale over 2 ice cubes in an Old-Fashioned glass.*

JUNE 29, 1746

Hugh Macdonald of Armadale, head of a militia force looking for Prince Charles Stuart after Culloden on behalf of the young Pretender's enemy the Duke of Cumberland, greatly obliged his stepdaughter Flora by signing an official laissez-passer for her to carry on a visit to relatives on Skye. For this morning the 18-foot sailboat containing Flora and her new maid, Betty Burke, tied up at Kilbride, the home of Flora's cousin Lady Margaret Macdonald. A militia officer on the dock scrutinized the laissez-passer and glanced with some interest at Betty Burke, who sat demurely in the stern. She stayed sitting, for had the six-foot-tall lass clumped around in her ill-fitting headdress, the militiaman might have claimed the £30,000 offered for the apprehension of Bonnie Prince Charlie.

*There's only a touch of the Highlands in the **Bonnie Prince**: Combine with ice 1½ oz. gin, ½ oz. Lillet and ½ tsp. Drambuie. Strain into a small Old-Fashioned glass containing 1 ice cube.*

JUNE 30, 1859

Jean-François Gravelet today swallowed his annoyance with the Porter family. They owned Goat Island, N.Y., upstream from Niagara Falls, and had forbidden the young Frenchman to walk his tightrope from there to Canada. J-F, or "Blondin" as he liked to be known, had strung his two-inch rope downstream, where a 350-yard trip above a 200-foot gorge would be exciting enough. More than 100 guy ropes supported all except the central 40 feet of line. At 4 o'clock the aerialist entered White's Pleasure Grounds on the U.S. shore, where visitors had paid 25 cents admission, and soon stepped onto a platform to start the unprecedented trip. Halfway across, Blondin lay down on the rope, lowered a cord to the *Maid of the Mist* and hauled up a drink of Niagara water. Ten minutes later he was on Canadian soil; only $750 richer today, but with a fortune to come.

*Toast his success in your **Border Crossing**: 1½ oz. tequila, ½ oz. each cranberry and lime juice, 1 tsp. sugar. Shake well with ice and strain into an Old-Fashioned glass over 2 ice cubes. Add a slice of lime.*

JULY 1, 1883

Never downhearted, the British workmen tunnelling below Shakespeare Cliff, Dover, in the general direction of France gave a final three cheers this afternoon for entrepreneur Sir Edward Watkin. Work on their underground shovelling toward the European continent had been temporarily halted by a nervous government, which thought that 21 miles was about as close as it wanted France to get. The men had dug 2026 yards — a little more than the 1839 metres achieved by their French counterparts at Sangatte, whose leader Michel Chevalier had been obliged to stop them at his nervous government's behest. Five years later Sir Edward, now an MP, tried to recoup by introducing a Channel Tunnel Bill but Parliament voted the project down. His employees' layoff notice didn't specify when the job would resume. That was just as well: it turned out to be 100 years later.

*You can cheer up 25 workers with **Dover Rum Punch**: Combine 1 quart each dark rum, ginger ale and soda with 8 oz. each lemon juice and sugar syrup, and 2 oz. each brandy and Cointreau. Pour the mixture over ice in a punchbowl.*

JULY 2, 1863

James J. Pettigrew, the dashing Confederate brigadier, still had no proper boots for many of his troops today, and he regretted ever having read the advertisement for them in the Gettysburg *Compiler*. Of course, the Carolinian hadn't intended to pay for the boots. They were to be spoils of war, for he had happened onto a copy of that newspaper while taking part in Robert E. Lee's surprising advance into southern Pennsylvania. But approaching Gettysburg, Pettigrew's little group of raiders was spotted by a large Union army on the other side of town. Although the Southerners quickly withdrew, Lee was now obliged to give battle before he was ready. Instead of nearly isolating Washington and Baltimore from the rest of the North, the Confederates suffered 20,000 casualties at Gettysburg and were never able to mount such an offensive again.

*No doubt Pettigrew wished he were back in **Charleston**: Shake well with ice 1 oz. each light rum, dry gin and sweet vermouth; strain into a cocktail glass.*

JULY 3, 1850

Predictions of ill-luck accompanied Queen Victoria after her acceptance today of the immense Koh-i-Noor diamond, nominally a "present" from Duleep Singh, former autocrat of the Punjab, which the British occupied last year. But removing it from India attached a curse to the 278-carat gem, which was said to have descended from Aurangzeb through the Moghul emperors before the Sikhs took over that part of their turf. There was also a practical reason for promoting the curse. Indian diamonds were then the world's most valued (South Africa's underground treasure still being unkown) and the princes of the subcontinent preferred to keep the best ones for themselves. Anyway, Queen Victoria didn't like the shape that Aurangzeb had chosen: the Koh-i-Noor was recut and reduced to 102 carats (she thought 106, but see below). This must have undone the curse, for Victoria kept the diamond for another half-century and ended as Empress of India.

Queen Victoria's Tipple was strictly for diamond-weighing occasions: Pour 4 oz. red wine into a tumbler and top with 1 oz. Scotch. Warm the glass in your hand and be amused.

JULY 4, 1874

Henry Morton Stanley today christened the collapsible boat which he would shortly transport from Britain to Central Africa for the first-ever trip around Lake Victoria. He called it *Lady Alice* after the American girl who had just agreed in writing, though in secret, to become his wife. Alice Pike said that she would wait faithfully for the 33-year-old explorer's return. She and Henry exchanged letters that took three months to arrive; but soon it was borne in on Alice that her fiancé was going to be thousands of miles away for at least three years. Toward the end of that period one of Henry's loving letters crossed a classic Dear John in the mail. Alice admitted that she was about to marry someone else. She ended with who knows how little sarcasm, "You are so great that you will scarcely miss your devoted admirer, Alice Pike".

*Disappointment or no, July 4 calls for a **Fourth of July**: Place ½ oz. each bourbon and Galliano in a warm cocktail glass, then flame the mixture while sprinkling ground cinnamon on top. In a different container shake ½ oz. each Kahlúa, orange juice and whipping cream. Strain onto the hot mixture and add a cherry.*

JULY 5, 1841

Flourishing his white wand, symbol of total abstention, young Thomas Cook tonight escorted 570 other temperance supporters back to Leicester, England, from Loughborough, all of 10 rail miles away. He had good reason to be satisfied with the success of the world's first Group Inclusive Tour, which he had arranged as an encouragement to attend the quarterly regional sobersides meeting and thus help "Crush the Monster Intemperance". Entertainment on board the train was provided by Thomas' half-brother Simeon Smithard, a reformed drunkard who sang temperance songs with the excessive zeal of the convert. Perhaps that was the reason why such large packaged tours from Leicester to Loughborough declined in popularity among the drinking classes of Leicestershire.

Poor Simeon missed his **Drinker's Delight**: *Shake with 2 ice cubes 1½ oz. golden rum, ½ tsp. each curaçao and grenadine, and 1 white of egg. Strain into a cocktail glass.*

JULY 6, 1685

One-thirty this morning was a hell of a time to start the Battle of Sedgemoor, and young James, Duke of Monmouth, was among the most embarrassed. First, he had trusted a Somerset countryman to guide his little invasion force through a thick mist, to wait and surprise troops loyal to his uncle, King James the Second. The guide led Monmouth's infantry and cavalry both into the same deep irrigation ditch, where they crashed into each other in the dark. Then in the confusion Captain Hucker of Lord Grey's Horse unintentionally fired his pistol; this revealed them to the regulars, only 50 yards ahead on the bank of the ditch. The invaders quickly lost the match, 16 to 300. This became 301 nine days later when James, Duke of Monmouth, having lost by Bill of Attainder his right to a trial, lost his head to the axeman's fifth chop.

You should have better luck with **Combined Forces**: *Put 3 ice cubes in a jug. Pour over them 2 oz. vodka, 1 oz. dry vermouth, 1 tsp. white curaçao and juice of ½ lemon. Stir vigorously and strain into 2 chilled martini glasses.*

JULY 7, 1762

Catherine the Great of Russia found this one of her most relaxed days in a long while: she learned that her husband Czar Peter Feodorovitch, after ruling for only six months, had lost his life in a drunken brawl after dinner last night. This immediately relieved her of the necessity of always telling him what to do. The official notice to the public, however, avoided revealing Catherine's feelings. It also omitted to specify that her good friend Gregory Orlov had arranged from the winning side the brawl in which his brother did the dirty deed. Instead it proclaimed that all efforts by the most learned doctors had "regrettably failed to save His late Majesty, who had suffered an acute attack of colic during one of his frequent bouts of hemorrhoids".

*Far happier is the ending for your **King Peter**: Into an ice-filled highball glass pour 2 oz. Cherry Heering, 2 dashes lemon juice and 4 oz. tonic water. Stir gently and enjoy.*

JULY 8, 1889

As if being beaten up by John L. Sullivan for 75 rounds weren't enough, Jake Kilrain tonight was arrested on a charge of assault and battery for defending himself. After 2 hours 16 minutes in sweltering Mississippi heat, Jake's second had thrown in the sponge to recognize the Boston Strong Boy as "Champion of the World". Then the police had moved in: prize fights were illegal, even if this one had taken place on the private property of Charles Rich of Richburg. "Ain't I always voted right?", asked Sullivan. Maybe he had, as he got off with a fine. Jake Kilrain was sentenced to two months, but under Mississippi's convenient rent-a-convict law Charles Rich was able to hire him, to help dismantle the stands from which thousands had watched him lose the last bare-knuckle heavyweight title match.

*This **Summer Punch** should keep you going for 2 hours 16 minutes: stir three bottles chilled dry white wine and 12 oz. crème de cassis in a punchbowl; add a block of ice, then float 24 strawberry halves and 12 slices of orange.*

JULY 9, 1838

The spirit of Sir Robert Grant, Governor of Bombay, walked abroad in his stead this evening since Sir Robert was indisposed, having died earlier in the day. He had been in the habit of taking an evening stroll along a particular route of paths in the garden of the governor's official summer residence at Dapuri. After sundown today Sir Robert's pet cat left the house, passing the front-door sentry who watched it follow precisely the same route. He and the other guards agreed that the soul of the deceased governor had entered the body of the cat; so thereafter for several years, whenever the cat left by the front door, the sentry on duty would present arms in salute. But because Sir Robert, author of the hymn "O Worship the King, All Glorious Above", would have no truck with reincarnation, the cat refused to acknowledge the guards' salutes.

*Honour Sir Robert's **Cool Cat** by stirring gently together in a highball glass, ¹/₂ oz. each schnapps and brandy, 2 oz. lemon juice and 1 oz. lime juice cordial. Add 2 ice cubes, top up with soda and garnish with a slice of lime.*

JULY 10, 1865

Because he had lost two days getting medicine for a fellow-Englishman travelling in Switzerland, the 25-year old mountain climber Edward Whymper also lost the services of his chosen guide today, but he ended by being glad of it. J.A. Carrel, who had agreed to accompany Whymper on his seventh try at the unconquered Matterhorn, now pretended he was committed to "a party of ladies" — in reality, two male founders of the Club Alpino d'Italia who meant to beat the Englishman to the top of the border-straddling mountain, from the Italian side. Whymper persuaded three Britons and their guides to join him; reaching the summit first, he jubilantly threw stones down at Carrel's party. Only one thing spoiled his perfect day: on the way down a rope snapped and four of the party fell to their death. Whymper was not one of them: he wrote of his triumph in *Scrambles in the Alps*.

*Let nothing spoil your **Swiss Sunset**: Shake with cracked ice 1 oz. each brandy and mandarine liqueur, and 2 tsp. each lemon and grapefruit juice. Strain into a cocktail glass.*

JULY 11, 1755

A successful ambush by a far smaller force of French and Indians had knocked out of action 63 of General James Braddock's 89 British officers, and not all of the survivors were unhappy today to see their commander carried away badly wounded from the battlefield by the Monongahela River. Bribes had to be distributed among the private soldiers to persuade them to take turns carrying General Braddock's stretcher, so that the strict disciplinarian would not suffer the loss of his gold braid, dignity and scalp to the enemy. He muttered to an aide "We shall know better how to deal with them another time", but didn't make it clear before dying whether he was referring to the enemy or his own troops.

*For a more successful **Commander**, put 4 ice cubes in a cocktail shaker and pour over them 2 oz. vodka, 1 oz. Grand Marnier and the juice of ½ each lemon and orange. Shake until a frost forms, then strain into a Sour glass.*

JULY 12, 1809

Robert Barclay Allardice had to walk only 16 more miles today to win a wager, and he completed the distance handily, at just one mile per hour. Of course, that was the same slow pace he had maintained all yesterday, and the day before, and the day before that. In fact, "Captain Barclay", as he liked to be billed, had been walking for 41 days and nights, fulfilling the condition of completing one mile each hour for 1000 hours. The professional pedestrian lost a lot of sleep and 32 pounds in weight, but he had the satisfaction of knowing that nobody during the next 180 or so years would take the trouble to try and break his record.

*Before hustling lost its cachet, Captain Barclay would have been known as a **Hustler**: Shake well with ice 2 oz. bourbon, 1 oz. orange curaçao, 1 oz. sweet vermouth and 2 tsp. lime juice. Strain into a chilled Sour glass.*

JULY 13, 1793

This Friday the Thirteenth was even more uncomfortable than usual for physician Jean Paul Marat, a leader of the left-wing Jacobins in Paris during the Terror. Swathed in towels, he was sitting in a high copper bathtub to soothe the itching of a chronic skin disease, while associates in the next room ran off copies of a broadsheet. Then a young convent-educated fellow-native of Caen in Normandy entered, saying she had news of counter-revolutionary agitators there. "They shall all go to the guillotine!", cried Marat. "But — not you", replied the girl coolly, driving a sharpened two-franc dinner knife into his chest. That quickly stopped Marat's itching. His heart was interred in a porphyry vase at the Jacobin club, the Cordeliers, about the same time that Charlotte Corday's was being stopped by the guillotine.

*One **Cool Lady** makes a cool drink for four: Shake well with ice 8 oz. each calvados and orange juice; strain into highball glasses containing 2 ice cubes. Top up with ginger ale, stir gently, and decorate with cinnamon sticks and orange slices.*

JULY 14, 1789

This was a professionally satisfying day for Philippe Curtius, the renowned Parisian modeller in wax who was training his niece in the business (she became Madame Tussaud, of waxworks fame). First, Philippe had turned out with the militia and seen its governor, de Launay, dragged away. Later in the day, how flattering to have the late governor's head offered to him, to make a death-mask. Philippe improved on this by modelling the whole head and then making a deal with his next-door neighbour in the Boulevard du Temple, retired British sergeant-major Philip Astley. Astley happened to own an amusement centre near London's Westminster Bridge, so Philippe moulded him a duplicate wax head to send to England. It became a timely attraction, and as Astley's advertisements claimed, it was indeed a "striking likeness" of Governor de Launay.

*Your **Wax Melter** is a healthier attraction: Shake well 1 oz. each dry gin and anisette with 1 white of egg and 1 tsp. sugar syrup. Strain into a warm cocktail glass.*

JULY 15, 971

Swithin, a former Bishop of Winchester, was removed bodily today from the place he had chosen and there wasn't much he could do about it, having been dead for 109 years. Humble to the end, the old cleric and adviser to the West Saxon court had insisted that his remains be placed in the muddiest angle of the cathedral yard: the building lacked gutters, so rain funnelled from the roof onto his grave. Ironically, Swithin's humility led the locals to venerate him and rebury him today in a splendid tomb. But the last laugh was the bishop's: when Henry the Eighth plundered religious sites more than 500 years later, the gold and jewels of Swithin's shrine were found to be fake.

*Feeling humble, or damp? Try a **Bishop**: Half fill a highball glass with crushed ice. Stir in 2 oz. orange juice, 1½ oz. lemon juice and 1 tsp. sugar. Now almost fill the glass with red wine and stir again. Float 1 tsp. rum on top and stick a slice of orange on the rim.*

JULY 16, 1847

The young physicist James Joule had caused quite a stir three weeks ago, at the annual meeting of the British Association for the Advancement of Science, with his paper about the effect of friction on water temperature. So it was a happy chance, here in Chamonix with a travelling companion, to meet fellow-scientist William Thomson and be able to plan a practical experiment on location. They spent enjoyable days measuring the temperature at the top and bottom of the nearby Cascade de Sallanches. James had foresightedly brought thermometers from England, but the tests proved disappointingly inconclusive. To make matters worse, his travelling companion was getting restive. She reminded James that they were on their honeymoon.

*For a honeymoon hangover, try this **Lune de Miel**: Pour into a sherry glass, in this order, ½ oz. white crème de cacao, ½ oz. Parfait Amour, yolk of 1 egg and ½ oz. Kümmel.*

JULY 17, 1717

Possibly choosing today because of its four lucky 7's, composer George Frideric Handel finally succeeded in regaining the favour of the fellow-German who had now become King George I of England. Handel had earlier deserted his royal patron, who was then ruling little Hanover, to make more of a musical mark in Britain. Then, by a stroke of hereditary luck, the other George was invited to take over the island kingdom, and Handel had to ingratiate himself by composing special pieces for royal occasions. One of these, a portion of what we now call the Water Music, enjoyed a good reception in 1715, so Handel expanded it for today's outing on the Thames between Whitehall and Chelsea. The king liked it so much that he made the musicians repeat it twice during the round trip, whatever the other passengers might think.

*This **King** may also call for a repeat: Pour over ice in a jug 1½ oz. gin, ½ oz. sweet vermouth and 2 dashes each Angostura and orange bitters. Stir, then strain into a chilled martini glass.*

JULY 18, 64

It was a grand night for singing, according to the rumour spread by Nero's enemies, with the moon riding high over burning Rome as the emperor strummed his lyre. From the window of a tower in the palace, they said, came the sound of his favourite composition, "The Sack of Troy" (score by Nero). But the truth was that when the emperor, at his exurban retreat of Antium, heard of the fire he hastened to the city to help direct the bucket brigade. Still, the pattern of destruction was a trifle suspicious: 120 acres in the city centre were laid so waste that Nero decided the whole area had better be expropriated. It happened to be just the right size for his projected personal amusement park, so any buildings which had escaped the fire were bought — at knockdown prices, of course.

*Put out a dozen personal fires with **Roman Punch**: Place punchbowl in the sink and surround it with ice. Dissolve 1½ lbs. white sugar in the juice of 10 lemons and 3 oranges; add the rind of 1 orange. Beat well 10 egg whites and pour them on. Now add 1 bottle light rum and 1½ oz. orange bitters; stir well. Just before serving, pour in 1 bottle champagne.*

JULY 19, 1821

The single coronation was finally to take place today, after last August's scheduled ceremony had been abruptly cancelled "for divers good and sundry reasons". The main reason was King George's annoyance that his wife, estranged for 24½ years of their 25-year marriage, had suddenly turned up to claim her seat on the adjoining throne. German-born Caroline, however, couldn't take a hint: this morning she arrived uninvited at Westminster Abbey. The Lord Chamberlain himself shut the main door in her face. Rushing to another entrance, she was told it was for ticket-holders. The usual guard was reinforced by such experienced bouncers as the boxing champion Tom Cribb, so a disheartened Caroline went away. Her heartache descended to become inflammation of the bowel, and two weeks later she was on the way to a German burial plot. Supporters fixed a plate to the coffin reading "Caroline of Brunswick, the injured Queen of England"; not far out of London, the government had it removed.

*Don't miss this **Coronation**: Stir well with ice 1 oz. each dry gin, sweet vermouth and dry vermouth; strain into a chilled small Old-Fashioned glass and top with a twist of lemon.*

JULY 20, 1912

Rather a comedown today for Lord Ashby St.Ledgers to have the public learn that his family motto, *Ferro non Gladio* ("with the plow, not the sword") was all too appropriate. Only a week ago the noble lord, clad in full armour, had been proclaimed the best jouster in the medieval tournament at London's Earls Court arena. But was it he who had raised his vizor to kiss the Queen of Beauty's hand in exchange for the champion's gold cup? Foul rumor swept the peerage that Lord Ashby, preoccupied in real life with House of Lords business, had encased someone else in his elegant steel suit. Indeed yes: he had asked his young brother, the Honourable Freddie Guest, to do the tilting. Freddie had ridden with great élan, splintering his wooden lance against the breastplates of five other gallant knights. Today's *Times* did not divulge which aristocrat had battled and tattled, but it did explain to non-sporting readers that "the rules do not permit tilting by proxy".

*Award him the booby prize, a **Broken Spur**: Shake well with shaved ice 1 oz. white port, ½ oz. each gin and sweet vermouth, 1 tsp. anisette and 1 egg yolk. Strain into a small Old-Fashioned glass.*

JULY 21, 1793

Highland-born Alexander Mackenzie was justified in his irritation today as he sat listening to a native chief at a village on the North Pacific coast of what is now British Columbia. The Indians at the mouth of the Bella Coola river had insisted that the Scotsman and his 10-man crew hear tales of the other Europeans who had been seen along the coast. Mackenzie's arrival had been somewhat different, and to prove it he wanted to find cinnabar-bearing rock from which he could grind some bright orange powder. After a 24-hour delay the Bella Coolas let him go to mix the powder with grease, and to paint on the largest rock in sight, ALEX. MACKENZIE, BY LAND. Then, at last, he could turn around and paddle back across Canada.

*Only an adulterated memory of the lone sheiling is this **Bella Cooler**: Pour 2 oz. Scotch onto 1 ice cube in a highball glass, followed by juice of ½ lemon, 2 dashes Angostura and 1 tsp. white sugar. Stir well and top up with ginger ale.*

JULY 22, 1894

The other promised entries in today's grand race from Paris to Rouen included automobiles driven by clockwork and by gravity, so Albert de Dion, the *comte mécanicien*, guessed that his steam-powered carriage had a fair chance of beating them. Indeed, he arrived at Rouen first and might have made history by winning the first automobile race to field more than two cars. But the judges disagreed, awarding the prize instead to a Monsieur Dorion as the first competitor to fulfil the requirement of "a single driver". Although the wealthy count had skilfully steered with the tiller, a companion had ridden with him to make the continual mechanical adjustments. Meanwhile a reporter for the New York *Herald*, instructed by publisher J.G.Bennett not to risk being delayed on an unreliable horseless carriage, had tried to keep up with the racers by bicycle. Albert de Dion, averaging 11½ miles an hour, managed to outrun him.

*Keeping up with bicycles is no trouble after a **Bennett**: Shake with ice 1½ oz. gin, ½ oz. lime juice and 2 dashes Angostura. Strain into a chilled cocktail glass.*

JULY 23, 1886

Generally regarded as unemployable, 21-year-old Steve Brodie found a career ready-made for him after being fished out of New York City's East River tonight and hauled aboard a conveniently located barge. Steve, or more precisely a human-shaped lump of his general dimensions, had been spotted dropping the 130 feet from the centre of the Brooklyn Bridge. There was no doubt in the minds of those who had bet heavily on his success, most of whom turned out to be acquainted with him. The proceeds went to help young Brodie establish a saloon, above the bar of which hung a huge painting of the exploit. But when patrons urged him to repeat it, Steve always had the crisp reply: "I done it once, ain't I?"

Make, do not buy, the **Brooklyn Bridge**: *Shake well with ice 1 oz. Canadian whisky, ½ oz. sweet vermouth, and 1 dash each Amer Picon and Maraschino. Strain into a chilled cocktail glass.*

JULY 24, 1915

Geheimrat Dr. Heinrich Albert, commercial attaché at the German Embassy in Washington, was daydreaming today as the Sixth Avenue elevated train pulled into New York's 50th Street station. Jumping up, Heinrich stepped out onto the platform, then turned back as he realized he had left his briefcase on the seat. Too late: someone had whipped it! Dr. Albert spotted him and gave chase, but the man jumped aboard a speeding open-sided crosstown streetcar. Not coincidentally, it was Frank Burke of the U.S. Secret Service. Within days, documents from the briefcase reached the White House, still neutral in World War I. They showed that Albert's boss, Ambassador Johann von Bernstorff, was fomenting anti-U.S. feeling in Mexico. The public was soon reading the documents in the newspapers, and opinion turned decisively against the German side.

To enjoy a **Deep Secret**, *stir with ice 1½ oz. Old Tom gin, 1 oz. dry vermouth, ¼ oz. Pernod and 1 dash orange bitters. Strain into a martini glass and drop in a twist of lemon peel.*

JULY 25, 1908

British amateur runner and army lieutenant Wyndham Halswelle finally won today the Olympic gold medal which, by his reckoning, he had been done out of two days ago. He was competing against three Americans in the 400 metres at London's Shepherd's Bush stadium. Right up to the last curve they were closely bunched; then Cornell athlete J.C.Carpenter forged ahead. But one official leaped onto the track shouting "Foul!", and another broke the finish-line string before any of the runners could reach it. Halswelle said "someone" had jostled him in the turn. After a quick huddle, Olympic officials declared the race void and ordered today's re-run. The U.S. competitors refused rather than acquiesce in an allegation of fouling, so Halswelle ran the 400 all by himself, and won.

*Spectators need this **Stadium Warmer**: 1 oz. each Scotch, sweet vermouth and pineapple juice, well mixed and served in a cocktail glass.*

JULY 26, 1812

By drinking too much this evening Prince William, Duke of Clarence, muffed his chance at catching a rich Russian bride. Having wooed the Czar's sister by mail, he was delighted to find a fellow-guest at dinner in Brighton who might help — Princess Lieven, the Russian ambassador's wife. Afterwards he followed her outside, jumped into her carriage and as a conversational opener blurted "Are you too hot?". "*Non, monsieur*". "Are you cold?". "*Non, monsieur*". Unable to get around to the reason he wanted a private chat, the nervous suitor then jumped out of the carriage. Princess Lieven wrote to the Czar's sister that the Englishman was an imbecile and she had better marry someone else. Taking that advice, however, did her out of becoming Queen of England when the "imbecile" became King William the Fourth.

*Show your sympathy for **Sweet William**: Shake well with ice 1 oz. each pear brandy, apricot liqueur and 35% cream. Pour into a pre-chilled small Old-Fashioned glass and sprinkle with nutmeg.*

JULY 27, 1913

Aboard *Sapphire*, one of the last and grandest of private yachts, the Duchess of Bedford (not to mention her maid, her Pekinese dog and most of the 49 crew members) slumbered peacefully at 3 o'clock this morning. But the newly hired radio operator, Eric Sharp, was straining his ears to catch a weak Morse signal from Cornwall, 600 miles to the south. The duchess thought it would be nice to hear regularly from her husband while she was off scouting seabirds among the Shetland Islands. She had omitted to tell young Sharp that the Marconi station at Poldhu sent out personal messages only after finishing with shipping business. So it was his duty to wait up in the wee hours and copy out "All well here. God Bless and good night", ready for the duchess' breakfast tray. The Duke of Bedford welcomed this way to avoid leaving terra firma: once his splendid 285-foot yacht had been launched, he never set foot aboard.

*Tune in to **Marconi Wireless**: Stir gently with ice 2 oz. applejack, 1 oz. sweet vermouth and 2 dashes orange bitters; strain into a cocktail glass.*

JULY 28, 1902

Several national teams of three cars each had been entered in today's Gordon Bennett Trophy race over public roads from Paris to Innsbruck, but by evening these were whittled down to just two automobiles. Heading into Austria, the Panhard of Belgium's Chevalier de Knyff led a British Napier driven by the big Australian-born car dealer Selwyn Edge. But in the rugged Arlberg Pass the Napier slewed to a stop with a flat tire. Its non-detachable wheels had beaded rims which normally called for a heavy tire lever, but now Edge and his cousin Cecil, acting as mechanic, discovered that their toolbox had been shaken off the running-board. With their bare hands they tore the casing off the rim, fitted a new tube and replaced the cover. By then blood was running from Edge's hands, but his only thought was to drive like hell and catch de Knyff. On the final stretch they found him sitting by the road: the Panhard had broken its differential casing. Selwyn Edge roared into Innsbruck the winner after 11 hours at the wheel.

*Change tires and enjoy a **Dunlop**: 1 oz. golden rum, ½ oz. medium sherry and 1 dash Angostura bitters. Stir with ice and strain into a cocktail glass.*

JULY 29, 1588

Intelligence from Lisbon had warned that the dreaded Spanish Armada should be arriving toward the end of the month, so Admiral Sir Francis Drake suffered a small surprise this afternoon. As he and his commander-in-chief rolled lawn-bowls outside Plymouth in southwest England, they thought that today was only the 19th. Unlike Spain and other Catholic countries, England had not taken Pope Gregory's advice to move the calendar 10 days ahead. Now Captain Flemyng of Drake's squadron hurried over to report that the Armada had been sighted from the Lizard headland only 50 miles away. Though hull down to the watchers, the great fleet had been identified by its gaudily painted sails. But Drake was unshaken, knowing that the local tide would not be ready for him until 10:30 that night. "We have time to finish the game and beat the Spaniard", he declared. Did, too, by the time July 29 turned up on the English calendar.

*Your **Admiral**, by contrast, is well shaken when you have combined with ice 1 oz. bourbon and 1½ oz. dry vermouth. Strain into a small Old-Fashioned glass containing 1 ice cube, squeeze ½ lemon over and garnish with a sliver of lemon peel.*

JULY 30, 1908

Leutnant Hans Koeppen, on leave from the General Staff to represent Germany in a 12,000-mile road race, was understandably upset today when he saw crowds massing outside the offices of Paris' *Le Matin*. They were responding to the news that the Thomas Flyer, an American entry, would be welcomed at the finish there within hours. The newspaper had co-sponsored the race from New York to Paris the long way around — via Siberia. Koeppen was the first to arrive, bringing in the big Protos tourer three days ago, but anti-German feeling resulted in a tepid reception. The French entries had withdrawn earlier and the last car, an Italian, wasn't expected for weeks, so now Koeppen waited to be honoured as winner. But after penalty points were totalled the Thomas was placed ahead, having covered the most road miles. It turned out that Leutnant Koeppen had put his car on the train from Pocatello to Seattle.

*Riding the Union Pacific rails was strictly **Verboten**: Shake well with ice 1 oz. gin and ½ oz. each Forbidden Fruit liqueur, orange and lemon juices. Strain into a chilled cocktail glass and garnish with a brandied cherry.*

JULY 31, 1889

This jubilant day for young Kaiser Wilhelm II of Germany began at 7 a.m. as the royal yacht *Hohenzollern* led his 12 most impressive warships out of Wilhelmshaven enroute for British waters. Nominally this would be a courtesy visit to his old granny, Queen Victoria, on the Isle of Wight. But really the emperor wanted to show off his ships to the equally proud British fleet, anchored for inspection off nearby Spithead. Wilhelm had recently been created an honorary admiral in the Royal Navy — a distinction of which he gushed to the British ambassador, "it makes me quite giddy to wear the uniform that Nelson wore". The giddiness vanished 25 years later to the day, as he issued an imperial decree declaring Germany to be in a state of war. The British reciprocated, and unkindly withdrew his commission in the Royal Navy.

*The **Imperial Highball** can be a great consolation: Stir well with cracked ice in a highball glass 2 oz. old Canadian whisky, juice of ½ lemon and 1 tsp. sugar. Add 4 oz. ginger ale.*

AUGUST 1, 1910

It was ever so comfy for Ethel LeNeve, the London typist, to wake up in a pretty Québec City bedroom and be able to dress as a girl again -- until she remembered that she was the guest of Chief Constable McCarthy. He wanted to be sure that Ethel would be delivered to justice as a presumed accessory in the murder of her employer's wife. The employer, Dr. Hawley Crippen, had buried the remains in the basement of 39 Hilldrop Crescent, in London's lace-curtained Muswell Hill. Then they had enjoyed dressing Ethel as a boy and crossing the Atlantic together, until one of the "pilots" who came aboard at Pointe au Père turned out to be Inspector Dew of Scotland Yard. Ethel had indeed been much more than a typist to the doctor, but an astute barrister persuaded the jury to let her return to the keyboard. Dr.Crippen, however, was sent where no medicine would bring him back.

*It is highly improbable that Inspector Dew said "**GOTCHA!**": Pour 1½ oz. tequila over 2 ice cubes in a highball glass. Add 1 tsp. sugar and ½ oz. each grenadine and limejuice. Fill with tonic water, stir gently and garnish with a wedge of lime.*

AUGUST 2, 1830

Although there was no time for a proper coronation, 51-year-old Thérèse did today achieve her longtime ambition, to follow her late mother's career as far as becoming Queen of France (but no further — mother was Marie Antoinette). While the family watched, her father-in-law, King Charles X, signed his abdication in the library of the Château de Rambouillet outside Paris. The time was 9:50 a.m. Thérèse's husband Louis Antoine, Duc d'Angoulême, was Charles' elder son; but he had agreed to yield the succession to whomever else parliament might proclaim king "by the grace of God and the will of the People". With Thérèse, he enjoyed a brief reign. Then at 10 a.m. sharp, a representative from the Chambre des Députés entered the library, and it was Louis Antoine's turn to sign away his rights. Thérèse thus experienced at no risk the thrill of anticipation, the majesty of queenship and the calm of retirement — all in ten minutes.

*Commemorate her reign with a **Queen's Cocktail**: Shake with ice 1 oz. each dry gin, dry vermouth, sweet vermouth and pineapple juice; strain into an Old-Fashioned glass.*

AUGUST 3, 1492

Christopher Columbus's response to Queen Isabella's question "When do you go?" ("after breakfast, usually") has often been misinterpreted. This morning he really was setting sail from Palos, six years after finally finding sponsors for his trip to Japan. Chris had failed to persuade competing monarchs -- João II of Portugal and Henry VII of England — to stake him, and even the city fathers of his home port, Genoa, backed away. Then Isabella and her husband Ferdinand took him on as Admiral of All the Ocean Seas, but held up the money until they had run Boabdil's Moors out of Granada. Leaving Palos at last in the *Santa Maria*, Columbus had the right idea in sticking to the 28th Parallel, even if he underestimated the distance to Japan by two-thirds. Nobody else had any better idea.

*The Court toasted the admiral's departure in **Good Luck Punch**: Stew 2 lb. chopped rhubarb with 1 lb. sugar in water to cover, for 10 minutes. Strain through fine cloth; combine the juice with 1 bottle each light rum and soda, 6 oz. lemon juice and 4 oz. pineapple juice. Pour over a block of ice in a punchbowl and let cool before serving.*

AUGUST 4, 1892

Lizzie Borden of Fall River, Massachusetts was relieved of her burden of guilt this morning when she found that her stepmother Abigail had been done to death with an axe. For only last evening, the prussic acid which Lizzie had bought from a downtown druggist had turned up in Abby's soup; Lizzie was afraid that the subsequent stomach upset might be blamed on her. It was true that her father had remarried rather soon after Lizzie's own mother had died, but the girl assured the police that the resentment which this had caused would not have moved her to commit murder. In fact she was distressed to learn that her beloved father, president of a local bank, had been hacked about with a similar axe and that nobody could find it. Lizzie also explained quite reasonably that she had burned a dress a couple of days afterwards only because it was splattered with paint. Now orphaned, she inherited half a million dollars and so was able to live happily in Fall River for another 35 years.

*Nothing to fear from this **Dizzy Lizzie**: Stir with ice 4 oz. sweet vermouth, 1 tsp. each cognac and framboise, and ½ tsp. Angostura. Strain into an Old-Fashioned glass.*

AUGUST 5, 1858

Cyrus Field, president of the New York, Newfoundland and London Telegraph Company, rejoiced at his transatlantic cable being hauled ashore today in Newfoundland's Trinity Bay. It was the first one ever completed; Field couldn't know that he had only a few weeks to enjoy success. P.T.Barnum offered a huge payment to be able to send the first intercontinental message, but there were bigger suckers waiting on the line — the Queen of England and the President of the United States. On the 16th, Victoria and Buchanan did indeed exchange platitudes, transmitted by professional telegraphers using Samuel Morse's dot-and-dash code. They were lucky to do so, for two weeks later the undersea transmissions became indistinct and then faded out completely. It would be eight years before another cable was completed.

*Avoid failures in the **Deep Sea**: Shake well with ice 1 oz. each Old Tom gin and dry vermouth, and 2 dashes each Pernod and orange bitters. Strain into an Old-Fashioned glass over 1 ice cube; add an olive.*

AUGUST 6, 1840

Louis-Napoléon Bonaparte, nephew of the late great general, had mixed feelings about being rescued from a lifeboat outside Boulogne harbour today. At 5 a.m. he had invaded what was now France's Second Republic, from an excursion steamer rented at a seaside resort in southern England. Among the invasion force of 55 were his chef, tailor and valet, whom he led to the barracks of the 42ème Régiment to gather support. However, the Boulogne garrison seemed uninterested in helping him regain the French throne for the Bonapartes, so Louis went back to the jetty. There he found his steamer had been impounded by the customs authorities. The invasion force stole a lifeboat but, because Louis had been studying emperorship rather than seamanship, it shortly capsized. As a result, he was able to spend the next seven years continuing his studies in jail.

Occasionally one welcomes a **French Pick-Me-Up**: *Blend with a little chipped ice 1 raw egg, 1 oz. cognac, ½ oz. each Pernod and lemon juice, and 2 tsp. sugar. Pour into a lowball glass, sprinkle with nutmeg and drink for breakfast!*

AUGUST 7, 1503

Shortly after attending a dinner in honour of his son Cesare, the portly, high-living Pope Alexander VI (a.k.a. Rodrigo Borgia) confided to his principal aide today that "so many in Rome are sick now, We are disposed to take more than accustomed care of Our Person". Seized with fever and vomiting, he retired to the six-room Vatican apartment which had been lavishly decorated for his family's use. Three years ago the embellished plaster ceiling in a principal room had fallen, or been pushed, narrowly missing the Pope. Now rumours spread about poison having been slipped into his food at the farewell bash thrown by Adriano di Corneto for young Cesare, who was leaving to command military forces in the north. In actuality, the same malaria which was striking down the common people wiped out Pope Alexander; but it was excusable to suspect poison when the victim was the father of Lucrezia Borgia.

Could Alex have been the victim of an **Italian Stinger**? *Try it and see: Pour 1 oz. brandy and ½ oz. Galliano over ice cubes in an Old-Fashioned glass; stir and drink.*

AUGUST 8, 1802

Captain William Codling, master of the *Adventure*, knew what he was about as he hove-to this afternoon off England's south coast. There would be plenty of witnesses, for a holiday crowd strolled along the seafront at Brighton, recently made fashionable by the Prince of Wales and his hangers-on. Most of the *Adventure*'s heavily insured cargo had been quietly offloaded the previous night, and Captain Codling now expected her to spring a leak and sink. A loyal crew member gallantly drilled several leaks and the ship descended to the bottom of the English Channel. Unfortunately, the bottom turned out to be a sandbar not far below the surface. The perforated *Adventure* was left sticking embarrassingly high out of the water. The penalty for making false insurance claims was so severe in those days that we'd rather not discuss Captain Codling's fate before your drink.

Down the hatch with a **Brighton Punch***! Shake well 1 oz. each bourbon and cognac with ½ oz. Bénédictine and 2 tsp. lemon juice. Pour over 2 ice cubes in a highball glass and fill with soda.*

AUGUST 9, 1872

Charles Gounod, the composer who had taken French leave from his wife to board in England under the wing of the domineering soprano Georgina Weldon, began this day satisfied that he would be going to prison at the end of the month. He looked forward to embarrassing his ex-publishers, Novello's, who had sued Gounod after he described them as thieves. The composer lost, and though fined only two pounds was assessed another £ 100 for legal costs. Gounod, rather enjoying the publicity, declared that he would go to jail first. This evening, however, he was outraged to learn that his bourgeois mother-in-law had saved the family honour by paying his debt. He shouted expressions supposedly so unfamiliar to Georgina Weldon that she had to leave the room.

Gounod's language would have made a **Maiden Blush** *and you can make one too: Stir well 1½ oz. dry gin, 3 dashes each curaçao and grenadine, and 1 dash lemon juice. Strain into a cocktail glass.*

AUGUST 10, 1628

King Gustavus Adolphus of Sweden watched proudly this Sunday afternoon from the Lodgatan quay below his Stockholm palace as the navy's new 64-gun flagship *Wasa*, bearing his family name, left on her sea trials. With four sails set, the great warship moved quickly out into Lake Mälaren, gleaming with gilt wood and bright paint. Captain Hansson had left her two tiers of gunports open so that the crowds on shore could appreciate her firepower. But barely a mile from the quay a sudden gust of wind caught the *Wasa*'s huge sails. Underballasted and topheavy with armament, she heeled over and sank to the bottom of the cold Baltic as water rushed in through the gunports. Only the Dutch master-shipwright who had designed her, Henryk Hibbertzoon, could profit by the experience: henceforth he tested scale models in advance.

*This **Sea Breeze** is more bracing than dangerous: Stir together 1½ oz. vodka and ½ oz. each dry vermouth, blue curaçao and Galliano. Pour into an ice-filled goblet and add a twist of orange.*

AUGUST 11, 1888

After living with the eccentric painter James McNeill Whistler for 14 years, Maud Franklin had agreed to spend a few weeks away from London to convalesce from a nervous ailment. Today's ceremony was likely to bring it on again. Whistler, having arranged with his MP friend Henry Labouchère for the Parliamentary chaplain to speed a wedding license, turned up promptly at Kensington's fashionable St.Mary Abbots church. But invited to join him at the altar was not Maud, but pleasingly plump Trixie Godwin -- widow of the architect whose design for Whistler's expensive house had helped to push him into bankruptcy. The newlyweds took off for three months, hoping that time might cool the fury of a woman scorned. Instead, they returned to find Maud calling herself "Mrs.Whistler" and selling his etchings. This enabled her to move to Paris, marry a rich South American and live happily ever after.

*Come into the garden, Maud, and drink to Trixie, the **Wedding Belle**: Shake well with cracked ice 1 oz. each dry gin and sweet vermouth, and ¼ oz. each orange juice and cherry brandy. Strain into a martini glass.*

AUGUST 12, 1762

Whether through greed, haste or ignorance of anatomy, the Earl of Huntingdon did himself out of 500 pounds this evening. Britain's Queen Charlotte was about to give birth to her first child, and George III had promised that sum to the first person to bring him news of the safe arrival as he waited in another room of St.James's Palace. If it were a son, he added, the reward would be doubled. At 7:24 the Queen was safely delivered; the noble earl, who had been on the scene by right of his function as Groom of the Stole, hotfooted it to the King's presence. "Your Majesty is the father of a fine princess!", he cried. The nation had 68 years to reflect on this piece of misjudgment, as the princess soon became Prince of Wales and eventually King George IV.

*Outsmart the earl with a **Little Prince**: Over 3 ice cubes in a tumbler, pour 1½ oz. gin and 1 oz. each kirsch and sweet white vermouth. Stir, top up with bitter lemon and strain into 2 small Old-Fashioned glasses.*

AUGUST 13, 1875

It took a long time, in the wee hours of this morning, for British merchant marine officer Matthew Webb to get rid of all the porpoise grease with which he had smeared himself at the suggestion of Frank Buckland, editor of the naturalist magazine *Land and Water*. By that time his companions had brought the intrepid 27-year-old swimmer nearly back to the Admiralty Pier at Dover. Dressed for the occasion only in grease and goggles, Captain Webb had reached the middle of the English Channel when rough weather ruined his chances of attaining the French coast. "We are strongly of the opinion", pontificated the following week's *Illustrated London News*, "that the Channel will ever prevent any man from swimming across without artificial aid". But four days later Matthew Webb, re-greased, gave them the lie with a heroic effort lasting more than 15 hours.

*Toast the waterproof mariner in a **Sea Captain's Special**: Muddle 1 tsp. sugar and 3 drops Angostura in the bottom of a champagne tulip. Add 1 oz. rye with cracked ice. Stir; top up with champagne and 3 dashes Pernod.*

AUGUST 14, 1822

Sir Walter Scott, who had appointed himself emcee of King George IV's first visit to Scotland, decided this evening that toadying to royalty had its disadvantages. Invited on board the king's yacht, named (you guessed it) *Royal George*, which was anchored in the Roads of Leith outside Edinburgh, he had persuaded the overweight and dignity-conscious monarch that it would be proper for the royal Person to be seen in Highland dress at a public function. The royal knees, he explained, could be covered by flesh-coloured tights. Then, over a drink, Scott obtained permission to take away the king's glass as a souvenir. When he reached home in Edinburgh, with the glass stuck in the pocket of his loose cloak, he found the old poet Crabbe on the sofa. Scott immediately sat down next to him, damaging both glass and ass.

You can mix this nearly as quickly as Sir Walter's **Bottom Rose**: *Stir briskly with ice 1½ oz. Genevers gin and ½ oz. each apricot brandy and sweet vermouth. Strain into a cocktail glass.*

AUGUST 15, 1901

Writing home from their Paris hotel today, the two English college principals found they were both recounting the strange feelings they had experienced in the gardens of Versailles a few days before, seeming to spot ghosts from the time of Marie Antoinette. As they walked the paths, "royal gardeners" disappeared into the shrubbery, and a shadowy "courtier" waved from behind a window in the Petit Trianon, then vanished too. Feeding on each other's recollections, the Misses Jourdain and Moberly developed their story over the next 10 years and published it, to the delight of enthusiasts of psychic phenomena. It took several more years for the likely explanation to emerge: Rich, exquisite Comte Robert de Montesquiou, who lived nearby at the time, delighted in dressing his friends in aristocrats' costumes of the 1700's. Marcel Proust wrote later to ask him, "When will you return to that Versailles of which you are the pensive Marie Antoinette?"

Was it only their **Dream**? *For similar effects, mix 1 oz. brandy with ½ oz. curaçao and 1 dash Pernod over ice. Strain into a cocktail glass.*

AUGUST 16, 1822

Accompanying Lord Byron to the Mediterranean shore near Viareggio today, the writer E.J.Trelawny kept in mind his companion's characterization as "mad, bad and dangerous to know". Last month Percy Bysshe Shelley had drowned off that beach when his boat capsized. Now his friends had come to exhume the remains from a shallow sandy grave and cremate them. Suddenly the free-spirited Byron suggested that he would like to save Shelley's skull, as a memento from one poet to another so to speak. This was agreed until, as Trelawny wrote, he remembered one of his companion's idiosyncrasies and "thereupon determined not to give up the skull." He recalled that at Byron's country seat, Newstead Abbey, a casual guest who accepted the offer of a glass of wine would find it served in a skull which the host had unearthed on the site. So Trelawny insisted that the cremation proceed with all of Percy Bysshe Shelley.

*Drink your **Abbey** from a more symmetrical container: Shake well with ice 1 oz. gin, ½ oz. each Lillet and orange juice, and 1 dash Angostura bitters. Strain into a cocktail glass.*

AUGUST 17, 1661

Well pleased this evening with the success of his estate-warming party for 6,000 intimate friends, Nicolas Fouquet, France's minister of finance, failed to note that he had aroused the suspicions of one of them — the boss, Louis XIV. The king admired Fouquet's Château Vaux-le-Vicomte and enjoyed the elaborate dishes prepared under the perfectionist eye of Vatel, Fouquet's Swiss-born maître d'hôtel; but he wondered where his minister found the cash. It turned out that Fouquet had been on the take. Three weeks later he was on his way to 16 years in jail. Chef Vatel was snapped up by the king's brother for his Château Chantilly, but it didn't last. When some fish ordered for a banquet failed to arrive, Vatel stabbed himself and expired before the guests had finished their soup.

*Little preparation is needed for your **Garden Party**: Pour ½ oz. raspberry liqueur into a champagne saucer and gently stir in 4 oz. chilled sparkling white wine.*

AUGUST 18, 1839

Lord Palmerston, Her Majesty's Secretary of State for Foreign Affairs, found himself in a domestic affair very early this Sunday morning. It was not long after midnight when the jolly 55-year-old bachelor, Queen Victoria's guest at Windsor Castle, padded along the corridor to the bedroom of a lady who had welcomed him in the past. But there had been a late change in the accommodation arrangements for the ladies-in-waiting: Palmerston found himself being resisted by the young and resonant-voiced Mrs. Brand. Luckily he was engaged to marry the sister of Prime Minister Melbourne, who managed to keep everyone quiet because of the embarrassment that might ensue to the 20-year-old maiden queen. In fact, Victoria didn't learn of it until after marrying stuffy Albert, when he reproved his secretary for suggesting in a note that "perhaps through force of habit Lord P. floundered into the usual bedroom".

*Tonight's remembrance of doings up at the castle is the **Castle Special**: Shake with ice 2 oz. dark rum, 1½ tsp. sweetened lime juice and 2 dashes curaçao. Strain into a cocktail glass; top with a mint leaf.*

AUGUST 19, 1745

Charles Edward Louis John Casimir Silvester Severino Maria Stuart sat gloomily today in a hut at Glenfinnan on Scotland's west coast. Only 150 Highlanders had turned up to rally to his invasion of the British Isles, now governed by German-born George the Second. But then, from over the hill, came the sound of the pipes as 700 Camerons thronged into the glen. They were led by the brave Lochiel (who was to die at Culloden cursing the same men as they turned and fled). Inspired by these reinforcements, the old Marquess of Tullibardine, who had fought for Charles' father James 30 years before, raised the standard and proclaimed him Resident Regent for "King James III of England and VIII of Scotland". The invasion was on ! Unromantic historians have stripped Bonnie Prince Charlie of such virtues as generalship and common sense, but at least you may toast the high hopes of that day at Glenfinnan.

*May the **Camerons' Kick** be as cheering to you: Shake well with cracked ice 1 oz. each Scotch and Irish, and ½ oz. each lemon juice and sugar syrup. Strain into a small Old-Fashioned glass containing 1 ice cube.*

AUGUST 20, 1883

The spirit of Atahuallpa, the last free Inca of Peru, must have looked on with dismay today as the city council of Cuzco had a new statue from Italy uncrated. In a few days, on the 350th anniversary of his garrotting by Spanish *conquistadores*, Atahuallpa would be unveiled in bronze atop a fountain in the Plaza de Armas. But the Italian foundrymen had economized. They were working on a North American order for a statue of Chief Powhatan, whose daughter Pocahontas had befriended the early settlers of Virginia; and here came another order for an Amerind chief. So Atahuallpa, wearing a feather and buckskin leggings instead of a gold crown and ornaments, was duly installed. His statue remained in place until public ridicule forced the city to hide him from view.

*A toast to the chief in **Sangre Peruana**: 1 oz. pisco (or tequila), 1 oz. dry vermouth, ½ oz. tomato juice, 3 dashes Angostura and 3 tsp. sugar syrup. Mix well, pour over ice cubes in a lowball glass and add an olive.*

AUGUST 21, 1888

At the request of his visiting Uncle Edward, newly-crowned German Kaiser Wilhelm II went out today from Berlin to suburban Spandau to watch different machineguns being tested. His uncle had been praising the British Maxim gun. When the competition started, the four-man team handling a Gatling rang off 333 rounds in just under a minute. The Gardner and Nordenfelt followed, both slightly slower. Then Hiram Maxim himself sat on the trail of his invention, and in half a minute fired as many bullets as any of the others had managed in twice the time. The Kaiser walked over, put his hand on the trail and said "This is the gun; there is no other". Uncle Edward, who happened to be Prince of Wales, fortunately didn't live to see the end result of his recommendation. By World War I Germany's 50,000 Maxim-licensed guns far outnumbered Britain's own supply; on the first day of Haig's Somme offensive they helped to mow down 19,000 Tommies labouring across No Man's Land under their heavy packs.

*Test the **Maxim** with a single round: Stir with ice 2 oz. gin, 1 oz. sweet vermouth and 2 dashes white crème de cacao. Strain into a chilled cocktail glass.*

AUGUST 22, 1851

The 83-year-old Marquess of Anglesey couldn't believe that the yacht didn't have an engine. He leaned so far over the stern looking for a propeller that Commodore John Stevens of the New York Yacht Club had to grab the old nobleman's wooden leg, won at Waterloo, to prevent him from falling overboard. But it was too true: the schooner *America* had fairly beaten 14 of Britain's fastest vessels in a 60-mile race around the Isle of Wight. Captain Dick Brown got the 110-ton craft away slowly but moved into the lead when the wind freshened, to take the race with eight minutes in hand. Commodore Stevens carried away the baroque silver ewer known (from its cost) as the 100-Guinea Cup. His consortium sold the world's fastest yacht at a loss, but had the satisfaction of bringing the championship to the United States for 132 years and having the trophy renamed The *America*'s Cup.

*This **Fresh Wind** will clear two heads: Stir 3 oz. vodka, 1 oz. dry vermouth, ½ tsp. Cointreau and juice of ½ grapefruit in a jug containing 5 ice cubes. Strain into martini glasses.*

AUGUST 23, 1784

Sir Joshua Reynolds, the eminent portraitist, reacted with ambivalence on learning today that he had been appointed Principal Painter in Ordinary to His Majesty King George the Third. Reynolds already knew that this was a lucrative job, if rather boring: instead of his usual 150-pound fee for a full length portrait, he would be getting 50 pounds each for many repetitive pictures of the King and Queen. These would be distributed among foreign monarchs and presented to visiting dignitaries. But Sir Joshua only discovered now the offensive part of his grand appointment. The yearly stipend attached to the office would be just 38 pounds — considerably less than the 48 pounds, three shillings and four pence which represented the salary of Alexander Schomberg, the Royal Ratcatcher.

***George's Beauty** is priceless, and only 96 calories: Shake well with ice ½ oz. brandy, 1 egg white, 2 tsp. lemon juice and 1 tsp. grenadine. Strain into a Sour glass.*

AUGUST 24, 1913

The world's first cabin airplane, standing in a well-guarded space enclosed by an eight-foot-high wooden fence, met its unlikely end today. The four-engined creation of Igor Sikorsky, brilliant 24-year-old chief aviation engineer of The Russian Baltic Company at St. Petersburg, was so big that the workmen named her *Bolshoi*, The Great. Now, after 58 flights in her first three months and a thorough inspection by Czar Nicholas II, whose summer palace was nearby, *Bolshoi* was sitting on a military airfield for the annual flying competition. Overhead, demonstrating a new biplane, was Gabor Vlinsky, whom Sikorsky had bested during the previous year's contest with his own light *S-6-A*. At about 1000 feet Vlinsky's craft began to come apart. Pieces flew off, the engine tore loose and plummeted to the ground — straight through *Bolshoi*. Vlinsky, who then showed his skill by landing uninjured in his engineless plane, always denied that his perfect shot had been intentional.

*What's going on **Upstairs**?: Shake well 3 oz. sweet vermouth with 1 oz. lemon juice. Strain into a highball glass containing 2 ice cubes, stir and top up with soda.*

AUGUST 25, 1759

This was the most disappointing day of his imprisonment for the ungentlemanly but cocksure Jacques Casanova de Seingalt. He had passed almost a year of his five-year sentence in the most secure jail of Venice, atop the Doge's palace. The day before yesterday, after five months of nightly digging a circular channel in the thick wooden floor beneath his bed, and refilling the hole with sawdust each morning, Casanova had decided that the job was about done. He set the 27th for his escape into the public room below and then out into the world. But this morning brought a cheery visitor — Laurence, the helpful jailer. "I bring good news. You're being moved today to a larger, brighter cell!"

*Casanova's tool, on this occasion exceptionally, was a **Gimlet**: Stir together with ice 2 oz. gin and 1 oz. lime juice cordial. Strain into a champagne saucer and top with enough chilled soda to fizz.*

AUGUST 26, 1346

Observing the battle from the upper floor of a windmill today, King Edward III of England was reassured about the new idea of training his peasants in tactics. Their longbow detachments kept repelling charges by French knights on horseback outside the Norman village of Crécy. Philippe II, captain of the home team, regarded battle as an exercise in chivalry and class warfare. Soon he was surprised by another of Edward's tricks -- the first field test of three roundelades. These jug-like cannon fired bundles of four iron bolts, with minimal accuracy but plenty of noise which scared the hell out of the French horses. Combined with the efforts of the underclass archers, this enabled Edward's 10,000 troops to put 60,000 French and Genoese to flight.

*A **Coup de Taureau** the morning after usually makes a Frenchman feel better: Overnight keep the cognac bottle, an Old-Fashioned glass, lemon juice and non-jelly type beef bouillon in the refrigerator. Next morning pour 4 oz. bouillon, 1½ oz. cognac and ¼ tsp. lemon juice into the glass. Stir; float a slice of lemon.*

AUGUST 27, 1896

Khaled bin Barghash, who had declared himself Sultan of Zanzibar two days ago on the death of the incumbent, this morning put his little country through an uncomfortable 37-minute war. The British, who were "protecting" the island nation, decided to protect it against Khaled and substitute their own choice. When a two-hour ultimatum expired, Rear-Admiral Harry Rawson's five Royal Navy vessels promptly blew holes in the Sultan's palace and sank the entire Zanzibari navy. It consisted of the aged wooden-hulled steam frigate *Glasgow*, which the British had sold to Zanzibar after she outlived her usefulness. This action effectively scuppered the royal soothsayer, who had predicted that the British ships would only fire jets of water. Khaled took refuge in the German consulate, leaving the soothsayer to do the explaining.

*Quieten six admirals with this **Zanzibar**: Shake well with ice 12 oz. sweet vermouth, 4 oz. dry gin, juice of 1½ lemons, 2 tbsp. sugar syrup and 1 tsp. orange bitters. Strain into small Old-Fashioned glasses and top each with a spiral of lemon peel.*

AUGUST 28, 1895

This evening produced a temporary embarrassment for Mrs. William K. Vanderbilt, throwing the "ball of the year" at Marble House, her Newport summer place. Hints had reached most of the 500 guests that tonight Mrs.V. would definitely announce the engagement of her daughter Consuelo to the slightly dissipated Charles Spencer Churchill, whose offsetting attraction was being the Ninth Duke of Marlborough. But the two orchestras played until well past midnight and still there was no announcement. An admirer noted that Consuelo's "doll-like beauty was unmarked by animation". Her mother knew what was wrong. Young Winthrop Rutherfurd had been invited along on the family's yacht cruise to India, and now the prospect of becoming a duchess meant nothing to the girl. Still, the duke was undismayed, for he knew that his title counted for something with the rich Americans. After a few weeks he got it: a trust fund of $2½ million in old Mr.Vanderbilt's railroad stock, an annual allowance of $100,000 cash — and Consuelo.

*Your **Duke** comes cheap: 2 oz. each dry sherry and sweet vermouth, stirred with 3 dashes orange bitters. Pour into a small Old-Fashioned glass and top with a zest of orange.*

AUGUST 29, 1860

Although Sir George Simpson was 73 and ailing, he had insisted that the Prince of Wales's official visit to Canada should include today's trip to his island estate outside Montreal. Sir George knew he would soon have to end his career as Governor-in-Chief of Rupert's Land, the top post in Canada for the fur trading Hudson's Bay Company. Only last month illness had curtailed his annual canoe-borne tour of inspection to the Northwest; yet for personal and political reasons he must put on a show for the 18-year-old prince. A hundred Iroquois paddlers escorted the royal visitor to Dorval Island for his official lunch. Then Simpson invited the prince to join him for a 1½-mile trip in a birchbark canoe to Hudson's Bay House at Lachine. But this proved too much for the "Little Emperor" of the HBC: three days later he took to his bed in the official governor's residence across the canal. By the time the Prince of Wales left Canada, Sir George Simpson was dead.

*This **Voyageur Reviver** might have helped: Dissolve 1 tsp. sugar in the same quantity of lemon juice. Add 1½ oz. dark rum, ½ oz. curaçao and cracked ice. Shake well and strain into a cocktail glass.*

AUGUST 30, 1816

Weary in body but with his British ambassadorial pride intact, William Pitt Amherst was turned away today from the court of the overbearing Chinese emperor Yuen Ming to begin the five-month journey home. Arriving yesterday in the emperor's antechamber, Amherst learned from the courtiers that he would have to perform the Kowtow — a series of three genuflections and nine prostrations in which his head would have to touch the floor each time. The ambassador protested that he was too ill and tired: the emperor obligingly sent his court physician, who soon twigged and told. This morning Amherst got the message that he was no longer welcome. So, 11 months after leaving London he returned, to report that he had been unable to establish diplomatic relations consistent with personal or national dignity. The government responded by sending him out to try again, this time in Burma.

*This **Oriental** demands no genuflection, just a gentle bending of the elbow: Shake with ice 1 oz. rye and ½ oz. each sweet vermouth, white curaçao and fresh lime juice. Strain into a small Old-Fashioned glass.*

AUGUST 31, 1839

Frightening the villagers of Irvine, Ayrshire for the last time by galloping through the streets tonight in full armour, the young Marquis of Waterford made up for some recent disappointments. First, a railway company had curtly refused to make two engines run into each other at full speed, even at the marquis' expense, "to see what would happen". Then, almost continuous rain had fallen during this week's Eglinton Tournament nearby. Its re-creation of medieval chivalry was designed to show that Britain's inbred aristocrats were as lusty and manly as ever. At least the young marquis had no doubts on that score: having rented space from the local dominie, who was moving out to avoid the moral contamination of the tournament, the marquis happily installed his mistress in the manse.

*A lusty drink indeed is the **Sir Knight**: Stir well in a mixing glass ½ oz. each cognac, Cointreau and yellow Chartreuse with 2 dashes Angostura. Pour into a cocktail glass and top with a twist of lemon.*

SEPTEMBER 1, 1870

French emperor Napoleon III rode up and down under Prussian artillery fire this afternon, hoping to be hit; but without success. An ex-politician known to his adversaries as "*Napoléon le Petit*" to distinguish him from his famous uncle, he had launched a glorious war and was now on the losing end. His army of 100,000 was surrounded near the town of Sedan in the Ardennes, so the emperor was courting death to save himself from further humiliation. But then, since the Prussians seemed unable to hit him, Napoleon decided he might as well stay alive. He penned a message to the king of Prussia: "My dear brother monarch: not having been able to die at the head of my troops....." The 3,000 Frenchmen killed in the battle were saved from knowing that their emperor would retire to a resort town in southern England.

*France surrendered and had to cede **Alsace-Lorraine** but you can win it back: ½ oz. each anisette and kirsch, mixed in the glass and then topped with water to taste.*

SEPTEMBER 2, 1909

Dr. Frederick Cook astonished the readers of the New York *Herald* today with his account of how, 17 months before, he had been the first person to reach the North Pole. Since then, Cook cabled from Shetland, he had been wandering in northern latitudes. But within five days Commodore Robert E. Peary, for whom Cook had been ship's doctor in the 1890's, was in print with the news that he had reached the Pole himself in April and found no trace of man or beast. To this Dr. Cook, who had stuck the *Herald* for over $3000, allowed that "there is no one living that I would prefer to the brave Peary — to follow in my footsteps". He was, however, to encounter a lifetime of scepticism, which was not allayed when he went to jail for using the mails to defraud.

*At least Peary and Cook agreed on the **Twinkle of the Pole Star**: Stir in a mixing glass 1 oz. each dry gin and green Chartreuse, ½ oz. each Drambuie and dry vermouth, and 1 dash orange bitters. Strain into a cocktail glass.*

SEPTEMBER 3, 1835

This evening ended most discouragingly for Joseph Livesey, the stammering printer from Preston in Lancashire, who had founded the Teetotal movement when he told a temperance meeting that he was a "t-t-t-total abstainer". Today, about to start a proselytizing lecture in a hall he had rented in London's Theobalds Road, Livesey suddenly realized that the entire small audience was composed of people who had accompanied him on the trip. He went out into the street ringing a handbell and calling on the citizenry to come to his lecture. Soon a police officer tapped him on the shoulder and threatened to take him in charge if he didn't stop the noise. As a result the lecture hall remained almost empty. Livesey's temperance message therefore went unheard by the public, and drinking has since continued in London right up to the present day.

*Most of the expected audience were **Absent**: Fill an 8 oz. glass with cracked ice. Pour in 1½ oz. Pernod, ½ oz. water, 3 dashes sugar syrup, 2 dashes orange curaçao and 1 dash Angostura. Stir well and add a twist of lemon peel.*

SEPTEMBER 4, 404 B.C.

Lucky, lucky day for Mrs. Kallistira of Rhodes, who just missed being thrown off a cliff overlooking the river Alpheus in the Peloponnese. Widow and daughter-in-law of former Olympic competitors, she had coached her son Pisirodos in boxing after her husband died, and last week accompanied the boy to the 94th running of the all-male Olympic Games. Dressed as his trainer, Kallistira escaped particular notice until today, when Pisirodos won his fight. Overcome with pride, she rushed into the ring to embrace her big boy. The usual punishment for women discovered at the Games was death, but the successes of her family saved Kallistira. To make sure it never happened again, the committee decreed that trainers should attend future Olympics dressed just like the athletes — in their birthday suits.

*Honour the heroes of the steroid-free Olympics with a **Greek Buck**: Shake with ice 1½ oz. Metaxa brandy and 2 tsp. lemon juice; strain into a highball glass over 2 ice cubes. Nearly top up with ginger ale; add 1 slice lemon and float 1 oz. ouzo.*

SEPTEMBER 5, 1859

Isambard Kingdom Brunel, the "Little Giant" of British railway and marine engineering, compensated for his short stature with an exceptionally tall hat today. He was to be photographed before one of the five funnels on his *Great Eastern*, which was five times larger than anything else afloat. She was still untried, but after 18 months the Great Ship Company had finally fitted her out to a standard that satisfied Brunel. None too soon, for a few moments after his photograph had been taken the great engineer collapsed. Carried to his home, he learned a few days later that the *Great Eastern*, on trials in the English Channel, had burst a boiler and would be out of commission for longer than the six days which were all that he had left.

*Outdo old Isambard with not one, but **Two Hats**: If feeling rocky, heat 6 oz. red burgundy almost to boiling; add 3 oz. cognac, 1 tsp. honey and 2 whole cloves; simmer for 5 minutes. Pour into a mug which has been scalded. Put a hat at the foot of your bed and get into bed. Sip the mixture. When you can see two hats, your illness is fading away.*

SEPTEMBER 6, 1769

James Boswell prepared today to make an absolute ass of himself at Stratford-on-Avon, where the town burgesses were only three years late with their sesquicentennial celebrations of Shakespeare's death. Tired from a long coach ride, Boswell stopped in at the inaugural ball just to size up the crowd and decide on a costume. Then to call attention to his current external enthusiasm, the independence of Corsica from France, he attired himself in Corsican style. Boswell hoped to attract some enquiries, but he was judged simply an eccentric tourist. Next day he had a large sign painted and stuck it in his hat. It read BOSWELL-CORSICA. Still nobody took any notice, and it was only out of self-interest that the British, 25 years later, did help the Corsicans to become very briefly independent.

*Boswell competed against this mixture to be **Dr.Johnson's Choice**: Heat 2 bottles Bordeaux, 24 lumps of sugar and 12 cloves to near boiling; add 1 qt. hot water and 2 wineglasses each of brandy and orange curaçao. Pour into heated mugs and sprinkle with grated nutmeg. Serves 10.*

SEPTEMBER 7, 1838

A great letdown today for young William Darling and six other volunteer boatmen of North Sunderland, County Durham. After learning by a messenger from Bamburgh Castle that the 300-ton paddlewheel steamer *Forfarshire* had run onto the rocks five miles away, they rowed through heavy seas to reach her. There they found nobody: the nine survivors had already been rescued by William's older sister Grace and their father, the keeper of Longstone lighthouse. Grace had spotted the wreck at first light and persuaded her father they could get there in the family coble. But having come this far, the Sunderland boys rowed along to the lighthouse, where Mum gave them all tea. Young Wiliam would rather have won the Humane Society's gold medal, which was presented to his big sister.

Grace's Delight was to cheer on the seven-man lifeboat crew with 3½ oz. Scotch, 4½ oz. sweet vermouth and 1½ oz. raspberry brandy, poured over shaved ice in a jug. Add juice of 1 orange, 3 juniper berries, and 1 pinch each powdered cinnamon and nutmeg. Stir well with a silver spoon, strain into a cocktail shaker and refrigerate for at least one hour. Shake before serving.

SEPTEMBER 8, 1883

Chief Sitting Bull of the Western Dakotas, only seven years after his epic victory over Custer's Seventh Cavalry at the Little Big Horn, had retired to the Standing Rock reservation and become a figure of more interest than fear to the American public. Today's visit to Bismarck gave him an opportunity to satisfy their curiosity. The Northern Pacific Railroad's new line from there would bring supplies for Standing Rock, and the old warrior was asked if he would say a few words of appreciation at the opening ceremony. A young Army officer, assigned as interpreter, sat with him and worked out a short statement. When the chief's turn came, he stared out at the crowd and declaimed in Siouan Dakota: "I hate white men; you are all thieves and liars". The audience listened politely, then burst into cheers as the officer translated: "I am greatly honoured to be in your fine city". The Northern Pacific people were so pleased they insisted that Sitting Bull do a repeat performance in St.Paul.

*This **Warrior** may make you cheer: Shake with ice 2 oz. white rum, 2 tsp. grenadine syrup, and a pinch each of black pepper, cinnamon and nutmeg; strain into a cocktail glass. Decorate the rim with a lemon slice.*

SEPTEMBER 9, 1890

It was an unpleasant thought for members of the smart Yorkshire houseparty — surely Sir William Gordon-Cumming, owner of a 40,000 acre estate with income to match, wouldn't cheat the Prince of Wales out of a few 10-pound wagers at baccarat? Yet it seemed that the occasional extra counter was finding its way across the chalk line when the bank had to pay out, and it was the prince's turn as banker in tonight's card game. "There's another tenner, Sir, to come over here", Sir William called out. "I wish you'd put your counters where they can be seen better", came the royal retort. But Sir William never got the chance to sharpen, or perhaps to blunt, his handling of the chips. Fearful of publicity about the Prince of Wales's gambling, the others made the wealthy baronet agree never to play cards for money again, in exchange for their pledge of secrecy. That pledge was soon broken, so Sir William was ready to gamble — but nobody in Society would play.

*What more appropriate for those highfalutin' guests than an **After-Dinner Charade**? It takes 1 oz. Sciarada liqueur and ½ oz. each peppermint schnapps and 35% cream. Shake well with ice and strain into a cocktail glass.*

SEPTEMBER 10, 1898

All over Europe, crowned heads wobbled when the man who stabbed Empress Elisabeth of Austria-Hungary this afternoon in Geneva declared her a suitable target "because she wore a crown". (The assassin had planned to start with King Umberto of Italy, but couldn't raise 50 lire for the train fare to Rome). No crown wobbled faster than that atop Sultan Abdul Hamid of Turkey. This Emperor of Mighty Empires, Sole Arbiter of the World's Destiny, High King of the Two Seas and Shadow of God on Earth was actually a nervous little fellow. Abdul reacted to the news by ordering a vest of chain mail, which he wore henceforth on his way to and from Friday evening service at a public mosque. When President McKinley was shot, the sultan had the newspapers ascribe his death to anthrax. That still sounded rather severe, so when the King and Queen of Serbia got theirs a bit later, the Turkish public read that they were suffering from indigestion.

*This **Crown** should be shaken, not wobbled: Mix 1 oz. Scotch, 2 oz. lemon juice and 1 dash grenadine syrup. Strain into a small Old-Fashioned glass.*

SEPTEMBER 11, 1847

This was a big evening for young Stephen Foster of Pittsburgh as the local amateur glee club sang his "Oh! Susanna" in Andrews' Ice Cream Parlor. It was the first public performance, after rehearsals at the 21-year-old Foster's home. The song began to attract attention, and the commercially ignorant young man sent the music to anyone who asked for it. One recipient, the British-born former military clarinettist William Peters, sent Foster $100 in return. Then he copyrighted "Oh!Susanna" and published it "as sung by G.N.Christy" of the Christy Minstrels, a celebrated blackface troupe. By 1851 Peters had grown rich on the proceeds, while during that period his payment to the composer would have earned an average interest of $6.50 a year. When Stephen Foster died, in a roominghouse for derelicts on New York's Bowery, he left 38 cents.

At that level, no worries about **Income Tax**: *Stir with ice 1 oz. each dry gin and orange juice, ½ oz. each sweet and dry vermouth and 1 dash Angostura. Strain into a chilled cocktail glass.*

SEPTEMBER 12, 1683

Proudly proclaiming that he had captured the Grand Standard of the Prophet Mohammed in the battle outside Vienna, Poland's King John Sobieski sent it south today to be presented to the Pope as a souvenir. In several days of fighting, the Christian forces under John and the Duc de Lorraine had managed to turn back a Moslem advance at the very gates of the city, which was not bothered by Infidels again. An equerry showed the captured flag to the Doge of Venice and then in every city on the route to Rome. After its display to admiring crowds, princes and mayors wrote letters of congratulations to John Sobieski, who had them bound in a book. Only after several months did the proud Pole admit that the Moslems had made off with their real Grand Standard; his trophy was a minor regimental banner. But of course he kept the bound volume of congratulations.

Here's a **Polish Bull** *you can swallow: Dissolve 1 tsp. Bovril in a mug of boiling water; stir in 1½ oz. vodka, 1 squeeze lemon and 1 shake pepper.*

SEPTEMBER 13, 1759

At 7 this morning, encamped on the northern outskirts of Québec City, General Louis Joseph Saint-Véran, Marquis de Montcalm, received today's first nasty surprise. Having judged the heights above the St. Lawrence river, 10 miles southwest of his headquarters, as the least likely place for the British to attack, Montcalm had entrusted their defence to old Captain duChambon de Vergor, who had been reprimanded for cowardice after surrendering Fort Beauséjour. So when news arrived that the British had climbed those heights, Montcalm guessed correctly that the captain had already been taken prisoner. The general hastened south-westward and ordered 25 cannon to follow him, but only three had arrived by the time of his second nasty surprise, which was to be hit by a cannonball. Then another cannonball dug a hole in the floor of the Ursuline convent, coincidentally just the right size to hold the late Marquis de Montcalm.

*For a taste of **Québec**, Shake well with ice 1½ oz. Canadian whisky, 2 tsp. dry vermouth and 1 tsp. each Amer Picon and maraschino. Strain into an Old-Fashioned glass containing 2 ice cubes.*

SEPTEMBER 14, 1812

"At Moscow" was the new heading on today's letter from General Armand de Caulaincourt to the Arch-Chancellor of France in Paris. Napoleon, after entering the gates of the almost deserted city, told de Caulaincourt to start letting the world know that he would soon be master of Russia. Exactly 15 days later the word would reach Paris, by the relays of express couriers established to carry back news of the Grande Armée's triumphal progress. An advance party was in the Kremlin compound to raise the *tricolore*. This was just what the Mint at Paris had been waiting for. One side of its new medal design showed the Emperor Napoleon's head wreathed in the garland of victory; on the other, the French flag waved from the Kremlin's highest steeple. The legend read "Entrée à Moscou, XIV septembre MDCCCXII". But even as the medals were being prepared, Napoleon was finally turning his troops around to struggle back through the gathering winter. No medal was struck to commemorate the Retreat from Moscow.

__Winter's a-Cumin__ won't bother you: ½ oz. each Kümmel and lemon juice are well shaken with 1 oz. dry gin and shaved ice; strain into a chilled martini glass containing 3 cumin seeds.

SEPTEMBER 15, 1830

At the end of today's inaugural railway trip from Liverpool to Manchester, it was considered an immense success by everyone except William Huskisson, the local member of Parliament, who had recently been dropped from the Duke of Wellington's cabinet. Eight trains were lined up; the Prime Minister rode in the first one but Huskisson was allocated to another. He still wanted to be noticed talking to Wellington, so when the locomotives all stopped at Parkhurst to take on water he jumped down and ran ahead. Suddenly the Prime Minister's train started off. Huskisson tried to clamber aboard, fell off and was promptly run over by the next locomotive. The *Northumbrian* tried to make up for this by being the first train ever to take anyone to hospital, but it was no use. A bye-election had to be held for the vacant Parliamentary seat of Liverpool.

*Your **Hot Locomotive** should be accident-free: Put in a pan 1 egg yolk, ½ tbsp. sugar and 1 tsp. honey. Add 1½ wineglasses burgundy and 1 tsp. curaçao. Stir well, heat nearly to boiling and pour into a mug over a cinnamon stick and slice of lemon.*

SEPTEMBER 16, 1714

Gottfried W. Leibniz, holder of the plum job of Court Philosopher and Librarian to George, Elector of Hanover, returned today from a stay in Vienna to discover that his patron had left yesterday for permanent residence in England. (It was not that the island off the coast of Europe attracted him particularly, but its inhabitants had offered him the crown and this could be politically useful). Leibniz, who had expected to be asked along, found that he had been bumped from the retinue in favour of two mistresses, two Turkish valets and one dwarf. Repeated enquiries to the Elector only produced instructions to stay in Hanover and work on the history of the House of Brunswick. Nobody likes a loser, so when the rheumatism-wracked philosopher died two years later the only mourner at graveside was his secretary.

*If restricted to communicating by **Royal Mail**, shake together with ice ½ oz. each sloe gin, Van der Hum, orange and lemon juices with 1 dash ouzo. Strain into a chilled cocktail glass.*

SEPTEMBER 17, 1799

James Briggs, master of the American trader *Nancy*, thought he had cleared his name today in the vice-admiralty court at Kingston, Jamaica. The ship had been seized by the British on suspicion of having carried arms to the Dutch colony of Curaçao while Holland was at war with Britain. Captain Briggs swore that no papers had been "burnt, thrown overboard, destroyed, cancelled, concealed or attempted so to be" — which seemed to cover most eventualities. But then Lieutenant Michael Titton of HMS *Ferret* burst into the courtroom, waving a packet of papers. These, crumpled but legibly damning of Captain Briggs' activities, had been found in the stomach of a shark which the *Ferret's* crew had caught for lunch. The *Nancy* became a prize of war and Captain Briggs had to hitch-hike back to the States.

*Tasty for two before a shark lunch is the **Shark's Tooth**: Shake well with ice 3 oz. golden rum, ½ oz. each lemon juice, sweet vermouth, passionfruit juice and sloe gin, and 2 dashes Angostura. Strain into chilled, sugar-frosted highball glasses containing 3 ice cubes. Top each drink with a twist of orange peel and a cherry.*

SEPTEMBER 18, 1836

A horse-van disguised as a coach trundled away from Goodwood racetrack in Sussex today, putting into action the sneaky plan of Lord George Bentinck. Inside was Elis, one of Lord George's throroughbreds and a consistent winner. Elis would be a good bet for next Sunday's St.Leger race at Doncaster, up in Yorkshire — if the team of six horses hauling the van could cover the 223 miles of country roads in time, and in secret. Horses were habitually walked from one venue to the next, after which they would rest for several days. So after midweek Lord George had his agents place bets on Elis, with bookmakers who were watching the scene at Doncaster. Since Elis hadn't arrived yet, the bookies guessed he would be too tired to place well. But the anonymous van arrived on Saturday evening, and on Sunday there was the well-rested Elis, winning the St.Leger by two lengths — a real eye-opener.

*Your **Eye-Opener** comes from a shaker. Mix 1 egg yolk in with 2 oz. golden rum, 1 tsp. each curaçao and crème de cacao, and ½ tsp. each Pernod and sugar. Shake with cracked ice and strain into a martini glass.*

SEPTEMBER 19, 1846

At 3:30 this afternoon, frail Elizabeth Barrett Browning first made sure that her father and sisters were still stuffing their faces at Sunday dinner downstairs. Then, although not considered robust enough to leave her chaise longue, Elizabeth slipped out of the house in Wimpole Street to meet her secret husband for the first time since their marriage a week ago. She had not dared admit to her widowed father that she had broken the house rule of celibacy for his daughters. But now Robert Browning was waiting outside Hodgson's the booksellers, with a cab which would take them across London to the Vauxhall station. In his excitement Robert had got the cross-Channel ferry schedule wrong, but they were just able to get aboard at Southampton, enroute to Italy, before the Barretts found out. Elizabeth's father refused to write or speak to her again.

For your own secret **Rendezvous** *you both need a drink, so mix with cracked ice 3 oz. gin, 1 oz. kirsch and ½ oz. Campari. Strain into cocktail glasses; add twists of lemon.*

SEPTEMBER 20, 1493

It had taken a lot of flesh-pressing by the Pope, but the vote today in the Sacred College of Cardinals was 11 to 10 in favour of accepting Cesare Borgia, of the well-known food processing family, as a member of the club. Pope Alexander VI was intent on packing the Sacred College with friendly nominees. He had certified in a public document that Cesare was legitimate issue of a virtuous Roman couple, but a secret Bull made it clear to the cardinals that the young man was Alexander's own illegitimate son. The new cardinal had other qualifications, of varying merit: he was Archbishop of Valencia, brother to Lucrezia Borgia, and all of 15 years old.

Celebrate Father & Son Day at the Vatican with a **Bastardo**: *Pour over ice in an Old-Fashioned glass 1 oz. each dry and sweet vermouth, ½ oz. brandy and 2 dashes Angostura. Stir well, add a dash of soda and top with a slice of lemon.*

SEPTEMBER 21, 1802

An accident of nature rather spoiled the effect of André-Jacques Garnerin's heroic parachute jump today as he landed near London's St.Pancras Church. The young Frenchman had nearly five years' experience in other countries of jumping from the baskets of hot-air balloons, but today for the first time a strut broke in the top of his parachute's umbrella-framed canopy. The balloon ascent from Grosvenor Square went smoothly enough, but as the parachute came down André-Jacques oscillated violently from side to side. When spectators rushed forward to greet him, poor Garnerin, described as "trembling excessively", suffered a violent nosebleed and vomited at their feet. This set back for more than a century the attraction of parachuting as a sport.

*A **Parachute Punch** would have put A-J back on his feet: Shake well together 1 oz. each brandy, kirsch and black coffee with ½ of an eggwhite. Strain into a goblet containing cracked ice, and top up with soda water.*

SEPTEMBER 22, 1842

Charles Babbage, the sharp-tongued Cambridge maths professor who had founded the Statistical Society but kept losing other people's money with his betting system, couldn't resist today's opportunity to point out someone else's error. In a new volume of poems Alfred Tennyson had included this couplet:
"Every minute dies a man
Every minute one is born."
The poet was rather fond of these lines, which he had taken from a superseded manuscript of *Locksley Hall* and found room for in the newly-published *The Vision of Sin*. But Babbage could not agree to the world population remaining constant: "The erroneous calculation to which I refer," he wrote Tennyson today, "should be corrected as follows:
'Every minute dies a man
And one and 1/16 is born'."
But Tennyson continued to ignore the population explosion. In the next edition he simply changed "minute" to "moment".

*Not a fraction of doubt in the **Hundred Percent**: Combine with ice 1 oz. Swedish Punch, 1 tsp. each lemon and orange juices, and 2 dashes grenadine. Shake well, strain into a Sour glass and add chipped ice.*

SEPTEMBER 23, 1777

Brigadier-General George Clinton, rebel governor of the colony of New York, enjoyed reading the British enemy's plans tonight after having been confused with his namesake, Major-General Sir Henry Clinton. <u>That</u> Clinton, who commanded the opposing forces up the Hudson, hoped to link up with General Burgoyne further north. He had sent an officer to find him, dressed in civilian clothes to remain inconspicuous. A little way through the rebel-infested countryside the officer, Lieutenant Taylor, was accosted by some gentlemen who told him General Clinton had an additional message, if he would just accompany them to a forward post. There Taylor found himself in the presence of the wrong general; he snapped a tiny silver ball from his powdered queue and swallowed it. Guessing that the ball contained useful information, Clinton had a surgeon administer a powerful emetic. Since Lieutenant Taylor wore no uniform and therefore counted as a spy, the emetic brought up what had to be his last meal.

*Let's hope your **Silver Bullet** has a happier result: Pour into an ice-filled glass 1½ oz. vodka, followed by 1 oz. kümmel.*

SEPTEMBER 24, 1854

One-armed Field-Marshal Fitzroy Somerset, First Baron Raglan, was glad to be wearing a discreet blue frock coat, rather than his uniform, when he encountered the enemy this afternoon. Although he commanded the entire British force in the Crimea as it approached Sebastopol, the 65-year-old usually appeared in mufti except on parade. Now he spurred his horse out of some woods and found himself at the rear of a halted Russian wagon train. The arrival of this country gentleman caused mild surprise among the enemy. But before they could question him, a vanguard of the British horse artillery came crashing through the woods behind Raglan, accompanied by his staff. The Russians took off, having muffed the chance to make an amazing capture.

*If **Mufti** suits you too, stir well with ice 1½ oz. Pernod, and 1 tsp. each maraschino and lemon juice. Strain into a cocktail glass.*

SEPTEMBER 25, 1513

Hacking and sweating his way across Panama's jungly Isthmus of Darien at slightly more than a mile a day, Vasco Nuñez de Balboa insisted on wearing his armour (perhaps in an effort to lose weight and belie his rather confusing nickname, "Stout Cortez"). Today at last he led his remaining 66 Spaniards up a rise from which they could see the Pacific. Balboa plunged ahead and waded into the water, waving his sword to claim for Spain the entire ocean and all lands around it. Returning to the settlement on the Caribbean side of the isthmus, he was rewarded with the opportunity to marry the new governor's daughter, sight unseen. This escaped him, however, due to a misunderstanding with his prospective father-in-law, Pedro Arias. Accused of wanting to renege on the engagement, poor Balboa was put to death — a difficult sentence for historians to evaluate, since no portrait survives of Señorita Arias.

To cool hot passions, try a **Pacific Pacifier**: *Combine over ice 1 oz. Cointreau and 1 tbsp. each banana liqueur and light cream. Shake, then strain into a small Old-Fashioned glass.*

SEPTEMBER 26, 1687

Not such a rewarding day, eventually, for General Francesco Morosini of Venice. He was as devout as the next Christian general, so he found himself in a bit of a quandary while attacking Athens under occupation by the Turks. Atop the Acropolis stood the most easily identifiable artillery target for several hundred miles around. The Parthenon had been transformed into a church by the Greeks, but Morosini knew that the Turks in turn had found a better use for it, as a warehouse for explosives. He gave the order to shell it. Up went the stored gunpowder and down came most of the centre section of the Parthenon. But the Turks did not yield the city. In fact, after the war they took advantage of the new open space in the church to build the highest mosque in Athens.

A hundred gunners sat down afterwards to enjoy **Artillery Punch**: *Extract the juice from 6 large pineapples. Slice 1 qt. strawberries; combine with the pineapple juice and 1 qt. orange juice in a large punchbowl. Add 1 gallon hard cider and 1 fifth each bourbon and dark rum; stir well and let stand overnight. To serve, add lots of ice and 12 bottles sparkling white wine.*

SEPTEMBER 27, 1842

General Antonio Lopez Santa Anna, enjoying one of his five stints as President of Mexico, intended today's ceremony as an example and inspiration to the nation's youth — even if others regarded it as a politician's ego trip. Since losing his left leg four years ago while defeating a French invading force at Santa Cruz, the general had preserved it at Manga de Clavo, his country retreat. On his 48th birthday earlier this year, however, he had announced that the historic limb would be dug up and placed in a ceremonial urn. So today it was solemnly interred atop a pedestal in Mexico City's Santa Paula cemetery, while a military band played the salute. A perfervid orator cited Santa Anna as the hero who had sacrificed his leg to save his country. But two years later the fickle populace, objecting to the president's dictatorial powers, pulled down the urn and dragged it through the dusty streets of the capital.

Salute the recurring hero with **Pegleg's Peg**: *Put 2 dashes orange bitters in a sherry glass, and swirl to coat the sides; add 1½ oz. tequila and ½ oz. water; stir before drinking.*

SEPTEMBER 28, 1811

Tom Molyneaux, the freed American slave who had worked his passage to England in order to meet his obligation of a return boxing match, soon regretted having tucked into such a big breakfast this morning. After licking Tom Cribb, the British coal porter who was that country's bareknuckle champion, last year, "Black Tom" took life too easy. By the time he reached Thistleton Gap in County Rutland for today's bout, he was far over his fighting weight. After 19 minutes Tom Molyneaux's jaw cracked, and he lost the title in 11 rounds. His breakfast, in case you need to be warned against fighting in such circumstances, included a boiled fowl and an apple pie, washed down with half a gallon of porter.

When in form, Tom could throw an **Old South Punch** *for 25 backers: Cool 1 fifth Southern Comfort, 8 oz. each pineapple and grapefruit juice, 4 oz. each golden rum and lemon juice, and 1 bottle each soda and sparkling white wine. Mix in a punch bowl, add a block of ice and float 25 slices of orange.*

SEPTEMBER 29, 1899

Admiral George Dewey rode up New York's Fifth Avenue today acknowledging the hero-worship being poured over him for smashing the Spanish fleet in Manila Bay. At Madison Square, where the route crossed 23rd Street, the procession passed under a huge triumphal arch. The admiral's hosts explained that it was just a plaster model of the real thing — its replacement would be in marble and granite, paid for by contributions from his grateful countrymen. They omitted to add that the money was coming in so slowly that construction hadn't yet started. Over the next few months public interest evaporated, while the plaster arch began to crumble. Finally garbagemen were sent out discreetly to dismantle it and haul it away to the city dump. The real Dewey Arch never was built.

Stir, do not build, the **Dewey:** *Into a mixing glass containing cracked ice, pour from chilled bottles 1½ oz. each gin and dry vermouth. Add 1 dash orange bitters, stir briefly and strain into a chilled martini glass.*

SEPTEMBER 30, 1661

The Comte d'Estrades considered himself the dean of London's *corps diplomatique* and a good friend of the Court, having suggested a choice of French princesses for bachelor King Charles II. So today he drove to the Tower watergate to welcome and escort the new Swedish envoy. But his arch-rival for diplomatic precedence, the Spanish ambassador, was there too; when d'Estrades tried to lead the parade uptown he found that his horses' traces had been cut. Louis XIV persuaded Spain to yield precedence, but it was too late: a new English law prohibited diplomatic escorts for new ambassadors, "to ensure the peace and security of the City of London". Anyway, Charles turned down the French princesses and planned to marry a Portuguese one instead. The Comte d'Estrades, piqued, resigned his embassy.

The **Charles** *is fit for a king: Stir well together, at room temperature, 1 oz. each brandy and sweet vermouth with 1 dash Angostura. Pour into a cocktail glass.*

OCTOBER 1, 1908

Samuel F. Cody, undeterred by the British Admiralty's stingy counter-offer of 100 pounds sterling to his request for 25,000, again put his life in their hands today as he climbed into a breeches-buoy on the deck of HMS *Recruit*. Four sailors held a huge kite; when they let go, it rose slowly to the end of a 500-foot line with Cody suspended from it. His choice of the breeches-buoy resulted from his last experience, when the line broke and he descended rapidly in a basket into the English Channel. This time the man whose notepaper was headed "INVENTOR OF THE CODY WAR KITE" landed on deck amid a group of officers, who agreed that his invention could be a great observation aid to naval gunnery. But Head Office was not convinced. "My Lords Commissioners of the Admiralty", a functionary wrote to Cody, "consider it premature." He never heard from them again.

*No need to be high as a kite to enjoy the **Skyride Fizz**: Shake well with ice 1½ oz. sloe gin, ½ oz. cream, juice of ½ lemon and 1 tsp. sugar. Strain into a highball glass containing 2 ice cubes; fill with soda and stir gently to fizz.*

OCTOBER 2, 1930

Pride came not long before a fall for retired Air Marshal Sir Sefton Brancker, Britain's director of civil aviation, as he agreed today to accompany his boss to India aboard the government-sponsored airship R-101. Brancker doubted its air-worthiness, but when Lord Thomson, Secretary of State for Air, sneered "Well, would you like to surrender your place on the maiden voyage?", the director took it as a slur on his courage. Thomson was intent on showing that his pet project matched its rival, the privately-built R-100, which had already crossed the Atlantic. But he was also promoting his candidacy for Viceroy of India, and insisted on his immense ministerial red carpet being added to the airship's load so he could receive in style on arrival. Neither man ever walked that red carpet: three nights later R-101, nose-heavy by half a ton, failed to answer the controls and burst into flames on a French hillside.

*This **Red Carpet** won't weigh you down: Stir well with ice 1 oz. each red Bordeaux and sweet vermouth, and ½ oz. strawberry liqueur. Strain into a large wineglass, add the same amount of soda and drop in a slice of lemon.*

OCTOBER 3, 1574

Louis de Boisot, Admiral of Zeeland, made slow progress today toward some besieged Netnerlanders rebelling against Spanish occupation. Floating flat-bottomed boats across flooded fields was not his style, but it was the only way to relieve the starving town of Leyden, hemmed in by the 8,000 soldiers of General Valdez. Leyden's mayor had told his prince, William of Orange, that the town's defenders would soon have to surrender. Because the prince was known as William the Silent, nobody really expected an answer, but he sent a carrier pigeon with the message "Be of good cheer, the water is coming". Orders were given to breach the dikes and let in the North Sea. When Valdez saw de Boisot's mirage-like fleet approaching he thought it advisable to withdraw. Leyden was relieved by a mere 800 Netherlands troops; the next day a lucky wind blew de Boisot's fleet, and the North Sea, back where they belonged.

*Drink to **Old Holland**: 1 oz. each Genevers gin and white curaçao, with 1 tsp. orange bitters. Shake well with ice and strain over rocks into an Old-Fashioned glass.*

OCTOBER 4, 1797

Whether or not the poet Samuel Taylor Coleridge had been tripping out on opium, he was certainly embarrassed to be interrupted today after setting down only the first few lines of *Xanadu*, which he later claimed had come to him in a dream. Holed up in a lonely farmhouse in England's West Country, Sam had just gotten off to a swinging start:

"In Xanadu did Kubla Khan
A mighty pleasure-dome decree,
Where Alph, the sacred river, ran
Through caverns measureless to man
Down to a sunless sea."

But then a tradesman from Porlock knocked on the door. By the time Coleridge had paid the man's bill, his "dream" had vanished and he had to work hard to continue the poem by actually composing. The remaining lines seemed so unsatisfactory that he didn't publish *Xanadu* for 19 years.

*Pass your own judgment on this **Poet's Dream**: Mix well ½ oz. each of dry gin, dry vermouth and Bénédictine. Pour into a cocktail glass and add a twist of lemon.*

OCTOBER 5, 1894

The wedding today of Prince André Poniatowski was not the one that San Francisco heiress Maud Burke had had in mind for him. André, a great-grandson of the last king of Poland who seemed amenable to making Maud his princess, had spent some time with her in New York but had irritatingly withheld the precious question. Maud's reaction on returning to San Francisco was to spread the word that they were practically engaged, it was just a matter of time; the newspapers turned this around to have the prince making the announcement. His reaction was to propose marriage to quite a different San Francisco heiress. Maud rebounded with a one-week engagement to middle-aged British shipping magnate Sir Bache Cunard. Then she moved to England, changed from Maud to Emerald and created a London salon for the rich, famous, and anyone not called Poniatowski.

*For a more effective **Bachelor Trap**, shake with crushed ice 1½ oz. gin, ½ tsp. grenadine, 4 dashes orange bitters and 1 egg white. Strain into a chilled cocktail glass.*

OCTOBER 6, 1873

Of the three gallant aeronauts sitting in the lifeboat this morning Alfred Ford, a reporter for the New York *Daily Graphic*, was undoubtedly the least confident. Only because his publisher was sponsoring this first transatlantic flight was Ford resigned to leaving the ground at 9:19, in company with the skipper, Captain Washington Donaldson, and ballooning enthusiast George Lunt. Their huge balloon, not surprisingly named *Daily Graphic*, rose from Brooklyn's Capitoline Gardens with the lifeboat suspended from it by slings. Then it drifted slowly northeast across the border of Connecticut and, running into a rainstorm, came down to catch on some bushes near New Canaan. At Captain Donaldson's suggestion the three men jumped from their lifeboat, ending the transatlantic flight right there at 1:15 p.m. Alfred Ford was quite relieved to wire the story to his paper and catch the afternoon train back to New York.

*To become more of a **Daredevil**, stir 1 oz. each ruby port and oloroso sherry with 1 egg and 1 dash Angostura, but no ice. Chill well, stir again and pour into a Sour glass.*

OCTOBER 7, 1571

The Spanish sub-officer Miguel Cervantes distinguished himself today at the head of a 12-man troop aboard *Marquesa*. The 206 ships of a combined Spanish and Venetian fleet had come up with 250 Turkish and allied Infidel vessels between the Greek mainland and the Peloponnese peninsula. Now, off the fortified city of Lepanto, the Turks were attacking. Young Cervantes, though invalided below with a fever, heard the enemy boarding *Marquesa* and struggled up on deck. The Christian forces won the biggest naval battle of the century, but only after a bloody hand-to-hand combat. One of the hands which was damaged was Miguel's left one, in fact it fell off. Luckily right-handed, he was able to go away and write *Don Quixote*.

*To feel thoroughly **Iberian**, mix in advance and chill well 1½ oz. each dry sherry and Bittall (if unavailable, white port with a spiral of lemon rind). Serve straight up in a small Old-Fashioned glass and top with a slice of orange.*

OCTOBER 8, 1815

Fancy gold-plated spurs proved the undoing of ex-King Joachim Murat today when he tried to regain the throne of the Two Sicilies. After being appointed by Napoleon (who happened to be his brother-in-law) the former French cavalry commander had ruled from Naples but fled after Waterloo. Now, landing with only 30 supporters at the southern Italian fishing port of Pizzo, he marched to the central piazza in his gorgeous gold-braided uniform. An aide called for "Three cheers for King Joachim Murat!", but the citizens remained silent. Thinking better of it, Murat turned and headed back to the waterfront, followed by a growing crowd shouting insults. Then, just as his party reached their boat the ex-king caught a spur in a fishing net and stumbled to the ground. Instantly he was set upon, and an old woman tore out half of his long moustache. Although rescued by the police, Murat survived only for the five days that it took his successor, a returned Bourbon, to order up a firing squad.

*No stumbling allowed after this **Golden Spur**: Put 4 ice cubes in a cocktail shaker; pour on 1½ oz. Scotch, ½ oz. Cointreau, 1 tsp. sugar and juice of 1 lemon. Shake until a frost forms, then pour ice and all into a highball glass. Serve with a straw.*

OCTOBER 9, 1869

Charles Augustus Howell, the unscrupulous commission agent who hung around the Pre-Raphaelites, persuaded the poet Dante Gabriel Rossetti that there was money to be made from tonight's dirty digging. Accompanied by a doctor and two hired assistants, Howell first unearthed the coffin containing Rossetti's wife Elizabeth, who had died of an overdose of chloral seven years before. Then he had to reach in and find a manuscript that the poet had dramatically thrust into the coffin as it was being closed. Rossetti recently discovered that this was the only complete set of his poems, and now he had forgotten some of them. When Howell found the slightly mouldy volume he handed it to the doctor to disinfect, then went home for a stiff drink. His effort brought recognition to the poet and prosperity to publisher Frederick Ellis: the first printing of Rossetti's collected poems sold out within a week. But Howell's commission didn't save him from a sticky end, in the gutter outside a Chelsea pub, with a gold half-sovereign clenched between his back teeth.

*Here's a more pleasant way to revive **Sweet Memories**: Stir with ice 1 oz. each white rum, orange curaçao and dry vermouth. Strain into a chilled cocktail glass.*

OCTOBER 10, 1886

Tired of raising the long tails of his dinner coat every time he sat down, Griswold Lorillard, an ornament of New York society, raised the eyebrows of fellow-ballgoers at the Tuxedo Park Club this evening by wearing instead a short black jacket with satin lapels. Because his father, a tobacco millionaire, had been a founding member of the club, Griswold escaped censure. In fact, once they got over the shock the other members copied his adaptation of the velvet "smoking jacket" and their tailors christened it the Tuxedo. Griswold Lorillard, when issuing informal invitations to his home, began telling guests "we don't dress for dinner", meaning black tie rather than tails. He had to put up with some who misunderstood and turned up in business suits.

*Whether dressed or not, make enough **Black Tie** for yourself and dinner partner: Pour 2 oz. Pineau de Charentes over one ice cube in each small Old-Fashioned glass; top up with sparkling white wine.*

OCTOBER 11, 1399

Due to be crowned King of England the day after tomorrow, Henry Bolingbroke invited his three sons and a few faithful followers to spend this Saturday night in the Tower of London. Besides its more sinister uses, the Tower served as a kind of royal guesthouse; each room had a private bath, quite a rarety and, on this occasion, actually used by the guests. It was not that the nobles' persistent B.O. bothered anybody, least of all themselves: the bath represented a spiritual cleansing. Then they stayed up all night, in a symbolic guarding of their King-to-be Henry the Fourth. In recognition of their new cleanliness, Henry on Sunday morning knighted each of them, thus instituting the Companionship of the Bath. Since that time, it is said, Saturday night has become the traditional bath night for the British nobility.......

*For your own **KCB**, combine over ice 1½ oz. gin, 2 tsp. kirsch and ½ tsp. each lemon juice and apricot brandy. Shake the mixture, strain into a lowball glass over an ice cube and top with a twist of lemon peel.*

OCTOBER 12, 1492

Early this morning, with the fading moon in its last quarter, Rodrigo de Triana, a lookout on Christopher Columbus' flagship *Santa Maria*, looked out, then looked forward to receiving the 10,000 maravedis that Queen Isabella had promised to the one who first sighted land beyond the Ocean Sea. But when this news reached the skipper, Columbus disclosed that a few hours earlier he himself had seen lights bobbing up and down; Rodrigo only got a consolation prize. This was tougher luck than anyone realized, for only recently have marine biologists called attention to a natural phenomenon in the shallows off the Bahamas' Watling Island. During the moon's last quarter the luminous marine worms *Odontosyllis Enopla* set about breeding, bobbing with enjoyment. The biologists theorize that *Santa Maria* passed Watling overnight, and that Rodrigo's was the real landfall sighting, of nearby Cat Island.

*For a better view from the **Poop Deck**, stir with ice 1 oz. blackberry brandy, ½ oz. each port and brandy. Strain into a chilled cocktail glass.*

OCTOBER 13, 1878

Sarah Bernhardt, a free spirit and self-promoter, considered rides in the captive balloon at Paris' International Exposition pretty tame. The 33-year-old actress' idea of fun was to pester the aeronaut Giffard to label his orange balloon "Doña Sol" after her current role in Verdi's *Hernani*, and then to soar out of town today from the exhibition grounds. Stripping petals from her corsage, Bernhardt scattered them as the balloon cleared Père Lachaise cemetery. It drifted 30 miles before landing near Verchères, where Bernhardt had to spend most of the night in the little railway station. In Paris she found that the Comédie Française was fining her 1,000 francs for leaving town without notice. Resigning on the spot, France's favourite actress threw the culture establishment into a tizz: the Minister of Fine Arts had the fine rescinded. Bernhardt soon quit anyway for a lucrative contract in the United States.

*Up, up and away in the **Red Balloon**: Shake with ice 2 tsp. maraschino and ½ oz. each white rum, Campari, Mandarine liqueur and lemon juice. Strain into a cocktail glass; clip the rim with a sliver of orange peel.*

OCTOBER 14, 1066

Ever since the Spring, courtiers had been warning Harold Godwinsson, king of parts of southern England, not to look at the sky — he might see the comet over Normandy which obviously portended something terrible coming from that direction. But today, from the security of his little hilltop outside Hastings on the south coast, Harold thought he was doing quite well against the Norman invaders under Duke William (whose slogan, "A new Star, a new King!" had been hard to top). The Normans were retreating. But it was a trick: back they came with a company of archers. Intrigued by this novelty, Harold finally did look up, and promptly caught the sharp end of an arrow right in the eye. Hard luck, Harold, and the end of the Anglo-Saxon dynasty.

*Join Duke William on the **Norman Ferry**: Put crushed ice in a tall tumbler; add 1 oz. each Calvados and sweet lime cordial; stir and top up with ginger beer (not ginger ale!). Add a squeeze of fresh lime and decorate with a slice of the fruit.*

OCTOBER 15, 1869

Labourers digging a well on William Newells' farm near Cardiff, in upstate New York, today came upon an enormous fossilized human body. The farmer promptly pitched a tent over it and began selling tickets to view the 10-foot-tall Cardiff Giant at five cents apiece. As the news spread, he kept raising the price until it peaked at a dollar a peek. Then the showman Phineas Barnum offered $50,000 to lease the fossil for his travelling circus; on being refused he hired a sculptor to carve a copy from gypsum. This proved both economical and scientifically sound, for the young Yale palæontologist O.C.Marsh went against popular opinion by showing that the original was made of gypsum too. It had been planted by one of Farmer Newells' close relatives, in a profitable sermon on the Genesis text, "There were giants in those times".

*Less profitably, they could have left the old giant **Six Feet Under**: Shake with cracked ice ½ oz. each golden rum, Swedish Punch and calvados. Strain into a cocktail glass and twist a zest of orange on top.*

OCTOBER 16, 1906

Berlin shoemaker Wilhelm Voigt dressed with extra care today, for he was tired of being a nobody and was determined to attract some respect. A sure way to do that was to outfit oneself as a Captain of Grenadiers. Striding out of the shop, he encountered four private soldiers and ordered them to follow him. Voigt then led his little troop to the nearest railroad station, where they boarded a train to the outer suburb of Köpenick. There the self-promoted captain proceeded to the office of the suburb's burgomaster and, after some resistance, commandeered 4,000 deutschmarks. The burgomaster was then arrested for insolence and taken to the police station. But after six hours of this sort of thing the shoemaker's façade began to crack. After prosecution he lost both the respect he sought, and six months' freedom.

*Any visit to the suburbs is improved by a **Berliner**: Shake well with ice 1½ oz. gin, ½ oz. dry vermouth and ¼ oz. each kümmel and lemon juice. Strain into a cocktail glass.*

OCTOBER 17, 1907

Cassandra Chadwick, who had temporarily improved her finances by forging multimillionaire Andrew Carnegie's signature and shyly "admitting" that he was her unwed father, couldn't escape the news media even after her burial today in Woodstock, Ontario. The Methodist clergyman, F.W. Thompson, was trying to conduct a dignified service for the 58-year-old widow, whose body had been shipped up from an Ohio prison. But reporters were not about to let the former Betsy Bigley (she had found the name Cassandra more toney) depart in peace. One news photographer, handling a heavy tripod-mounted cinécamera, missed the lowering of the coffin. He had been changing reels, so he asked the minister if the coffin could be raised and lowered again. Dr. Thompson was outraged: "Go on with you!", he shouted, pushing him in the chest. They were standing in mud thrown up by the gravediggers, and the photographer crashed with his equipment onto Cassie's coffin.

Truth to tell, the lady was a **Crook***: Shake well with cracked ice 2 oz. sweet vermouth, 1 oz. Pernod and 2 dashes orange bitters. Strain into a cocktail glass.*

OCTOBER 18, 1920

Red-bearded, short-tempered English artist Augustus John was angered today to learn from his agent that the portrait he had done of self-made soap magnate William Lever, First Lord Leverhulme, had been returned in its packing case. At least, most of it had come back — the head was missing. Faced with this, Leverhulme admitted that he had kept only the important part because he couldn't fit the complete painting into his safe. But returning the packing case had been his housekeeper's mistake; would Mr. John please send it back and consider the matter closed? Mr. John would not. As he backed into the limelight ("I did not want this publicity", he fibbed) the art community took up his cause. London students constructed a headless effigy of Leverhulme, while apprentices in Florence carried their version, appropriately carved in soap and tallow, to the Piazza dei Signori and burned it.

Stay friendly with the **Beaux Arts***: Shake well with ice 1 oz. dry gin, 1/2 oz. each dry and sweet vermouth, 1 tsp. each pineapple and orange juice and 1 dash anisette. Strain into a cocktail glass and drink straight-up.*

OCTOBER 19, 1781

Gentlemanly General Lord Cornwallis had promised that on surrendering today all his troops, would now cease fighting the French and American forces who hemmed him in by land and sea at York Town, Virginia. But Lieutenant-Colonel John Graves Simcoe, commanding the Queen's Rangers, had begged his general for permission to escape. Simcoe's men, Loyalists and United States deserters, were uncertain of their treatment. At the least they were determined not to give up the regimental standard to be displayed in Philadelphia with those of Cornwallis' six British regiments. So the Rangers' colour-sergeant left York Town rather bulkier than usual — the colours were wound around beneath his long jacket. Reconstituted in Canada, the regiment eventually became by amalgamation the Queen's York Rangers. Those ancient colours hang in its Toronto officers' mess .

*Wrap yourself in a **York Town Special**: Shake with cracked ice 2½ oz. dry vermouth, 1 tbp. maraschino and 3 dashes orange bitters. Strain into a chilled cocktail glass.*

OCTOBER 20, 1810

Jean-Baptiste Bernadotte, the ex-NCO Marshal of France, had been raised as a Roman Catholic by parents of Jewish descent, but today he found it expedient to become a Lutheran and thus get in line for the throne of Sweden. The ailing king of the northern country, Charles XIII, was anxious to seem friendly to the strongest tyrant of the time, so he asked Napoleon if he could spare someone to become Crown Prince. Actually the young marshal was so insubordinate that Napoleon had recently dismissed him from command, but he counted on Bernadotte's wife, a former fiancée of Napoleon himself, to keep him under control. It didn't work: after today's conversion to Lutheranism, Bernadotte became the king's adopted son, his regent and commander of the Swedish army. In that capacity the renamed Prince Carl Johan joined other European powers in bringing down Napoleon.

*One more switch and Bernie might have become a **Tall Presbyterian**: 1½ oz. Scotch and 1 dash lemon juice are thrown onto 2 ice cubes in a large Old-Fashioned glass; a twist of lemon peel is added and ginger ale gently stirred in to fill.*

OCTOBER 21, 1832

Today's lively discussion at Dr.Southwood Smith's house in Finsbury Square, London, ended with the decision to put most of the late social philosopher Jeremy Bentham into a glass-fronted mahogany case. One of Jeremy's proposals had been to stand people's embalmed bodies in their own gardens as a kind of memorial statuary. So the least he could do was leave his own remains to Dr. Smith, to be embalmed as a friendly memento. In that form Jeremy stayed with the Smiths for some time, dressed, seated and holding a walking stick. Then the doctor unloaded him on University College, of which Bentham had been a great benefactor. He's still there, in the anatomical museum, but topped off with a wax head. The real one, having "lost all expression", used to rest at Jeremy's feet but is now safe from pranksters in the college vault.

*Do his bones **Shake and Rattle**? Shake 3 oz. golden rum, 1½ oz. dry vermouth and 4 dashes Angostura with cracked ice until it rattles. Strain into cocktail glasses. Preserves two.*

OCTOBER 22, 1904

Only slightly paranoid in the early morning hours, Russian Vice-Admiral Zinovy Rozhdestvensky had his gunners on full alert as the fleet headed through the North Sea on its long journey to a war with Japan. Suddenly, hostile shapes were spotted and four of the battleships blasted away with their 12-inch guns. The enemy could be seen suffering heavy damage, but so could the Russian battleship *Aurora*, which was hit by a slight miscalculation and four Russian shells. Another miscalculation involved the Japanese warships, which proved to be trawlers out of Hull, Yorkshire. It was the fishermen's fault, wrote Chief Engineer Evgeny Politovsky: "They must have known our fleet was coming". Luckily the Czar was more forgiving. HAVE HEARD OF SAD INCIDENT, he began the telegram to his cousin King Edward VII of England, and signed it BEST LOVE, NICKY.

*A harmless explosive, this **TNT**: 1 oz. brandy and ½ oz. orange curaçao are stirred with ice. Add 1 dash each anisette and Angostura bitters. Stir again; strain into a cocktail glass.*

OCTOBER 23, 1707

Early this morning Admiral Sir Cloudisley Shovell decided he had been too proud of his huge emerald ring. It showed how far he had risen from his entry into the Royal Navy as a cabin-boy 43 years ago. But late last night the *Association*, flagship of his returning Mediterranean fleet, was driven onto the Bishop-and-Clerk Rocks off the Scilly Islands. When Sir Cloudisley struggled ashore, a local fisherperson noticed the ring and decided that the admiral was too badly hurt to be worth saving. Damage to Sir Cloudisley's pride was added posthumously by his colleagues at the Admiralty, who censured him for not having anchored in a storm. Meanwhile the woman who had borrowed his emerald realized that it was much larger than those usually worn by peasants in the Scilly Isles, so she hid it for 30 years and handed it to a priest on her deathbed.

*For a double-size **Emerald**, shake well with ice 2 oz. each cognac and green crème de menthe, and 2 dashes orange bitters. Strain into cocktail glasses.*

OCTOBER 24, 1901

Annie Edson Taylor, a dowdy 43-year-old widow and failed primary-school teacher, finished this afternoon bleeding from a cut behind the ear and generally feeling rather wobbly. This was to be expected in anyone who had just gone over Niagara Falls in a barrel. But as compensation, Annie was convinced that fame would be hers tomorrow. Unfortunately, she set about demonstrating the lack of flair which had marked her teaching career: she began a lecture tour in which the "lecture" consisted of a 10-minute recital of her experience, delivered in a monotone. Because audiences demanded something more dramatic, Annie returned to Niagara Falls for her iron-hooped barrel; but it had been reduced to a few unconnected pieces. A reproduction was made, and she sat next to it selling autographed photos. Annie died in a charity ward, still wondering why the world had not beaten a path to the door of the first woman to go over Niagara Falls in a barrel.

*At least pay tribute to Annie's **Caprice**: Shake with cracked ice 1½ oz. gin, ½ oz. each dry vermouth and Bénédictine, and 1 dash orange bitters. Strain into a cocktail glass.*

OCTOBER 25, 1854

Captain Lewis Nolan today regretted, if only for a minute, having pointed in the wrong direction. He had ridden down a precipitous slope into a valley with an order from Lord Raglan, commanding British forces outside the Crimean port of Balaclava. Nolan shouted to Lord Lucan, who had two brigades drawn up, "Lord Raglan wishes the cavalry to advance rapidly toward the front!" Lucan, unable to see the Big Picture, asked "Attack, sir? Attack what?" Nolan flung out his arm: "There, sir, is your enemy". After Lucan ordered his brother-in-law, Lord Cardigan, to lead 672 horsemen down the valley, Nolan saw that they were riding straight into artillery fire instead of attacking the Russian infantry. He galloped in front of Cardigan to try and stop the advance, but a Russian shell fragment stopped him instead. The Charge of the Light Brigade continued to its disastrous end. While this depressed many Britons it inspired Alfred Tennyson, whose verses about it bolstered his reputation as Poet Laureate.

Join 24 survivors in **Balaclava Punch**: *Stir juice and grated peel of 1 lemon, 4 tbsp. sugar and 4 oz. maraschino with 2 bottles red wine. Pour over block ice with 2 bottles each chilled champagne and soda.*

OCTOBER 26, 1369

Today, possibly foreseeing that he would die in a few years suffering from rotten teeth, diseased kidneys and gout, King Charles V of France dedicated an appreciative memorial stone to his late Flemish chef Benckels. But the gesture was not only in praise of the man's cooking: Charles was grateful for not having been poisoned recently. As Duke of Normandy in his early twenties, he had experienced falling hair and other symptoms of an arsenic-rich diet while staying at the château of his older cousin Charles of Navarre, who considered he had just as good a claim to the French throne. Thenceforth, as duke, dauphin, regent and finally monarch, Charles V employed a personal chef, thus rightly earning the sobriquet "Charles the Wise".

Commemorate the event with a **Stone Sour**: *Pour over crushed ice in a highball glass 1½ oz. bourbon, 1 tbsp. lemon juice, 1 tsp. white crème de menthe and ½ tsp. sugar syrup. Stir, then fill with soda and add a sprig of mint.*

OCTOBER 27, 1614

Twelve-year-old King Louis XIII of France, having watched the commoners of the Third Estate bow below stomach level as they passed him at yesterday's official opening of the Estates-General, was gratified today to find that they agreed with him about the monarchy. "The King is sovereign in France and holds his throne from God alone", read their resolution; "no power on earth, spiritual or temporal, has any right in his realm which can deprive the King's sacred person of it, on any pretext whatever." Having thus started on the right foot, the Commons then passed resolutions calling for various reforms. But as the young king's advisers pointed out, these proposals were so numerous that he couldn't be expected to come to an early decision on them. In fact, the heavy overload discouraged his successors from even convening the next meeting of the Estates-General. It didn't take place for 175 years, which was not quite in time to stop the monarchy going under altogether in the French Revolution.

*Take your time with the **Royal Screwdriver**: Pour the fresh juice of 1 large orange into a goblet half-filled with cracked ice. Add 1 oz. cognac, fill with chilled champagne; stir gently.*

OCTOBER 28, 1449

This morning the court astrologer of Ulugh Beg, late Prince of Samarkand, learned with a certain gloomy satisfaction that his master had died last night from a massive sword-stroke to the neck. Until coming to the throne two years ago at the age of 53, Ulugh had been less interested in government than in mapping the stars from his elaborate observatory at the edge of town. Its 100-foot-high sextants made possible the most accurate tables to that time of our Solar System. But when testing the astrologer by asking him to foretell the success of his reign, Ulugh learned that his death would be due to his son Abdal Latif. He promptly exiled the youth, who developed a certain resentment. Now Abdal had returned with an army and, after overcoming his father's troops, ordered him killed. With Ulugh died Arab astronomy, for religious fanatics destroyed his observatory.

*Your **Star** foretells a mild euphoria: Pour over cracked ice 1 oz. each applejack and sweet vermouth, with 1 dash Angostura. Stir well, strain into a cocktail glass and top with a twist of lemon peel.*

Ned Kelly, the usually prescient Australian outlaw, had misjudged the police, and this afternoon a Melbourne jury caught him up on it by finding him guilty of murder. During a shoot-out with the law at Glenrowan, Ned's body armour should have protected him so that he could make his planned getaway. Mistakenly predicting, however, that the police would not hit below the belt, Ned neglected to cover his legs, which proved difficult to run on when perforated. Still, his prescience came into play when he was sentenced today by Judge Sir Redmond Barry to be hanged on November 11: "I'll see you where I'm going, Judge", he declared. The 67-year-old Sir Redmond followed him by just 12 days.

*They might, before leaving, have toasted each other in **Melbourne**: Put 4 ice cubes in a jug, pour on 3 oz. brandy and 1 oz. curaçao, and stir vigorously. Strain into chilled martini glasses; drop in twists of lemon peel.*

Henri, Duc de Bordeaux and Comte de Chambord, believed himself a legitimate king, but today his insistence on a flag prevented him from becoming Henri V of France. The obstinate scion of the Bourbons was living near Vienna rather than in France, where yet another republic had succeeded the upstart Bonapartes' "Second Empire". The *tricolore* flew over Henri's ancestral palace of Versailles, and he vowed that only the white flag of the Bourbons would bring him back. Député Pierre Chesnelong journeyed to Austria to explain that the national flag could be changed only through agreement with the elected representatives. But the royal claimant wouldn't budge, in person nor in the letter he wrote to Chesnelong: "*Mon principe est tout*". Then he ordered it published in this evening's monarchist *L'Union*. France remained a republic, and Henri's white flag was kept to be laid on his tomb.

*It's easy enough to make a **Bourbon Sour**: Combine with ice 2 oz. bourbon, 2 tbsp. lemon juice and 2 tsp. sugar syrup. Shake well, strain into a Sour glass and decorate with a slice of orange.*

OCTOBER 31, 1720

The successful pirate Anne Bonny, who had left her husband in disgust after he retired to enter the steadier profession of informing, was let down today by her new man. "Calico Jack" Rackam was lying drunk below with his pals when a Royal Navy sloop caught up with them in Jamaica's Dry Harbour Bay. His flag boasted a skull over crossed sabres, but Jack failed to respond when Anne and her pirate friend Mary Reade called for help on deck. "If you had fought like a man, you need not have died like a dog", she told him on his way to the gallows — an ungracious farewell to the father of her unborn child. By law a pregnant woman could not be hanged; Anne, a lawyer's illegitimate daughter, persuaded her father to buy her freedom with a fine and a guarantee of good conduct. Friends claimed she then married under a pseudonym and became one of the first thieving bastards to join the English aristocracy.

The two girls used to share a **Pirates' Apéritif**: *4 oz. dark rum, 2 oz. sweet vermouth and 4 dashes Angostura. Stir well with ice and strain into chilled martini glasses.*

NOVEMBER 1, 1911

This was an exciting and innovative day for Second-Lieutenant Giulio Gavotti of Italy's Servizi Aeronautici. It began with having to carry four 4½-pound weights in his lap as he took off in a single-seater Etrich monoplane near Ain Zara, Libya. Finding himself right above some unfriendly Turks, Gavotti dropped one of the weights, which was really a standard Cipelli infantry grenade. It gave off a satisfying puff of smoke. The young officer was so pleased with this new game of aerial bombing that he flew to a nearby oasis encampment and threw down the other three grenades. The Turks were rightly upset. They protested that throwing grenades from the sky violated the Geneva Convention, but were faced with the questionable logic that the framers of the convention had not anticipated aerial bombardment.

The Turks might have called for an **Oasis Cooler**: *Stir in a goblet 2 oz. each gin and sweet vermouth, ½ tsp. lemon juice and 2 ice cubes. Top up with soda.*

NOVEMBER 2, 1824

Abraham Gesner, an impoverished 27-year-old researcher into ways of distilling kerosene from petroleum, began finding out today how difficult it was to attract support while locked in his farmhouse. When the sheriff of Cornwallis, Nova Scotia knocked at the door Abe, bankrupt but hospitable, asked him in. This was a mistake because, under the law, the sheriff had only to touch a bankrupt in order to put him under arrest. Gesner then had the choice of going directly to jail or remaining in the farmhouse until his debts were paid. He chose the latter course, but the debts gathered interest. Fortunately Abe's father-in-law, Dr. Webster, offered to bail him out if he'd learn something more lucrative, like medicine. Young Gesner failed at that too, but at least his kerosene process worked, so he emigrated to New Brunswick where people were more appreciative and made him a professor.

Petroléo is black gold: Pour over 2 ice cubes in an Old-Fashioned glass 1½ oz. tequila, 1 tsp. lemon juice and 1 tsp. Bovril [!]. Stir well and sip gently.

NOVEMBER 3, 1777

Sir William Howe, British commander in Philadelphia, couldn't see how the colonists could remain troublesome for much longer than two more years, but meanwhile he might need some help in putting down their rebellion. So today he had posters stuck up appealing for volunteers: any "intrepid able-bodied Hero" could apply to join the First Pennsylvania Loyalist Regiment. "Such spirited Fellows", the posters proclaimed, "will be rewarded at the end of the war .... with 50 acres of Land, where every gallant Hero may retire and enjoy his Bottle and his Lass". Sir William left no room on the poster for any mention of the possibility that the acres, bottle and lass just might have to be found in some less rebellious colony than Pennsylvania.

An offer of Philadelphia Spirit would have brought in the volunteers: Shake together with ice 1 oz. each applejack, port and orange juice. Strain into a Sour glass containing cracked ice; top up with soda.

NOVEMBER 4, 1605

Guido Fawkes, a Spanish army veteran now living in London, was looking forward to some excitement after spending this dull evening sitting with his 20 barrels in a basement. He and some friends had rented a little place in Whitehall so that they could smuggle the barrels, which contained gunpowder, into this adjoining basement under the house next door. The contents should call attention to their resentment at Catholics being denied civil rights, for Parliament would assemble tomorrow right above where Guido planned to light the fuse. But a leaked warning reached foxy old Robert Cecil, Secretary of State. He arranged for the plotters' arrest just before midnight — the eve of Parliament's opening by King James the First — so that he could claim to have saved the king's life. You wouldn't enjoy knowing how they treated poor Guido (private parts cut off and stuffed in his mouth, for instance), so just drink up!

*The conspirators' favourite tipple was the **Factory Whistle** (one blast and you're finished for the day): Stir with 4 ice cubes 1½ oz. Scotch, ½ oz. Bénédictine, juice of 1 lemon and 3 drops Angostura bitters. Strain into a Sour glass.*

NOVEMBER 5, 1895

George Selden thought the long-drawn-out struggle must be over today, as his patent for a gasoline-powered automobile was finally issued, 16 years after completing his model. But when, not being interested in manufacturing he sold control of the patent to the highest bidder, the arguments started all over again. Colonel Pope, builder of electric vehicles, understandably refused to license the patent to the makers of gasoline-powered cars who competed with him. A group of them, led by Henry Ford, spent another 16 years fighting the issue through the courts. In 1911 they won the challenge, on the basis that their engines were powered by four-stroke engines rather than the inventor's two-stroke. Then George Selden decided to manufacture cars himself, and failed.

*No arguments, please, about this extraordinary **Automobile**: Stir with ice 1 oz. each Scotch, gin and sweet vermouth, and 1 dash orange bitters. Strain into a small Old-Fashioned glass.*

NOVEMBER 6, 1632

When the fog rolled in today over Lützen, near Leipzig, nearsighted King Gustavus Adolphus of Sweden became fatally confused. Inadequately armoured as he led the Småland cavalry against the German General Wallenstein's forces, the 38-year-old monarch was shot through the leg. His horse bolted and carried him away from his escort, who then lost sight of him in the fog. Gustavus landed up in the middle of an enemy group. Because this was the last major battle scheduled before half-time in the Thirty Years' War, he would make a useful hostage if taken alive; but his captors were out of luck. The king was already mortally wounded; asked to confirm his identity, he replied "I was the King of Sweden".

*Mix your own **Foggy Day** in an Old-Fashioned glass. Combine 1½ oz. gin and 1 tsp. Pernod with ice and shake well. Rub a lemon slice around the rim of the glass, then drop it in. Strain in the drink over ice cubes.*

NOVEMBER 7, 1876

Terrence Mullen and Jack Hughes were about to hoist President Lincoln's coffin out of its marble sarcophagus tonight when their collaborator, who had gone to bring the wagon into the Springfield, Illinois cemetery, returned with some detectives instead. The pair were counterfeiters by profession, hoping to hold Lincoln's body to ransom for the release of a colleague, whose absence had reduced the quality of their product. They had chosen election night, when public attention would be elsewhere, but they had also chosen an assistant who moonlighted as an informer. In court there was some question as to the value of a dead president, so Mullen and Hughes got off with a year in jail for "conspiring to steal a coffin (property of the National Lincoln Monument Assn.)". It was priced at $75.00.

*The conspirators shared a double by **Moonlight**: Shake with 2 ice cubes 2 oz. gin, 2 oz. white wine, 1 oz. kirsch and 6 oz. grapefruit juice. Strain into lowball glasses and decorate with twists of lemon.*

NOVEMBER 8, 1871

Was it today, next week, or even late last month? David Livingstone, feeling failed as a missionary and unappreciated as an explorer, had been ill and on short rations in the Tanganyikan village of Ujiji. He marked this red-letter day in his journal as October 28; then he recalled the weeks of delirious fever when he had written nothing, and corrected it to November. On the other hand Henry Stanley, the reporter sent by the sensation-seeking *New York Herald* to find Livingstone, first thought today was November 3. But remembering an illness during his four-month journey from the coast he adjusted it to the 10th. Whatever the date, runners came to tell Livingstone he was about to meet another explorer, his first white visitor in six years. Not until the following day did Stanley ask whether he knew of the *Herald*. "Oh yes!", exclaimed the good doctor, "who has not heard of that despicable newspaper?"

*You too can say **Welcome Stranger**: With a shot glass, pour over ice ½ oz. each gin, brandy, grenadine, lemon juice, orange juice and Swedish Punch. Shake well and strain into a small Old-Fashioned glass.*

NOVEMBER 9, 1874

What a frustrating day this turned out to be for Dr. George Hosmer, a public-spirited Manhattan physician. Reading headlines in his morning *New York Tribune* that wild animals had broken loose from Central Park Zoo, had killed several people and were now rampaging through the streets, Dr.Hosmer prepared for action. The *Tribune* had said that citizens were forming posses to catch the animals, so he hurried downtown, marched into the editorial office and pulled out two pistols. "Well, here I am!", he cried. It took the editorial staff some minutes to calm Dr. Hosmer enough for him to read all the way through the article. The last paragraph explained that the headlines were an attention-getter, to make people read a serious article about decrepit zoo enclosures.

*Dr. Hosmer's local anæsthetic was the **Manhattan**: Stir 1 oz. sweet vermouth into 2½ oz. rye; stick with a maraschino cherry.*

NOVEMBER 10, 1556

A thoroughly depressing and damp day for Osip Nepeia, the new Russian ambassador to England, as his first sea voyage came to an end. The little 160-ton ship *Edward Bonaventure* on which he was travelling had lost touch with the rest of the convoy that had left Archangelsk almost four months before. She carried a rich cargo of presents for Queen "Bloody" Mary from Ivan the Terrible — promoting exports of furs, metals and other commodities in exchange for warm British woollies, to be brought to Russia by The Muscovy Company. Now the vessel had foundered on the flat rocks of the north Aberdeenshire coast near Castle Pitsligo. Osip was cold, wet and hungry but at least he was on shore. Many had drowned and there was no sign of the valuable presents. At Bloody Mary's insistence 160 Scots were closely questioned, but all that ever reached her of the cargo were five parcels of wax.

*Waxless is the **Bloody Mary** as she used to mix it: Put 3 ice cubes in a highball glass. Pour on 1 oz. vodka, ¼ tsp. Worcestershire, ½ oz. lemon juice and 1 drop Tabasco. Add 1 shake each salt and pepper. Nearly fill with tomato juice, stir well and stick a lemon wedge on the rim.*

NOVEMBER 11, 43 B.C.

Pretending to be good friends today as they met to split the Roman world into three zones of influence, Mark Antony, Lepidus and Octavian all had the same worry: the late J. Caesar's will would complicate matters. Big Julie had named great-nephew Octavian his heir; when the young man hurried home from Greece he found Antony in control. But it was widely rumoured that before his untimely death Caesar had meant to rewrite his will in favour of his infant son by Cleopatra. So Antony made friends with Cleopatra. Sadly, this meant ditching Octavian's sister whom he had agreed to marry. That sort of thing could only lead to war, resulting in Antony and Cleopatra committing suicide and Octavian changing his name to Augustus. All this might have been averted by Caesar adding a couple of tablets to his will, if codicils had been legal. They weren't recognized until 13 years after his death.

*Anyone able to get that story straight deserves this less complicated **Trio**: Stir with ice 1 oz. each dry gin, sweet vermouth and dry vermouth. Strain into a chilled martini glass.*

NOVEMBER 12, 1772

Prince Nicolaus Esterhazy, although he liked to be addressed as Most Serene and Noble Prince of the Holy Roman Empire (or among friends simply as Nicolaus the Magnificent), proved today that he could take a joke and a hint from the director of his court music, Joseph Haydn. The prince had extended a summer sojourn at his country palace into the late fall, and the members of his orchestra were stuck there without their families. Haydn composed a short symphony in the unaccustomed key of F Sharp Minor, to attract Nicolaus' attention when it was played in one of his drawing rooms. As each musician finished his part in the score, he blew out the candle illuminating his music and quietly left the room. When they had all disappeared, the prince listened to Haydn's explanation, granted the orchestra a paid leave of absence, and said "You must call this the Farewell Symphony!"

*Match Nicolaus' sense of humour with this **Dry Melody**: Shake well with ice 1½ oz. vodka and ¼ oz. each Fraises des Bois and Mandarine liqueur. Strain into a martini glass.*

NOVEMBER 13, 1887

While wealthy, middle-aged Mrs. Annie Besant strode toward Trafalgar Square at the head of today's Socialist march, the young drama critic to whom she had proposed a common-law marriage contract prudently drifted away. It signalled the end of a relationship which had generated hundreds of letters between red-bearded George Bernard Shaw and "Mrs B" as his diary always listed her. Next month, in a predictable Victorian gesture, Annie brought his letters to the door in a casket. Shaw threw them away. He'd never taken seriously a common-law contract which sounded "worse than all the vows of all the churches on Earth." But Annie Besant, author of the pamphlet *Marriage as it Was, Is and Ought to Be*, refused to change a word of the contract. "Scene with her", Shaw recorded in his diary; and it was the final scene.

***None But the Brave** deserve the fair, nor should they try this: Combine with cracked ice 1½ oz. brandy, 1 tbsp. Pimento Dram, 1 tsp. sugar syrup, 4 drops lemon juice and 1 pinch ground ginger. Shake; strain into an Old-Fashioned glass containing 1 ice cube.*

NOVEMBER 14, 1890

Confident of being able to sell his rope for a dollar an inch, Ontario provincial hangman J.V.Radcliffe built an extra-high scaffold for today's event, at which Reginald Burchall would be the unpopular star. In a swamp near Woodstock, Burchall had disposed of a recently-arrived British immigrant whose wealthy father had paid Burchall to find the youngster a good farm property. Hardly had the immigrant begun to query the value of the swampland than two bullets in the back of the head pitched him forward, shooting a cigar-case out of his breast pocket into the long grass. Burchall carefully cut identifying labels out of the chap's clothes, but failed to notice the cigar-case. It was, however, noticed by Detective John W. Murray of the Department of Criminal Investigation. After Burchall's execution he modestly wrote up the affair in *Memoirs of a Great Detective*.

*Your ropeless **Suspension** was created to mark the opening of Scotland's Forth Bridge: 1 oz. each Scotch, ginger wine and orange juice. Shake well and strain onto 2 ice cubes in an Old-Fashioned glass.*

NOVEMBER 15, 1807

Because Britain and France were at war, many of his countrymen were outraged, but 29-year-old chemist Humphry Davy was proud to learn today from the Institut National in Paris that he had won a valuable prize originated by Napoleon. Earlier this year publication of Davy's Bakerian Lecture, about chemical changes caused by electric currents, had attracted the attention of French savants. Napoleon, when he inaugurated the annual prize and medal for advances in the knowledge of electricity, had specifically enjoined the judges that "foreigners are to be admitted". Humphry Davy saw nothing wrong with that. "If the countries are at war," he told a friend, "the men of science are not". His reaction to critics was that "foreigners, unbiased by considerations of personality, reduce an object to its true value." But the medal never reached him.

*It may have ended up as a **Gold Coaster**: Shake with ice 2 oz. unsweetened pineapple juice, 1 oz. each brandy and dry vermouth, ½ oz. lemon juice and 1 tsp. maraschino. Strain into a highball glass, fill with ice and stir gently. Float a circle of fresh pineapple; sip through a straw.*

NOVEMBER 16, 1648

Having lost the English Civil War, King Charles I today missed his last chance at a long life when he balked at efforts by friends on the Isle of Wight to get him to a ship and away. The king was under gentlemanly surveillance at Newport while representatives of Parliament negotiated with him to give up most of his Divine Rights. But a few days ago a Royalist lady's smuggled letter told of an ominous new agreement between Parliament and the Army to "dispose of His M". All Charles would have to do was "walk out a mile or two as usual" and friends would get him out of the country. The king had encouraged previous escape plans, and even devised a code using names of vegetables; but this time he sent word that he was "verrie melancholie" and the time was wrong. Too bad: a few days later the melancholy monarch was put in close confinement, soon to lose the trial for his life.

*Simpler than the royal vegetable code is this **A-B-C** for 3 courtiers: Crack 3 ice cubes in a jug and stir in 3 oz. each armagnac and Bénédictine. Add 2 dashes Angostura. Crush 1 more ice cube for each champagne tulip; strain in the liquor and top up with champagne. Decorate with a lemon slice and a cherry.*

NOVEMBER 17, 1844

Michael Faraday enjoyed his royal command dinner invitation at Windsor Castle this evening, but he was to suffer spiritual indigestion. As an Elder of the simple-worship Sandemanian sect of Christianity, the famous scientist was due tonight at a prayer meeting of its tiny London congregation. But he had found it too embarrassing to use this regular Sunday evening engagement as an excuse for declining Queen Victoria's invitation. On returning to London Faraday discovered that his position as an Elder had been declared vacant, at just about the time that he had been enjoying a royal pudding. He refused to express penitence and was kept on the religious outs for the next 16 years, but he had been wise to accept the invitation because the Queen never sent him another.

*Could jollity have run riot at **Windsor**? Chill gin and green crème de menthe. Stir gently, without ice, 2 oz. and 1 oz. respectively; strain into a martini glass and top with a twist of lemon peel.*

NOVEMBER 18, 1895

George, Duke of Cambridge, who had correctly noted in his diary "my most glaring fault is that I desire to argue with everybody", this evening took one of his last chances to do so in public. After 48 years in the army — the last 43 spent as Commander-in-Chief — the 76-year-old cousin of Queen Victoria had just been eased out of his post in favour of a popular reform team led by Sir Garnet Wolseley, an experienced general. At a military dinner tonight he was placed near a man instrumental in arranging the change: St.John Brodrick, Secretary of State for War. When the toast to "The Services" had been drunk, the old duke remained standing, turned toward Brodrick and roared "the Army is not quite as inefficient as some people seem to suppose!" Nobody agreed, but he consoled himself by continuing to wear a uniform so covered with state decorations that the cloth could hardly be seen.

*The **Army** had one of the first variations on the 4-to-1 martini: Stir with ice 2 oz. dry gin and ½ oz. sweet vermouth. Strain into a chilled cocktail glass and top with a twist of orange peel.*

NOVEMBER 19, 1497

Because the late King João II of Portugal had believed so strongly in the PR power of positive thinking, Vasco da Gama today sailed on past the Cape of Good Hope and went on looking for India, which had been hiding. His fellow-countryman Bartoloméu Dias, the first European adventurer to reach the Cape, had for good reason wanted it named Cabo Tormentoso because of the local storms, and ventured not much farther. But old King João (the Good and Perfect, as his shaving mirror reminded him) had persuaded Dias to rename it "Cape of Good Hope", to encourage others to press on in search of Oriental trade opportunities. Vasco took the royal hint and continued on to reach India, but Dias was not so lucky. He died in a storm at sea, not far from the Cape of Good Hope.

*Those old port-drinkers arrived too early to stop off for **Cape Town Coffee**: Put 1 oz. golden run and 1 tbsp. coconut syrup into a coffee cup. Nearly fill with hot, strong coffee; stir and top with whipped cream.*

NOVEMBER 20, 1805

Polite applause from the small audience of French officers did little to assuage Ludwig van Beethoven's disappointment this evening as he conducted the première in Vienna of his only opera, which he had titled *Léonore*. Originally this performance had been scheduled for the Austrian empress' birthday, but a French invasion had culminated in the occupation of Vienna last week. Many of Beethoven's well-heeled clientele, including the empress herself, had sought safety elsewhere. The review *Freymütige* did nothing to help, commenting that the music "was really below the expectations of amateurs and professionals alike". But at least that first-night critic had company in the audience: on the next evening nobody came at all. Beethoven, humiliated, revised his opera and renamed it *Fidelio*.

*Your **Opera** should meet with more success: Shake well with ice 1½ oz. gin, and ½ oz. each maraschino and Dubonnet. Strain into a cocktail glass; top with a twist of orange peel.*

NOVEMBER 21, 1783

After today's episode it would be hard to imagine that the Marquis François d'Arlandes could be accused of cowardice. Since the summer, the Montgolfier brothers' new hot-air balloons had been used to carry animals. Now experimenter Pilâtre de Rozier suggested that it was probably safe enough for human beings to try, and King Louis XVI agreed: as a matter of abundant precaution, one could start with condemned prisoners. D'Arlandes, a young courtier with a clean record, objected to being thus discriminated against. With de Rozier as pilot, he climbed into the basket and they lifted off from the garden of the Château la Muette, in the Bois de Boulogne outside Paris. The balloon rose to 1500 feet and carried the daring first aeronauts for five miles. D'Arlandes knew how lucky he had been when, soon afterwards, de Rozier fell to his death from a burning balloon. But a few years later the dashing young marquis was cashiered for cowardice.

*Explore the **Stratosphere**: Shake with ice 1 oz. golden rum, 2 tsp. each brandy and lemon juice, 1½ tsp. sugar syrup and 1 tsp. cherry liqueur. Strain into a cocktail glass.*

NOVEMBER 22, 1682

If he couldn't sleep, newlywed Edmond Halley could surely have been more amusingly employed at 5:30 this morning than jumping out of bed to go peer through his telescope. But this was what Mary Tooke had been warned of before she married the 26-year-old astronomer. From his private observatory attached to their new house on the northern outskirts of London, Edmond was charting the path of the Moon when, at 6:30, something else caught his attention. He had spotted a comet, and later he was to predict with some accuracy its next approach to Earth. Celebrating the discovery may have started Halley on his other hobby, drinking, for which voyages of observation to the South Atlantic offered lengthy opportunity. Eventually, tired of doctors' potions and prohibitions, Edmond Halley took a forbidden glass of wine and died with it in his hand, thus missing the return of Halley's Comet.

*Two can make this **Discovery** at any time of day: Put 4 ice cubes in a cocktail shaker. Add 3 oz. brandy, ½ oz. each curaçao and sweet vermouth, ¼ oz. Amer Picon, ½ tsp. sugar and 3 drops Angostura. Shake until a frost forms, then strain into Sour glasses.*

NOVEMBER 23, 1689

As England's King James II opened a letter tonight from Lieutenant-General John Churchill, chief of his headquarters staff, he wondered where the fellow had disappeared to. The king had driven from London to Salisbury a few days ago, trying to decide what to do about Prince William of Orange, who had landed in an unfriendly way down in Devon. He knew that a large proportion of Englishmen would prefer the prince to himself. But today's meeting with advisers ended inconclusively and James put off deciding whether to abdicate or fight. Now, opening the letter, he discovered that General Churchill had despaired of his indecisive boss and left with 400 horsemen to join William of Orange. John Churchill never regretted switching kings: soon he was successfully leading the armies of King William and his successors across Europe, to be rewarded as Duke of Marlborough with a huge life pension.

*Be decisive and join **William of Orange**: Stir with ice 1 oz. brandy, ½ oz. orange curaçao and 1 dash orange bitters; strain into a chilled martini glass.*

NOVEMBER 24, 1639

It was lucky that the Puritan Horrocks family discouraged time-consuming church rituals, for today young Jeremiah Horrocks, curate of Hoole in Cheshire, was in a hurry to finish mattins and go sit with his telescope. Six years ago, at the age of 15, Horrocks had forecast that the planet Venus would pass across the sun sometime during these weeks, and so he had spent the past several days in a darkened room with the sun's image projected on the wall through his telescope. Sure enough, at 3:15 this afternoon Venus did transit the sun. Horrocks' loyal friend William Crabtree tried to verify the occurrence but, being stuck in Manchester, was stymied by clouds. Horrocks himself was never to see another eclipse: he died at 23.

*Horrocks would not have mixed an **Eclipse**, but you're no Puritan. Shake well with ice 1½ oz. sloe gin and 1 oz. dry gin. Pour 2 tsp. grenadine syrup over a cocktail cherry in the bottom of a small Old-Fashioned glass; carefully strain in the gin mixture so it floats on the grenadine. Top off with a twist of orange peel.*

NOVEMBER 25, 1871

His reception by the audience at tonight's première of *The Bells* convinced 33-year-old Henry Irving that he was about to be acclaimed as a great actor. For comic relief, he had followed the short melodrama at London's Lyceum theatre by playing the lead in *Pickwick*, and at the cast party thrown afterwards by family friends Henry was in high spirits. Only his wife Florence failed to catch the mood of celebration; she ended by suggesting aloud that Henry was boring the company. On the way home their cab had reached Hyde Park Corner, only a quarter of the distance to their house in suburban Fulham, when Florence turned to her husband: "Are you going on making a fool of yourself like this all your life?" Irving ordered the cabbie to stop, stepped out without another word and walked away. He never went home, and never spoke to his wife again.

*May your **First Night** leave no aftertaste: 1 oz. brandy, ½ oz. each Tia Maria and Van der Hum. Add 1 tsp. light cream; shake well.*

NOVEMBER 26, 1878

James McNeill Whistler was broke and angry today — so strapped that he had pawned his portrait of his mother, and particularly angry after being snidely cross-examined by British barristers about his views on art. His libel action against John Ruskin, who had written that nobody should ask 200 guineas "for flinging a pot of paint in the public's face", went to the jury. After an hour's deliberation they did find Ruskin guilty of libel, but the judge assessed the damage to Whistler's reputation at one farthing — the least valuable coin of the time. The artist sold his house and petitioned for bankruptcy, but he commanded his friends to "tell everyone it's a great triumph", and wore the farthing on his watch chain.

*Join Whistler in **Smiling Through**: Shake with ice ½ oz. each white rum, maraschino and Grand Marnier, and 1 dash each lemon juice and grenadine syrup. Strain into a cocktail glass and add a cherry.*

NOVEMBER 27, 1703

In the five years since the Eddystone Light started shining its 60 candles outside Plymouth Harbour, it had alarmed the lighthouse keepers. Their 120-foot Chinese-style wooden tower shivered in the westerly gales coming up the English Channel. So yesterday 59-year-old shipowner Henry Winstanley, whose loss of two vessels on the rust-red rocks had led him to design the lighthouse, went out with a party of workmen to see what strengthening might be needed. Henry had more than a professional interest in keeping the tower up: his investment of 5,000 pounds had so far returned only 2,000 through the penny-a-ton charge on incoming and outgoing cargoes. But more bad luck was on the way — the most cataclysmic storm in living memory. So this morning, watchers on shore spotted the usual eddies around the stone reef; but they would never again see the tower, or the workmen, or Henry Winstanley.

*Light yourself up to 60 candlepower with a **Lamp**: Stir well ½ oz. each brandy, crème de menthe and Cointreau with 2 tsp. crème de cacao. Pour into a pousse-café glass.*

NOVEMBER 28, 1895

Having brought their automobile by train all the way from Massachusetts, Charles and Frank Duryea were disgruntled to learn that finishing first in North America's first car race didn't automatically bring them the $5,000 prize. The brothers had shown that the roadster they had built — one of only four American gasoline-powered cars — was at least the equal of any of the 200 imports already in the U.S. But the Chicago *Times-Herald*, sponsor of the twice-delayed 53-mile race to Evanston and back, wanted to show its appreciation to all the drivers who had lined up in wet snow for the start. So technical reasons were found to disqualify the Duryea, which rolled in after less than 11 hours, as well as the Benz chasing it; another Benz limped in the following afternoon. The prize money was divided to suit, with the Duryeas getting $2,000. Two entries which had been pushed to the starting line, but had then failed to proceed, still shared $500.

*This **Roadster** is to be drunk only after driving: Shake well with ice 1 oz. each dry gin, Grand Marnier and orange juice. Strain into a cocktail glass and add a twist of lemon peel.*

NOVEMBER 29, 1870

Confidently, General Louis Trochu watched his troops today marching from besieged Paris to cross the Marne and attack the Prussians. Other French forces would come up from Orléans to catch the enemy in the rear, in accordance with orders that Trochu had sent out by balloon. Because the balloon mail was a one-way system there had been no acknowledgment of his message, but the general was an optimist. In reality, when daylight came after a night launch the balloon's crew discovered themselves over water instead of central France. They let out so much coal-gas to descend within hailing distance of shipping that the balloon sank dangerously low, so they jettisoned the heaviest package aboard. It contained General Trochu's plans. After 15 hours aloft they landed gently in a Norwegian pinetree and thereafter avoided the general. His attack and career both came to a sticky end.

*If you prefer being **Up in the Air**, shake well with ice 1½ oz. gin, ½ oz. lemon juice and 2 tsp. maraschino. Strain into a martini glass and add a cherry.*

NOVEMBER 30, 1830

What a nasty shock for one of the world's foremost statisticians, to discover this evening that he had miscalculated the voting for president of England's prestigious Royal Society. For generations its members had elected an amateur, usually from the royalty or nobility, but Charles Babbage and many of his fellow professionals thought the presidency should go instead to "a person of distinction in learning". They had put up the astronomer John Herschel, in an unprecedented challenge to the official nominee — Prince Augustus Frederick, the king's brother. The prince was a large friendly fellow, but known for liberal social views rather than scholarship. Babbage's vigorous campaigning before tonight's annual meeting in London gained so many promises of support for Herschel that he told several out-of-town members they needn't trouble to come and vote. But when the ballots were all in it was Prince 118, Herschel 111. Babbage, Herschel and friends went off and founded the British Association for the Advancement of Science, so there!

*Salute the **Royal Victor**: Shake well with ice 1 oz. each lemon gin and Liqueur d'Or, ½ oz. Cointreau and 1 dash lemon juice. Strain into a cocktail glass and add a cherry.*

DECEMBER 1, 1872

On this, the first sunny morning of the *Mary Celeste*'s transatlantic voyage, Captain Benjamin Briggs called the little cargo ship's entire crew to line up for a group portrait. His heavy Harkness "Tower" wet-plate camera stood on its tripod. The captain peered at the ground-glass and motioned the men backward and inward until they were posed, arms linked, on the port rail. Then Briggs dragged his unwieldy apparatus to the starboard rail and climbed up. At that moment a sudden squall stuck the ship ; captain and crew all fell overboard. The drifting *Mary Celeste* was boarded four days later by crewmen of the Nova Scotian *Dei Gratia*. As they told the Admiralty Court at Gibraltar, the last sign of life seemed to be the leavings of breakfast on the cabin table. No trace was ever found of the sailors, nor of the captain's camera.

*That new theory about a famous maritime mystery would probably be as comforting as any to the **Captain's Widow**: Put 5 ice cubes in a shaker and (for two widows) pour on 4 oz. gin, 1 oz. each golden rum and lemon juice, and 1 tsp. sugar syrup. Now fill two champagne tulips with crushed ice, shake the shaker until a frost forms and strain into the glasses. Sip through straws.*

DECEMBER 2, 1804

General Napoleon Bonaparte had organized today's Paris holiday outing, and he was not about to be upstaged by a cleric, even if the focal point of the ceremonies was Notre Dame cathedral. Some months ago the French senate had, rather paradoxically, decided to entrust the supreme government of their republic to an emperor. Napoleon had won by acclamation. Now the façade of Notre Dame was decorated like a triumphal arch; inside, 15,000 guests spent two chilly hours waiting for the about-to-be-royal general and his wife Josephine. Then they watched as Pope Pius VII held forward a magnificent crown. But just as he was about to place it on Napoleon's head, the "little corporal" snatched it and crowned himself. And when Pius VII later lost all patience and excommunicated him, Napoleon had the Pope put under house arrest for five years, just to show who was boss.

*The royal couple would get 9 glasses each out of this **Coronation Crystal**: Mix in a punchbowl 1 bottle white wine and 12 oz. madeira or marsala. Drop in 1 slice lemon and 1 sprig borage. Let stand for at least 2 hours. Add 1 block ice and 1 bottle soda; stir and serve.*

DECEMBER 3, 1886

"What the Butler Saw" became today's highlight in the long-running, simultaneous divorce suits brought by Lord and Lady Colin Campbell. Eager crowds packed London's High Court of Justice to hear James O'Neil describe what he had observed through the drawing-room keyhole. *The Times* preferred not to publish his description verbatim, but primly reported that if true it would "fully establish the charge" of adultery against Lady Campbell. It appeared that her effort to be equally gracious to all ranks of Society brought on the trouble, for the co-respondents included the Duke of Marlborough, General Butler, Captain Shaw and a Doctor Bird. Not to be outdone, Lady C. sued for divorce on account of her husband's own infidelity. But after hearing 19 days of titillating evidence, the jury announced that neither side had proved its case. So Lord and Lady Colin Campbell, who had spent two small fortunes trying to lose each other, were condemned to remain man and wife.

*These **Sour Kisses** disappear in your glass: Shake with ice 1½ oz. dry gin, ½ oz. dry vermouth and white of 1 egg. Strain into a martini glass.*

DECEMBER 4, 1926

Archbishop Neil McNeil of Toronto saved himself considerable embarrassment by having a letter delivered to the surrogate court just before it closed at noon this Saturday. The will of the late Charles Millar, a high-living bachelor, was coming in for probate, and Millar's executor had warned the archbishop that Clause 5 bequeathed him $500 to celebrate masses for the soul of one Major Joseph Kilgour. Regrettably Kilgour, a Protestant, was a well-known sporting man about town and still very much alive. The archbishop's letter begged the surrogate judge to "have Clause 5 expunged"; moments later the executor delivered Millar's will, and the surrogate judge acquiesced before reporters got wind of it. Archbishop McNeil thus escaped the fate of two pillars of the anti-gambling lobby: Millar's duly probated will obliged them to accept his shares in the Ontario Jockey Club, which they then had to unload to highly-amused members of the racing community.

*Suitably restrained is **The Archbishop's Punch**: Spike an orange with 6 cloves and bake at 300 degrees until it browns. Quarter it, remove the pips and put the orange in a saucepan with 1 bottle red wine and 1 tbsp. brown sugar. Simmer till steaming, then ladle into heated mugs.*

DECEMBER 5, 1832

On his hands and knees, the redoubtable Lord John Ponsonby still managed a proud entry today to the presence of the Grand Vizier of Sultan Mahmud at Constantinople. The Ottoman Empire's "Sublime Porte" was a high gateway leading to the Vizier's palace, but only a three-foot-high embrasure was offered for ambassadors to crawl through. Ponsonby, whose appointment had taken effect just three weeks before, wanted to start off on the right foot, or knee. So he resolved the conflict between respect and self-respect by crawling through backside first. Britain's Foreign Secretary, Lord Palmerston, encouraged Ponsonby by writing that the vizier was only a "greasy, stupid old Turk" anyway, and they had the last laugh six years later when the post of Grand Vizier was abolished.

*A true **Diplomat** follows this procedure: Stir well with 3 ice cubes 1½ oz. dry vermouth, ½ oz. sweet vermouth, ½ tsp. maraschino liqueur and 2 dashes Angostura. Strain into a chilled cocktail glass, then decorate with 1 cherry and ½ slice lemon.*

DECEMBER 6, 1414

When the outspoken reforming priest John Hus, Rector of Prague University, agreed to attend a church council in Constance, Switzerland, he did not anticipate spending tonight in a lakeside cell next to an open latrine. Sigismund, Holy Roman Emperor, had arranged a safe-conduct; but conservatives on the church council had John arrested. Claiming he was a heretic, they took him before one of the three self-styled "Popes" who were competing for recognition by the council. The one chosen as judge, who had rather prematurely styled himself "John XXIII", sought brownie points by sending the troublesome reformer as a prisoner to an island monastery just offshore. Still, he didn't win the election. John Hus's lodging has since been transformed into a luxury hotel which boasts flush toilets.

*You don't have to be Swiss to enjoy an **Alpine Stinger**: Combine 1½ oz. brandy and 1 oz. Fior d'Alpe in an Old-Fashioned glass, then stir with 2 ice cubes.*

DECEMBER 7, 1858

Dr. James Barry's appointment as Inspector-General of the British Army's Medical Department took effect today, and it is most unlikely that the Commander-in-Chief, the Duke of Cambridge, knew what he was doing in signing it. The strictly vegetarian and teetotalling doctor, capping a 46-year military career with this prestigious posting, also differed in a less public way from the general run of 19th Century medicos. There might have been people who found Dr. Barry a bit odd, but one should take care to show respect for the chief. The following year Dr. Barry retired. Not until an Army doctor signed the death certificate in 1865 did it turn out that the smartly-uniformed officer had been a woman. Nobody, obviously, had made more than a general inspection of the Inspector-General.

*No need for secrecy, just great care in mixing the **Barry**: Stir into a martini glass 1½ oz. gin, ½ oz. sweet vermouth and 1 dash Angostura bitters. Float 1 tsp. crème de menthe; garnish with a twist of lemon peel.*

DECEMBER 8, 1903

Charles Manly, the engineer and loyal assistant to the Secretary of the Smithsonian Institution, again ended the day wetter than he had started, after trying to pilot the boss's "Aerodrome" flying machine. On its maiden outing two months earlier, Samuel Langley's invention had flopped into the waters of the Potomac, downstream from Washington. This time a dozen reporters were on hand to record the "first powered flight in a heavier-than-air machine". Manly had designed a suitable five-cylinder engine, but it was installed in Langley's unsound airframe. The Aerodrome was tethered in the jaws of a mighty catapult atop a houseboat; when the spring was released, it again toppled over into the water 16 feet below, while Charles Manly gamely worked the controls. Ten years later a modified version of Langley's craft did fly, but by then the inventor was dead.

*Salute the damp pioneer with an **Aviation**: Shake with ice 1½ oz. gin, ½ oz. lemon juice and 2 dashes Maraschino. Strain into a chilled cocktail glass.*

DECEMBER 9, 1761

Aboard HMS *Deptford*, young William Harrison was greatly relieved this morning as an island in the Madeira group rose above the southern horizon. His father's latest chronometer showed correctly how far west they were of Greenwich. The Harrisons hoped to win the Board of Longitude's prize of £20,000 for extreme accuracy; the Board had entrusted the ship's officers with four locks for the chest holding the clock, so that William couldn't sneak in to adjust it. The ship's captain was equally pleased to reach Madeira: two days ago 1057 gallons of condemned beer had been thrown overboard, and a sad entry in his journal read "Oblidged to drink Water". When *Deptford* reached her destination in Jamaica, with the crew on an unfamiliar diet of Madeira wine, Chronometer No.4 was only 2½ minutes fast — or else way out of whack, according to whose astronomical observation you believed. It took 12 years for the government to give the Harrisons any money, and they never received the full prize.

*Properly adjusted, the **Clockwork Orange** is its own reward: Put 2 ice cubes in a large Old-Fashioned glass, pour in 2 oz. each Pernod and orange juice, and stir.*

DECEMBER 10, 1911

The journey had taken him nearly three months, and might indeed have been faster on horseback, but Calbraith Rogers did today complete the first aerial crossing of North America. A supply train, loaded with spare parts, had no trouble keeping up with the fragile biplane *Vin Fiz* as it hopped across the United States in short stages. These were punctuated by 12 major crash landings, followed by lengthy waits on the ground. Starting from Sheepshead Bay, Long Island on September 17, Rogers flew as far as 133 miles on a good day. The hardy aviator actually crossed the California border in mid-November, but a worse landing than usual caused the delay until today's final 10-mile hop to Long Beach on the Pacific.

*A Far Western version of the Vin Fiz is **California Lemonade**: Shake well with cracked ice 2 oz. rye, juice of 1 lemon and 1 lime, 3 tsp. sugar and ¼ tsp. grenadine. Strain into a highball glass nearly filled with shaved ice; top up with soda, and decorate with a cherry and slices of lemon and orange. Sip through a straw.*

DECEMBER 11, 1883

Charles Stewart Parnell, the Irish politician, was so deep in debt that he had put his country estate up for sale, and this evening's meeting would show how much the public sympathized with him. A subscription to benefit the "uncrowned king of Ireland" had brought money pouring in, and not only from that country, to reach the impressive total of 37,883 pounds, 15 shillings and 10 pence. Charles Dawson, the loquacious Lord Mayor of Dublin, was on the platform with Parnell to make the presentation, but first he wished to unburden himself of a few well-chosen words. After about five minutes, when the Lord Mayor was in full flood, Parnell interrupted him: "I believe you have a cheque for me?" The Lord Mayor admitted that he did. "Thank you very much", said Charles Stewart Parnell. He took it and left.

*Not often do you run into such **Cold Irish**: Put 2 ice cubes and 1 slice lemon in an Old-Fashioned glass. Stir in ½ tsp. each sugar and water. Then pour on 2 oz. Irish whiskey, stir lightly and drink.*

DECEMBER 12, 1822

There was a happy ending this Thursday to the marital troubles of the Brooks' of Ivy Bridge, near Plymouth in Devon. Mr. Brooks was slow at arithmetic — his wife gave birth three weeks after their wedding, but it took a while for him to decide that the child wasn't his. Now the couple had separated, but agreed to split the proceeds of a sale: Mr.Brooks would sell Mrs.Brooks to the highest bidder, at Plymouth cattle market. The ostler of the Exmouth Inn, where Mrs. Brooks stabled her horse, had already volunteered he'd go as high as 20 pounds. But today, market day, the bidding had only just started at three pounds when two constables stepped in and hauled the couple away. The magistrate could not agree with Mr.Brooks' contention that "this can always be done on market day", so the deal had to be concluded in private. The ostler paid three pounds down and the remaining 17 within ten days, making for a Merry Christmas all around at Ivy Bridge.

Smiling Ivy calls for 1 oz. each of dark rum, peach liqueur and pineapple juice. Add white of 1 egg and 2 dashes lemon juice; shake well and strain into a cocktail glass.

DECEMBER 13, 1896

Disaster struck young playwright Alfred Jarry on this unlucky 13th, following last night's Paris première of his iconoclastic *Ubu Roi.* As secretary to the manager of the Théâtre de l'Œuvre, Jarry had been given a free hand in the presentation. First he chose to stand on stage with such a verbose explanation of his intentions that the audience told him to get on with the play. Then the curtain went up on the leading man, who shouted the single epithet *MERDRE!* Although Jarry had reluctantly inserted an extra "R" in the word, many in the audience seemed to recognize it: they objected at length, not only then but each of the subsequent 27 times it was uttered. The theatre manager might not have minded, except that the delays carried the evening past 11 o'clock, when his stage hands began earning overtime pay. This morning he called Jarry in and fired him.

*Playwright and manager could share this smoother **Curtain Raiser:** Shake well with ice 3 oz. vodka, 1 oz. cranberry juice, juice of 1 lime and 2 tsp. sugar. Strain into cocktail glasses.*

DECEMBER 14, 1903

When he lost the toss of a coin to his brother today, Orville Wright uttered a mild imprecation at not being the first to try piloting their flying machine. But then Wilbur's efforts failed to urge it off the sands of Kitty Hawk, South Carolina. Orville's turn, and lasting consolation, came three mornings later. At 10:35 the *Flyer* took off under power with him at the controls, and stayed aloft for 12 seconds; a 59-second flight followed. Although a telegraphed report to their clergyman father only resulted in an item in the hometown newspaper "Wright Brothers will be Home for Christmas", other journals rose to the occasion. The Norfolk *Virginian-Pilot* stretched the truth with its headline "Flying Machine Soars Three Miles", and marvelled in a subheading "No Balloon Attached to It". After a judicious delay the *New York Times* reported it with an added detail: "Machine invented by O. and W. Wright flies without the aid of a Balloon or Gas Bag".

*The brothers are assumed to have shared a **Wright Special**: 2½ oz. each of rye and port are well shaken with 3 tsp. lemon juice, 2 tsp. sugar syrup and 1 white of egg. Pour into highball glasses nearly full of cracked ice, stir and sip through straws.*

DECEMBER 15, 1876

An anonymous letter brought good and bad news today to Thomas Agnew, patriarch of a fashionable London art dealership. The good news was the return of a tiny corner fragment of Gainsborough's portrait of the Fifth Duchess of Devonshire. One foggy night the painting had disappeared through a second-floor window of 18-B Bond Street. The bad news was that Agnew could only have the complete duchess back in return for 3,000 gold sovereigns. The dealer did not respond, and risk of police involvement must have made the thief avoid further contact. Agnews, confident of a rising market for Gainsboroughs, set about an unhurried private investigation. After 25 years Robert A. Pinkerton, the American private detective, was approached by a down-at-heel character to act as go-between. In a Chicago hotel room one of Thomas Agnew's sons got back the painting and handed over a sum — not disclosed, but doubtless rather less than what Agnews then received for Gainsborough's duchess from their valued customer J.P.Morgan.

*Your **Duchess** will be less costly: ½ oz. each of Pernod, dry vermouth and sweet vermouth with 1 dash orange bitters. Shake well with ice and strain into a cocktail glass.*

DECEMBER 16, 1857

Engineer Robert Mallet's immense 36-inch mortar, designed to lob shells weighing a ton, had to be withdrawn from field trials on the Welsh island of Anglesey today after yet another crack was discovered in its barrel. Mallet had proven that the weapon, nearly two years in development, could send its heavy shells 1½ miles at a 45-degree elevation — sufficient to accomplish its prime task of destroying the Russian fortress of Sebastopol in the Crimea. But now Britain's new Secretary of State for War meanly refused to allot more money to repair the mortar, not even the 150 pounds requested. He pointed out that Sebastopol had fallen more than a year ago, and that a peace treaty with Russia had now been signed.

*Mallet and his 24-man crew deserved a **Crimean Cup**: Muddle the rinds of 2 lemons with 3 oz. sugar. Add 10 oz. lemon juice and 2 bottles soda water, stirring until the sugar is dissolved. Add 3 cups sugar syrup and beat until foamy. Pour in 16 oz. cognac, 8 oz. dark rum and 8 oz. maraschino. Let stand for a few minutes, then add a block of ice and 2 bottles champagne.*

DECEMBER 17, 1906

The publication today of Percival Lowell's elegantly-bound *Mars and its Canals* was a bit of one-upmanship hard to debunk. Since siting his telescope atop "Mars Hill" in Arizona, the wealthy amateur astronomer had been promoting his pet theory. His Italian counterpart Schiaparelli had postulated that the streaks on Mars' surface might be *canali*, which translates equally as "channels". But Lowell seized on the idea of canals and marvelled at the Martians' skill. He paid engineers to work out where the pumping stations must be situated to irrigate the Martian landscape. The distinguished scientist Alfred Russel Wallace wrote of Lowell's monomania: "The innumerable difficulties which it raises have either been ignored or brushed aside". Still, the idea of life on Mars intrigued the public: it took the Mariner flypast, 50 years after Lowell's death, to prove that his ideas about canals didn't hold water.

*Share a double **Astronaut's Revenge**: Combine and freeze 4 oz. milk with ½ tsp. vanilla extract. Blend until fluffy with 4 oz. each golden rum and pear nectar; pour immediately into tulip glasses.*

DECEMBER 18, 1912

The British amateur geologist Charles Dawson enjoyed his moment of glory today before an enthralled audience at London's Burlington House. He explained how, near Piltdown Common in Sussex, he had discovered two pieces of ape-like human skull which pre-dated anything yet known. He had found the Missing Link! Over the next 40 years millions of students learned of Piltdown Man, before certain suspicions proved true. The bones of *Eoanthropus Dawsoni*, one of which belonged to a recently-deceased orangutan, had been stained with laboratory chemicals and the teeth filed down. But meanwhile Piltdown Man's creator had died, full of the recognition he had craved. Later it was suggested that Dawson himself had been the victim of a hoaxer — an Oxford professor known to have disliked the pushy amateur. He would have set up the "find" hoping that a short-lived sensation would end with him exposing Dawson; but then the hoaxer realized that his own personal reputation might suffer.

*Missing from the Missing Link, no doubt, was his **Monkey Gland**: in a small Old-Fashioned glass stir 1½ oz. gin, 1 tbsp. orange juice, and ½ tsp. each Bénédictine and grenadine syrup. Put in 1 ice cube and stir gently.*

DECEMBER 19, 1894

At the tiller of the Benz Vélo which he had imported last month, law-abiding Britisher Henry Hewetson of Catford showed today that he had heeded a police inspector's warning. As the driver of the only four-wheeled gasoline-powered vehicle on the nation's roads, Henry would have to comply with the Locomotives on Highways Act, passed by anti-steam parliamentarians some 30 years earlier. Some way in advance of his vehicle rode a boy on a bicycle, primed to spot any Catford policeman going his rounds. On the Benz itself sat another youth, who at the warning signal would jump off and run 60 yards in front, waving the required red flag. Hewetson's flag was quite easy to run with, since it measured only two inches square. Its flagpole was a pencil.

*Your **Flag**, made in a small Old-Fashioned glass, uses 1 tsp. Crème Yvette as a base. Pour on carefully 1½ oz. apricot brandy, and top off with 1 oz. red burgundy.*

DECEMBER 20, 1780

Henry Laurens, former president of the Continental Congress and now the unwilling guest of King George in the Tower of London, learned today that through his ineptitude Britain had just declared war on the country to which he had been assigned as ambassador. The brigantine *Mercury* had been captured off Newfoundland by the British while carrying him from Philadelphia to Holland. Laurens was discovered throwing overboard an unweighted package which was quickly recovered. It contained the draft of a secret anti-British treaty with Holland. So now a guilty conscience was added to the financial burden of having to pay for his room and board in the Tower. Still, after the surrender at York Town it all came right: Laurens was exchanged for the British commander, Lord Cornwallis, and then had the satisfaction of drafting the peace treaty with the defeated Mother Country.

*Nothing sneaky about your **Dry Ambassador**: 2 oz. dry gin, ½ oz. dry vermouth and 1 tsp. chilled dry white wine are gently stirred with ice, then strained into a cocktail glass containing a twist of lemon peel.*

DECEMBER 21, 1891

Young James Naismith, an instructor at the YMCA training college for athletic directors in Springfield, Massachusetts, met his novel assignment with an inspiration today. Dean Gulick had asked the recent McGill graduate from Bennie's Corners, Ontario to devise an inexpensive all-weather sport that would wear out a hyperactive gym squad. Naismith asked the janitor to find him two equal sized cardboard boxes, but when this failed he got two peach baskets. These he tied to the balcony railing in the gym, then divided his 18-man class into two teams and began the first game of basketball. Soon there were teams all over Springfield trying it out, including a girls' team on which Maude Sherman was the star. Naismith admired her style and married her.

*Short of **Inspiration**? Stir with ice ½ oz. each gin, dry vermouth, calvados and Grand Marnier; strain into a cocktail glass and add a cherry.*

DECEMBER 22, 1849

When the priest, shortly after dawn this morning, offered his cross to No.6 in the line of condemned prisoners, 28-year-old Feodor Mihailovich Dostoievsky kissed it with fervour. The first three young men were already bound to posts to face the firing squad, on a platform raised for the purpose in St. Petersburg's Semyonov Square. Like No.6, they had "circulated writings against the Supreme Power". But just as the rifles were being loaded, a government courier raced up bearing a pardon from the Supreme Power himself — Czar Nicholas I. He had agreed to the court's recommendation of mercy, but then ordered the imminent-death scene staged for its deterrent effect. Suspecting this, young Dostoievsky was still glad to accept the alternative — leaving in leg-irons for four years' hard labour. And he was able to turn his experience there to profitable use by writing *The House of the Dead, or Prison Life in Siberia*.

*If you agree that Dostoievsky was better read than dead, join him in a **Tovarich**: 1½ oz. vodka, ½ oz. kümmel and juice of ½ lime. Shake with cracked ice and strain into a cocktail glass.*

DECEMBER 23, 1874

Because London's Charing Cross Hotel, attached to a main railway station, was not used to royal visitors, there was slight embarrassment at its registration desk this evening for the heir to the Spanish throne. The Crown Prince of the Asturias was on his way home to be crowned as King Alfonso XII following his mother's abdication, and he was travelling rather light. This was quite understandable for a first-termer at Sandhurst military college who had just turned 17, but the front desk clerk saw only a youth signing the register with his subsidiary title, Marqués de Covadonga. In fact Alfonso and his equerry, Don Juan de Valasco, inspired so little confidence that the clerk obliged them to hand over one pound apiece before assigning them their rooms on the third floor.

*Nothing less than champagne for the under-age **Alfonso**: Place 1 sugar lump in a champagne tulip, add 2 dashes Angostura and 1 oz. Dubonnet; fill with iced champagne. Stir gently and add a twist of lemon.*

DECEMBER 24, 1801

This Christmas Eve Richard Trevithick, a 6-foot-2-inch amateur wrestler and professional engine builder, spent a few minutes too long celebrating Britain's first successful trial of a road steam-carriage. Seven men climbed aboard outside John Tyack's workshop in Camborne, Cornwall, where Trevithick's machine had been more than a year a-building. It started slowly up the hill toward Camborne Beacon; when one man jumped off to walk alongside, it kept pace with him. But on returning to town Richard Trevithick hurried his mates into an inn, leaving the carriage in a shed. When they came out, shed and carriage were both being consumed by fire. Although he built another vehicle and took it to London, Trevithick never could arouse public interest. He died deep in debt, probably to the local innkeeper.

*Save the situation with a **Fire Extinguisher**: Into a 12-oz. highball glass containing 2 ice cubes, pour in 4 oz. each pale ale and soda. Top with a pinch of salt just before drinking.*

DECEMBER 25, 1870

May this be as happy a Christmas Day for you as it was for Cosima Bülow Wagner, who happened also to be celebrating her birthday one day late, as usual. She and her bridegroom Richard, who was father to 18-month-old Siegfried (and, she believed, to certain others of her children), had agreed to economize this first Christmas by not exchanging presents. But at 7 this morning a string quartet assembled down the staircase from her bedroom, along with clarinets, horns, oboe, flute, trumpet and bassoon. They played a tender new composition, which Wagner soon named the Siegfried Idyll after their son. Cosima's four daughters had no such luck: Herr Bülow, who was bringing them up, was a conductor rather than a composer. He had studied conducting under Wagner while Wagner studied running away with Cosima.

*Warm the family with 30 glasses of **Christmas Cheer**: Stick a lemon with cloves; bake at 350° F. for 15 minutes. Heat 4 bottles of red wine with 16 oz. water and 6 oz. dark rum. Stir in ½ tsp. powdered cinnamon and 1 pinch nutmeg, and float the lemon.*

DECEMBER 26, 1776

Today started badly, and ended even worse, for the hard-drinking Hessian colonel Gottlieb Rall, commanding 1400 mercenaries on the Loyalist side at Trenton, New Jersey. After accepting Postmaster Abe Hunt's applejack hospitality into the wee hours, Rall was awakened at 7 a.m. by the arrival of rebel troops in the street outside. Last evening a Loyalist farmer had wanted to deliver a note warning of General Washington's approach, but Hunt's manservant had refused him entry and taken the note himself to Colonel Rall, who stuffed it in his pocket without reading it. Now, rushing out of the house half-dressed, the Hessian was hit by three bullets. When he was laid on a pew in the Presbyterian church the note fell out of his pocket, so he did have a chance to read it before he died.

*Your turn to be **Bloodshot** (it's only a name): Shake well with ice 1½ oz. vodka, 2 oz. each tomato juice and beef consommé, 2 dashes Worcestershire sauce and 1 dash lemon juice. Strain the mixture into a highball glass over 2 ice cubes sprinkled with 1 shake celery salt.*

DECEMBER 27, 1891

Young John Lingman, who had hoped to be paired with multimillionaire Cornelius Vanderbilt in a unique experiment, found half his wish granted this morning. Last evening John presented himself at the portals of Vanderbilt's palace, which stretched for a whole block along New York's Fifth Avenue. The butler who greeted him left the chain on the door — wisely, for John was quite insistent that he had come to take the chairman of the New York Central Railroad away to a medical school. "They can examine his brain and mine and see how they differ. Mr. Vanderbilt makes so much more money than I do." The butler regretted, Mr. Vanderbilt had some visitors upstairs. Meanwhile he was tipping off another servant to find a policeman. And today, Judge Grady found himself quite unable to help John with the Vanderbilt part of the project, but sent him to Bellevue hospital, where they could make a thorough examination of his brain.

*Your **Vanderbilt** takes little brainwork: Just 1 oz. each brandy and cherry brandy, stirred with 2 dashes each Angostura and sugar syrup. Add a twist of lemon and a cherry.*

DECEMBER 28, 1694

Sophia Dorothea, wife of a future king of England, was prevented by today's decree from ever seeing that country. Her intimacy with handsome young Count Philip Königsmarck had disgruntled her husband George, Electoral Prince of Hanover, although it was quite all right for himself to keep his mistress of the moment in a palace apartment. Sophia and the count had arranged to elope to friendly relatives in Brunswick, but then he was found face down in a ditch just as George started a divorce action. The resulting decree made life no brighter: henceforth Sophia's name would be omitted from the state prayers, and she would spend the rest of her life in the prison-like castle of Ahlden. While his "ex" gloomed out her remaining 31 years, George became Elector of Hanover and then King of England, whither he took two mistresses for variety. To quote an earlier leader of the West Britons: "It's easy when you're a king, you know".

*If you too must say **Fare-thee-well**: Stir with ice, for the two of you, 3 oz. dry gin, 1 oz. dry vermouth and ½ oz. each sweet vermouth and curaçao. Strain into cocktail glasses.*

DECEMBER 29, 1174

As he walked barefoot the last stretch to Canterbury Cathedral today to be pardoned for putting out a contract on the late archbishop, England's King Henry II wished he'd never started the whole chain of events. Thomas Becket, formerly a loyal courtier, had turned obstructive after donning church uniform. For instance, he thought an ecclesiastic should report to the Pope rather than to the King. Henry took advantage of Becket being on vacation in France to have the Archbishop of York carry out a few royal whims. After Becket complained at being bypassed, Henry asked aloud, who would rid him of this troublesome priest? Reginald FitzUrse and three others said "We will", and did, four years ago today. Henry sent messengers, at a slow walk, to stop them; it was too late. For political reasons he then needed a papal pardon, and today he paid the price. Not only were his feet bleeding from the rough road into Canterbury, but he had to submit to a flogging from members of Becket's clergy.

*A hot pilgrim needs a **Canterbury Cooler**: Pour over 3 ice cubes in a highball glass, 1 oz. each light rum, dry gin and sweet lime cordial. Top up with tonic water and a slice of lime; sip through a straw.*

DECEMBER 30, 1762

If Britain's recently-married King George III had wanted to see a leg show this evening, he likely would not have taken Queen Charlotte along to the play at Covent Garden. The dancer Jenny Poitier, offering a sailor's hornpipe as an entr'acte to "Love in a Village", gave the audience an eyeful when, by accident or otherwise, she kicked off a slipper. After stooping to retrieve it, reported the *Theatre Review*, "She lifted up her leg. This, had she worn drawers, would have been the more excusable, but she was not provided with as much as a fig-leaf." The king and queen, conscious that those members of the audience who were not looking up Jenny's skirts were observing the royal reaction, "turned instantly from the stage".

*That was a strong recommendation for **BVD's**: Shake well with ice 1 oz. each golden rum, dry gin and sweet vermouth; strain into a small Old-Fashioned glass containing 1 ice cube.*

DECEMBER 31, 1758

Colonel George Washington had had enough, so today his retirement from Virginia Regiment No.1 took effect. Despite outstanding performance in the field, the young militia commander had never been offered a regular British army commission, and he remained subordinate to any regular of the same rank. One of those had written of the Virginians, "their slothful and languid disposition renders them unfit for military service." George, disagreeing, foresightedly kept his uniform. When the first Continental Congress assembled he wore it into the hall, giving the other delegates the idea that he might be of some use were any unpleasantness to occur opposite the Mother Country. And seven years later at his siege of York Town, which obliged the British to sue for peace, Washington was delighted to count the Virginia militia among his victorious troops.

*Ring in the New Year with **George Washington's Eggnog**: Mix 20 oz. brandy in a punchbowl with 5 oz. each golden rum, rye and oloroso sherry. Dissolve 1 lb. sugar in the liquor. Separate 12 eggs, beat the yolks until foamy and pour in. Whip 2 qts. cream until stiff, fold into the mixture and cool it on porch if no raccoons around. Just before serving, sprinkle with nutmeg.*

INDEX OF DRINKS

INDEX OF DRINKS

INDEX OF DRINKS

INDEX OF DRINKS

END OF INDEX

ABOUT THE AUTHOR

Hugh Quetton is a Canadian, born in England and educated in the United States, where he graduated from Yale University. Military and civilian travel in several countries introduced him to much of the material in these pages. Now retired and living in Toronto, he is married with three adult children.